THE 13 SECRETS
OF POWER PERFORMANCE

ALSO BY ROGER DAWSON

BOOKS

You Can Get Anything You Want—Secrets of Power Negotiating
Secrets of Power Persuasion
The Confident Decision Maker

AUDIO CASSETTE PROGRAMS

Secrets of Power Negotiating
Secrets of Power Persuasion
Secrets of Power Performance
Confident Decision Making
The Personality of Achievers

VIDEO TRAINING PROGRAMS

Guide to Everyday Negotiating
Guide to Business Negotiating

The 13 SECRETS OF POWER PERFORMANCE

ROGER DAWSON

PRENTICE HALL
Englewood Cliffs, New Jersey 07632

Prentice Hall International (UK) Limited, *London*
Prentice Hall of Australia Pty. Limited, *Sydney*
Prentice Hall Canada, Inc., *Toronto*
Prentice Hall Hispanoamericana, *S.A., Mexico*
Prentice Hall of India Private Limited, *New Delhi*
Prentice Hall of Japan, Inc., *Tokyo*
Simon & Schuster Asia Pte. Ltd., *Singapore*
Editora Prentice Hall do Brasil, Ltda., *Rio de Janeiro*

10 9 8 7 6 5 4 3 2 1

Library of Congress Cataloging-in-Publication Data

Dawson, Roger.
  The 13 secrets of power performance / Roger Dawson.
    p. cm.
  Includes index.
  ISBN 0-13-123035-2
  1. Success. 2. Performance. I. Title. II. Title: Thirteen secrets of power per-
formacne.
BJ1611.D335 1994
158'.1--dc20   94-28407
                                                       CIP

ISBN 0-13-123035-2

Prentice Hall
Career & Personal Development
Englewood Cliffs, NJ 07632
Simon & Schuster, A Paramount Communications Company

PRINTED IN THE UNITED STATES OF AMERICA

Dedicated to Gisela

Who is wise
Who is wonderful
and
Who brought love back into my life

YOU CAN BECOME A POWER PERFORMER

Have you ever wondered how some people are able to get so much out of life?

Nothing ever seems difficult or complicated for them. Getting straight "A's" in high school and college? No problem! Move into a fast track career and zoom swiftly ahead? Nothing to it! Find a beautiful, intelligent human being to share their life and then raise a family of wonderfully talented children? Piece of cake!

If they ever agonize over anything, it never shows. If they ever run out of money before they run out of month, you'd never know it. It's hard to believe they've ever felt so overwhelmed by life's problems that they didn't want to get out of bed in the morning!

Who are these people? Martians? Or genetic accidents that never should have happened? No!

They are people who have made the principles that I'll teach you in this book so much a part of their lives that they have become habits. So many self-help books in the past have stressed changing the way you think. I say that the key to success is to study what power performers are doing and start doing it yourself. These people who make life look so easy have simply adopted some of the secrets of power performance and made them their own. In this book you're going to learn the 13 Secrets of Power Performance. Make these secrets yours and they will send you to the front ranks of top performers!

For the past ten years, I've been traveling the country speaking to top companies and leading trade associations. It has taken me to every major city and resort hotel in North America, and five times to Australia. Everywhere I've gone, I've taken the time to have lunch or dinner with the real winners at the game of life. I asked them all the same question: "What are you doing differently? What makes *you* successful, when so many others fail?" The answers they gave became the foundation of this book.

Also, I've been taking two months off each year to travel the world, so that I could find out what people in other countries are doing with their lives. I've climbed mountains in Europe, the Himalayas, Africa, and the Andes. I've been to the running of the bulls in Pamplona. I've sat with the rare mountain gorillas of Zaire, and the terra-cotta soldiers of Central China. I've white-water rafted, parachute jumped, and bungee jumped. I've been around the world six times, and traveled in ninety-five different countries.

Everywhere I go, I find the same thing—a few Power Performers who can meet any challenge, overcome every obstacle, and do great things with their lives. Sadly, though, the vast majority of people are living far, far below their God-given potential.

It's tragic because if they would learn 13 Secrets of Power Performance, they could be living life to the fullest also—savoring, loving, and thrilling to every moment of life, and raising their life to its fullest potential.

I remember meeting a man who had come to this country penniless from Newcastle in Northern England. He'd made tens of millions of dollars in real estate brokerage and development. He told me about the three stages of wealth. First you learn how to earn money. Then you learn how to make money. Finally you learn how to hire other people and get them to make money for you. "That's where most people have trouble," he told me. "They don't know how to get the best out of people."

"What's the secret?" I asked him.

He told me, "People can do so much more than they think they're capable of doing. The only way you'll ever get the best out of them is to push them too hard. The same goes for ourselves. We can all do more than we think we can do. The only way you'll ever get the best out of yourself is to push yourself too hard." Isn't that the truth? Aren't you doing so much more now than you ever thought you could before, back in the early days when you were just getting started? And, trust me on this, you are capable of doing so much more in the future than you think you're capable of doing today.

THE THREE STAGES OF WEALTH.

First you learn how to earn money.

Then you learn how to make money.

Finally you learn how to hire other people

and get them to make money for you.

We can all become superstars at living. We all have what it takes to become Power Performers. Over the years, however, time and circumstances have conspired to corrode our potential.

Within each of us is a hidden store of energy. Energy we can release to compete in the marathon of life.

Within each of us is a hidden store of courage. Courage to give us the strength to face any challenge.

Within each of us is a hidden store of determination. Determination to keep us in the race when all seems lost.

We can all become Power Performers, and that's what this book is all about. To identify and overcome those things that may have been holding you back in the past, and to cast them out of your life. By the time you've finished this book, you'll understand what's going on in your life better than ever before. You'll feel a new surge of energy that will boost you into the ranks of Power Performers. That's a promise!

The 13 secrets I'm going to teach you will be so important to you that you'll be saying, "Yes! Now I know what I have to do. Nothing can stop me now!"

We can all do more than we think we can do.
The only way you'll ever get the best out of yourself
is to push yourself too hard.

First I'm going to ask you to do something that you've probably never done in all your years on this earth. Plan now to set aside a day in which you can review what you've learned from reading this book, and think of nothing else but your life; your past, your present, and especially your future. I'd like to spend this day in spirit with you, thinking about your place in the scheme of things on this incredibly beautiful planet zooming around a small corner of the universe. I want to evaluate how you feel about the quality of those years between birth and death that we call "our life."

If you're willing to go out of your way to set aside this special day, I promise that you'll always look back upon it as a magical day. It will be a turning point for you in your journey to Power Performance.

Let us so live that when we come to die even the
undertaker will be sorry.

MARK TWAIN

Ideally, you'll need to get away to a place where you can be alone and away from the environment in which you normally live your life. Power Performers have found the day they set aside to do nothing but think about these habits is one of the most valuable days of their lives. Perhaps you have a friend who will lend you their condo down at the beach, or maybe you'd rather dig out your backpack and find a place of solitude up in the mountains.

My favorite place is a valley high up in the Sierra Mountains of Central California, called Mineral King. It's a remote place, some 80 miles from Fresno, so first you'll be driving across one of the greatest agricultural valleys in the world—the San Joaquin valley. Crops of cotton and figs stretch as far as you can see. It will probably remind you of John Steinbeck's classic book *The Grapes of Wrath* that depicted the harsh life of a family of Oklahoma farmers who came here in the 1930s to escape the savage drought that created the great American Dust Bowl. As you approach the foothills you'll pass through the miles of vineyards that make this the raisin capital of the world. Soon you'll be winding into a giant canyon that leads you into the magnificent Sierra Nevadas. Just beyond the town of Three Rivers, you'll turn at the ranger station and begin to wind your way up to Mineral King. The last 15 miles are by an unpaved one-lane road that curves around the shoulder of the canyon. The air will be colder now and fresher too. Far below you'll be able to see the ocean of smog that coats the Central Valley. Finally the road ends in a small alpine meadow dotted with cabins that a few fortunate families have been able to rent from the Forest Service. From the end of the road, you can hike up another five miles or so, to around 10,000 feet, and be in some of the country's most beautiful and remote scenery.

Many years ago the Walt Disney Corporation unveiled plans to develop a major downhill ski resort at Mineral King. It was to be a magnificent place that would rival any ski resort this country or Europe had to offer. They planned to replace the one-lane road with a monorail train to carry the skiers the 20 miles up to the valley, which they would fill with outstanding resort hotels and the finest of facilities.

> *Skiing combines outdoor fun with knocking down trees with your face.*
>
> DAVE BARRY

As an avid skier, I first made my way to Mineral King eager to see the area that would become a Mecca for skiers from all over the country. When I got there, however, I was instantly converted, like Saul on the road to Damascus. This was one of the most beautiful places I'd ever seen. Green mountain meadows, with an ice-cold river babbling its way down the valley, and snowcapped mountains all around. The Sierra Club was right to oppose the Disney development! We should leave places such as this pristine to delight and inspire future generations.

Although the Sierra Club lost their fight in the U.S. Supreme Court, they had delayed the development so long that development costs had soared out of sight. Disney could no longer make money on the project, and Mineral King remains today as it has been since the beginning of time.

So when you're through reading this book, please find your own Mineral King, whereever it may be, and we'll spend the day together contemplating the *13 SECRETS OF POWER PERFORMANCE.*

The objective of this book is to put you firmly and enthusiastically among life's Power Performers. You can compare most people to boats. Many are like the narrow houseboats that ply the canals of France and move only when they're pulled and then never deviate from a narrow course. Some people are like the huge barges that laboriously make their way up and down the Mississippi. Unless they're controlled they go adrift and crash wherever the current takes them. Some people are like the super tankers that plow the world's oceans with a determined course as they battle the elements. Some are like a cruise ship and exist only for fun. Power Performers are the great racing yachts that respond quickly to the elements, that leap from wave crest to wave crest, and inspire all who see them to do great deeds also. They relish the perfect days when the sun is bright and the wind takes them quickly to their destination. However, they also gleefully challenge the days when the elements conspire to defeat them and they must battle to make progress.

> *I find the great thing in this world is not so much where we stand, as in what direction we are moving: To reach the port of heaven, we must sail sometimes with the wind and sometimes against it—but we must sail, and not drift, nor lie at anchor.*
>
> OLIVER WENDELL HOLMES

You deserve to live your life as a great adventure. You deserve to conquer the adversities in your life and leap to take advantage of the days when fate conspires to see that you do great things with your life. You deserve to be a Power Performer. In your hands you have the pathway to greatness.

CONTENTS

1

POWER PERFORMERS MAKE THEIR LIFE AN ADVENTURE

There is no end to the adventures that we can have if only we seek them with our eyes open.

— *Jawaharlal Nehru*

Men spend most of their lives worrying about things that never happen.

— *Moliere*

One who has any faith in God should be ashamed to worry about anything whatsoever.

— *Mahatma Gandhi*

Good things don't happen to you. Bad things don't happen to you. Life is what happens to you. The more you examine the events in your life and categorize them into good things and bad things, the more messed up you're going to become.

— *Roger Dawson*

WOULD YOU DO IT ALL AGAIN?

Let's start our journey to Power Performance with a question: "If you could be given the chance to live your life again, an exact repeat of what you've experienced to this date, would you want to do it?" Imagine that if you say yes, you immediately go back to your fifth birthday and relive your life day by day exactly the way it has been, without any opportunity to change a thing and without knowing what will happen to you next. Also, you won't have the benefit of the wisdom you picked up the first time through. You must muddle through just as before. (Benjamin Franklin once addressed this issue. He said, "Were it offered to my choice, I should have no objection to a repetition of the same life from its beginning, only asking the advantages authors have in a second edition to correct some faults in the first.") Then when you catch up with today, your life goes on exactly as it would from this point on. Would you do it?

> *Life is like playing a violin in public and learning the instrument as one goes on.*
>
> SAMUEL BUTLER

It's an interesting question, isn't it? It directly relates to Power Performance for a very simple reason. The more fun you have at doing something, the better you'll do it. The more joy you see in being alive, the better you'll succeed—in your career, with your financial plans, and in your family and your social life. The more you see your life as an enriching experience instead of as a hassle, the more energy and passion for living you will have.

Try that question on your friends later, and you'll find a few will immediately say, "Oh yes, of course. I've loved every exciting minute of it, and I'd give my right arm to do it again." However, the vast majority will point out that although they enjoyed life, it was also quite a hassle, a struggle. Rather than repeat it, they'll take their chances with the future. At the start of this century Jules Reanard considered this proposition and came up with this conclusion: "If I were to begin life again, I should want it as it was. I would only open my eyes a little more."

If I had to live my life again, I'd make the same mistakes, only sooner.

TALLULAH BANKHEAD

THE BEST APPROACH TO LIFE

The experience of life should be like that of a child spending the day at Disneyland.

In 1960, soon after the original Disneyland opened in an orange grove in Anaheim, I was a photographer on board a British ocean liner that was visiting Los Angeles. There are dozens of exciting things to do during a brief visit to Southern California, so it amazed me how many of the passengers wanted to spend their entire time ashore at Disneyland. Because of this I became skeptical about the lure of this amusement park. What kind of person would rather spend a day riding roller coasters than seeing Beverly Hills, the Hollywood Bowl, or visiting a movie studio? It wasn't until 1963, after I had emigrated from England to California, that I finally got to go myself. As it had millions before, the Magic Kingdom captivated me. Far from being a mere amusement park, it was a wonderful re-creation of those magic moments in our childhood when everything seems so exciting that we want to burst with joy.

I was at the Tokyo Disneyland soon after it opened, and the expressions on the faces of the little children fascinated me. If children everywhere would remember the lessons they learn during their first visit to Disneyland, and apply them to life in general, they would always find life an exciting adventure:

◆ Children approach the park with excited anticipation, eager for the experience. Although the Japanese culture tells them to stay reserved and formal, they abandon all this the moment they enter the Magic Kingdom. They go wild with excitement.

◆ They overcome their fear of the unknown.

◆ They know there will be problems during the day such as rain and long lines, and they accept that not all of it will be pleasant.

◆ They know the fast rides will scare them.

Although these may not seem very challenging to you, to a five year old, they're formidable. Nevertheless, they love every minute of it, leave it only when their parents force them to, and they would do it all over in a minute.

Children always seem to get great pleasure out of what they do and would love to go back and do it again. It's as we get older and take on the cares and responsibilities of life that we begin to question whether life is that much of an adventure.

> *When she was 80 years old, Helen Keller said, "I have kept young trying never to lose my childhood sense of wonderment. I am glad I still have a vivid curiosity about the world I live in."*

HOW MUCH ARE YOU ENJOYING LIFE?

Isn't it shocking that surveys tell us that most of us don't like the work we do and would quit if it weren't for the money? The Los Angeles *Times* did a survey of workers in Orange County, California, which is one of the best places to work in the country (for me that means it must also be one of the best places in the world). The sun shines year round, everything is new and fresh, and you can ski in the morning and sail in the afternoon. Even in this paradise they found that only 24 percent of workers described themselves as very satisfied with their pay. Only 44 percent said that the work they did satisfied them. Isn't that something? Even in that great environment 56 percent of workers didn't like the work they did and were doing it only for the money. And 76 percent of them weren't happy with the money they were getting. No wonder we spend so much of our lives looking to the future for happiness and contentment, rather than relishing the moment— as a Power Performer always does.

Ask one person how he feels about life and he'll tell you it's a constant struggle, a hassle just to survive; he'll tell you people are always unfair to him; and even his bearing tells you that the most he hopes for is to reach the end of his life before some tragedy overtakes him. I remember sharing a ski lift with a person like this at Mammoth Mountain, a great ski resort on the east side of the Sierra Nevadas south of Reno. The lift ride was less than ten minutes long, but look at some of the negative things he shared with me during that time:

- ◆ One of the parallel lifts had been stopped and the skiers were sitting there patiently waiting for it to start again. My companion observed, "They're going to be there for a long time. They'll probably have to send someone out from Washington, D.C., to inspect it."

- ◆ "If the cable breaks it'll kill you even if you fall slowly. You don't have to fall fast." (The lift started up again a few minutes later.)

- ◆ We were watching some teenagers come swooping down on snow-boards, having the time of their life and whooping and hollering as they went. He said, "Snow-boards should be banned. I bumped into this kid once and I was furious. I said, 'Come here you little runt.'"

- ◆ A little further up I was admiring a paraplegic who was thundering down the slope on a sit-ski. These are like tricycles with snow runners where the wheels would normally be. Just as I thought what an inspiration this skier was to be out there even though he was paralyzed from the waist down, my companion said, "If I was that way I'd pull the plug. If you can't golf or make love [to use an expression that loses something in translation from his vernacular] I say pull the plug."

How depressing! As we approached the top he said, "Do you want to ski this run together?"

I said, "No, I don't want to ski with you. With an attitude like yours, you're a disaster waiting to happen." So he skied off alone

with his little black cloud hanging over him like a balloon tied to
the waist of an avalanche patroller.

> *A pessimist is one who feels bad when he feels*
> *good for fear he'll feel worse when he feels better.*

HOW POWER PERFORMERS LOOK AT LIFE

Power Performers' attitudes, however, couldn't be more different.
For them life is truly an exciting adventure. They never have
enough time for everything. For them every day brings new challenges and rewards. They're always meeting new people and discovering new ideas. If they should happen to think of dying, it sad-
dens them to think how death would deprive them of such joy of
living: never again to be overwhelmed by the beauty of a sunset or
a mountain peak covered with snow; never again to feel the thrill
of overcoming a challenge; and never again be moved to laughter,
ecstasy, or tears by someone they love.

To become a Power Performers, we must first get so excited
about life and what we're doing with these few precious years we
spend on earth that we can hardly stand it.

Power Performers all have one thing in common. They love
life! The very realization that they're alive charges them up so
much that they approach everything they do with a special gusto.
Whether they're working on a tricky business opportunity or
swinging through a golf ball or roaring down a freeway, they
approach everything they do with a terrific zest for living.

Have you ever noticed that it's hard to tell if a Power
Performer is working or playing? They give everything they have
to everything they do!

You'll find Power Performers everywhere: working seven days
a week to get a new business venture off the ground; or up in the
mountains putting finishing touches to the log cabin they built
from the ground up; or working past midnight in a laboratory
somewhere exploring the frontiers of new technology. And they do
it with all the fervor of Meriwether Lewis and William Clark
exploring the Louisiana Purchase.

Give everything you have, to everything you do!

Although Power Performers treat work like play, in their spare time you'll find them sailing in the Mediterranean, trekking in the Himalayas, clinging to a rock face in Peru, or scuba diving in the Caribbean, totally absorbed and exhilarated by the experience.

I remember scuba diving with my son Dwight off the West coast of Mexico just south of Puerto Vallarta. The local scuba diving shop has its own little beach there, with a few grass roofed huts where you can relax and picnic after your dive. We did a morning dive with the group that had come out from town on the launch, and then Dwight and I did a second afternoon dive. Our guide took us to an incredible cliff stretching from about 100 feet under the surface down into the depths of the ocean. We plunged down to where you can no longer see the surface and the water begins to turn black. I turned to the cliff and imagined that I was high on a mountain wall, with a mile of empty space beneath me and only a few more feet to go to the summit.

I'd had some experience of laboriously climbing such cliffs in the Himalayas and the Andes, where every move takes a supreme effort, but here I could float up and down the wall with the incredible feeling of weightlessness that scuba diving gives you. What an experience! I felt like an eagle floating and swooping and soaring at will. In my revelry I remembered that Jacques Cousteau and Emil Gagnan invented scuba equipment less than 50 years ago. Think of the great men and women of history who never had an opportunity to do what I was doing.

The experience so exhilarated me that I began to think of Alexander the Great, who wept because there were no new worlds for him to conquer. Of course, the wonders of the deep sea existed then, but Alexander had the misfortune to be a Power Performer born too soon, before he'd have a chance to explore them.

Alexander III of Macedonia is known as Alexander the Great because he killed more people of more different kinds than any other man of his time.

WILL CUPPY

Suddenly I realized that our guide was tugging at one of my fins. I rolled over and looked up at him. He was silhouetted against the bright light of the sun that was creating a circle on the surface far above us. Come up now, he urgently signaled. I checked my air gauge and saw that I had plenty of time left. I flashed him the okay signal and tapped my watch to let him know that I wanted to stay down longer. He waggled his finger at me and pointed urgently to the surface, so I reluctantly followed him and left behind one of the most euphoric experiences of my life. When we were back in the boat I found out why the guide was so insistent on my coming up. He didn't speak English well enough to explain it but my son, who has been to dive school, knew. (He does things like going to classes, unlike me. If I want to do something I tend to go do it and learn about the difficulties as I go. Take the sailboat out. If you sink it go back and get another one until you get it figured out. Slap the software in the computer and start playing with it. It shouldn't stump you, but if it does call the support line. Who has time to read all those manuals?) Dwight told me that when you stay down deep for long the nitrogen balance in your bloodstream changes and you experience an incredible high. It's dangerous because you're having so much fun that you don't want it to end.

> *So I'm scuba diving at 100 feet wearing $2,000 of equipment when I see this diver with no equipment at all. Thinking that the sporting-goods salesman had cheated me, I get out my underwater message board and ask him how he does it.*
>
> *He scribbles back, "You idiot! I'm drowning!"*

Whether is was nitrogen narcosis or natural euphoria, it stays in my mind as a wonderful experience. But even that must be nothing compared to the thrill of being in space. Imagine being in an environment where you can see to infinity and can float with more freedom than an eagle. Imagine floating through the airlock to do a space walk, knowing that you would go into orbit just like your space shuttle, your forward velocity perfectly synchronized to the pull of gravity so that the curvature of your fall exactly matches the curvature of the earth. To look at spaceship Earth and see our entire world in a single gaze. How it must change your soul! As Archibald MacLeish said, "To see the earth as we now see it, small and blue and beautiful in that eternal silence where it floats, is to see ourselves as riders on the earth together, brothers on that bright loveliness in the unending night—brothers who see now they are truly brothers." I can't wait to go!

YOU DON'T HAVE TO CHOOSE BETWEEN ADVENTURE AND SUCCESS

Power Performers understand that when you're doing something you love to do, you transform your energy level. When what you're doing excites you, and you're moving toward an objective with positive expectancy, there is virtually no limit to what you can accomplish. Then the energy and success drive that you nurture in pursuit of adventure will pay off in your career too.

Take Frank Wells for example. He was president of Warner Brothers, apparently at the pinnacle of his career in motion pictures. He was always reminiscing, however, of the days when he a student at Pomona College in California and used to dream of being the first man to climb Mount Everest. In those days that was what was going to make him famous. He could still remember the day in 1953 when somebody from his fraternity called and told him that he had waited too long. "Some guy named Hillary just climbed it," he told Wells.

The following year Wells was a Rhodes scholar at Oxford University and wanted to plan a grand adventure for his spring break. He knew a friend who had a pilot's license so they pooled their money, bought a $600 plane, and agreed to fly to Cape Town and back. Frank's job was to arrange the landing permits in the more than 20 countries in which they would have to refuel, because the tiny plane only had a 500-mile range. The day before they left his friend gave him a book on navigation and told him that he had been too busy to read it. Frank stayed up all night learning the fundamentals, and he learned the rest on the job. As they approached Mount Kilimanjaro, which straddles the Kenya/Tanzania border, Frank impulsively suggested that they climb it.

Nobody who has seen Kilimanjaro will ever forget the sight of this huge mountain that sits so close to the equator and yet is snow-covered year round. Driving south from Nairobi with my daughter, Julia, when we climbed the mountain, we were so stunned by the sight that we asked our driver to pull over so that we could absorb its magnificence. For miles around, the plains of Africa stretch off into the distance. It's the sheer size of the mountain that astonishes you when you first see it. It rises from only a little above sea level to 19,710 feet, but it is so huge it doesn't look as a mountain should with a sharp summit. Instead it grows slowly from the plains, converging on the squared-off summit (the top blew off in a volcanic explosion millions of years ago) from 50 miles in every direction.

The other astounding thing is the contrast between the heat of the equatorial plains below and the snow covered summit above. Climbers once found the carcass of a leopard near the summit but no one has ever been able to explain what drove it to make the enormous effort needed to get there. This fascinated Ernest Hemingway, and he made it the analogy of his short story about an adventurer who lay dying after a plane crash near the mountain. Before he dies he reviews his adventures in his mind and tries to make sense of the things he has done with his life. The conclusion appears to be that there may have been no reason why the leopard was at the top of the mountain, any more than there is a reason why we do many of the things we do with our lives.

Hemingway started to write the story when he lay in critical condition after a plane crash while sightseeing in Uganda. Hemingway was lucky to survive. Harry, the hero of his story, was not so fortunate and died of gangrene poisoning, although when Hollywood made a movie of *The Snows of Kilimanjaro* they had the nerve to give it a happy ending.

Having your book turned into a movie is like seeing your oxen turned into bouillon cubes.

JOHN LeCARRÉ

Frank Wells and his friend made it to the top of the mountain, and it became a seminal moment in his life. However, they never made it to Cape Town. Soon after leaving the mountain they were forced to make an emergency landing that destroyed their plane.

Back home he limited his climbing to going up the corporate ladder, something at which he was far more adept. Twenty-six years would pass before he would climb again, this time Mont Blanc in France. Thinking that he had climbed the tallest peak in Europe, a dream started to form in his mind. He had climbed the tallest peak on two continents (he thought)—why not go for all seven? He had found a new challenge: He wanted to be the first person to climb the highest peak in all seven continents. Even when he found out that Mont Blanc isn't the tallest peak in Europe (Mount Elbrus in Russia takes the honors), it didn't discourage him. He teamed up with 53 year old Dick Bass, the owner of Snowbird ski resort in Utah, who shared his dream, and set out on his grand adventure.

At first he didn't treat it seriously enough and was trying to squeeze the climbs in between his duties at Warner Brothers. He and Dick impulsively decided to attempt Mount Elbrus just a few weeks after they met, because Dick was going to be in Europe anyway researching new ideas for his ski resort. Mount Elbrus is 18,510 feet high, so it's not as high as Kilimanjaro, but Frank was now 28 years older. He collapsed in exhaustion 1,500 feet from the summit. When he returned to America he decided to get back into shape by climbing Mount Rainier in Washington. Because it is only 14, 410 feet high it shouldn't have posed a serious challenge to a man who was thinking of conquering Everest, but again he collapsed in exhaustion before reaching the top.

Finally Frank realized that if he were to realize his dream, he would have to make climbing a full-time obsession. But was it worth quitting his president's job at Warner Brothers? He had worked for decades to reach this pinnacle of success in the entertainment business and he doubted anyone would give him another opportunity to head up a major studio. After two days of agonizing, he made his decision and quit his job.

However, even this commitment was not enough to turn things around for Frank. He enthusiastically joined Dick for a climb of Aconcagua in Argentina and made it to 20,500 feet, his personal best, but he was still 2,300 feet from the summit when he collapsed.

In spite of these discouragements, he continued with the plan to climb Everest. He and Dick had bought their way onto a Lou Whittaker expedition that would attempt to climb Everest from the north side, out of Tibet. Two climbers died in separate accidents, including Marty Hoey, who had been a ski instructor at Bass's Snowbird Resort and had climbed on Aconcagua with them. Despite this the expedition continued, and although one climber made it to within 1,500 feet of the summit, Frank made only it to 24,000 feet, still his personal best.

Finally things started to turn around for Frank. In 1983 he and Dick returned to conquer Aconcagua, the highest peak in South America. Then they returned to the tallest of them all, Everest, at 29,028 feet, but failed to reach the top. By now Frank was achieving more with every climb and he reached the South Col—the saddle at 26,200 feet, less than 3,000 feet from the summit. If it hadn't been for another sick climber, he felt would have made it to the top. Undeterred, they lined up a third Everest expedition for later in the year and went on to climb Mount McKinley in Alaska and Mount Kilimanjaro in Africa. Then they returned to Mount Elbrus in Russia and reached the top in July.

Their next peak Mount Vinson in Antarctica, was a logistical nightmare. At 16,067 feet it was not very tall but was so remote and had such torturous weather that it presented the biggest challenge of them all. Then they went on to the easiest of them all: Mount Kosciusko in Australia, at only 7,310 feet a walk (they evidently decided not to consider 16,500-foot Mount Java in Indonesia part of the Australian continent, although it is in Australasia).

That left only one climb. The return to Mount Everest. Remember neither of these men were very experienced mountain climbers, and both were too old to be going over 20,000 feet, much less the 29,028-foot summit of Everest that had already killed more than 50 top mountaineers.

Frank's wife, Luanne, finally put a stop to it, convinced that Frank would kill himself on Everest rather than give up. Dick Bass went on to complete the seven summits, the first person to do that and the oldest person ever to climb Everest.

The fascinating part of this story, told brilliantly in their book *Seven Summits*, isn't so much the climbs as what happened to Frank Wells afterward. He'd given up his job as president of Warner Brothers thinking he was sacrificing his career for this one shot at adventure and glory. However, when he returned, Walt Disney Studios hired him to be their president, and he went on to do an incredible job leading that company to stratospheric success. Leaving Warner Brothers turned out to be the best career move he could have made. Although he was later killed in a helicopter skiing accident he would never have known how much he could accomplish in his career without the brave heart of an adventurer.

> *Power Performers understand that the energy and success drive they nurture in pursuit of adventure pays off in their careers too.*

What can we learn from the story of Frank Wells and the seven summits? You don't have to choose between adventure and success. Stop thinking that you have to sacrifice the things you really want to do in life because of your career. If that were true I would say the price is too high. Power Performers know that you don't have to choose between adventure and a career. They can have it all because the energy and success drive they nurture in pursuit of adventure pays off in their careers too.

You probably won't be choosing between adventure and career when you're at the pinnacle of your industry the way Frank Wells did. My golfing buddy Michael Crowe called me up one Monday. He wanted to fly to England to attend his brother's fiftieth birthday party that Friday and then stay over to see the Ryder's Cup golf match they were playing near his home town of Coventry. He really couldn't afford to take the time off work and he felt guilty about spending the money, but I was proud of him when he decided to go anyway. He will savor the memories long after he's forgotten how much it cost.

I remember when I was twenty and had started a promising career with a retail chain in England that sold televisions and appliances. Within a year I could have been a store manager. Then an opportunity came along to take a two-week cruise through the Mediterranean as a ship's photographer. If I did well the company would send me out on other ships and it would become a full-time job.

Now picture this: I was 20 at the time and living at home without any financial obligations. So on the one hand a good future in business lay ahead of me. On the other hand this was a once-in-a-lifetime opportunity to take off and see the world. Looking back, I can't believe it was a decision that would take more than 10 seconds to make, but at the time I was very hesitant about giving up my secure sales job. Eventually this fledgling adventurer decided to try his wings and I flew off to the adventure of world travel. It was the smartest decision I ever made, because it led to my visiting America and emigrating here a year later.

> *England is a beautiful country, with great theater and fine museums, and wonderful people. It's really quite amazing that nobody wants to live there anymore.*
>
> DUDLEY MOORE

Now I take two months off a year so that I can go adventuring, and I will turn down any speaking engagements during those months. The people in my office won't even take the time to tell me about any opportunities because they know what my response will be. Although sometimes they can't resist keeping track of the talks they turn down and calling me to say, "Roger, do you realize that trip you're taking has already cost you $30,000 and you haven't even left yet?" It doesn't matter to me. I want the speaking business to still excite me twenty years from now as much as it does today. Living a fulfilled, exciting, adventurous life is what keeps my energy and enthusiasm up.

You don't have to take a trip around the world to be an adventurer. It's a matter of attitude, not destination. Perhaps you've been dreaming of playing golf at Pebble Beach or renting a sailboat in the Virgin Islands. Go do it! I bet it won't cost as much as you think it will, and in the long run it won't cost anything, because you'll quickly recoup the outlay with your renewed enthusiasm and energy.

THE POWER OF SERENDIPITY

You don't have to climb the world's tallest mountains be an adventurer. You can turn the most mundane experiences into exciting adventures if you learn to harness the power of serendipity. English writer Horace Walpole made the word serendipity popular when he based his story *The Three Princes of Serendip* on a Persian fairy tale about the adventures of three princes who make accidental but fortunate discoveries. The word serendipity has come to mean good luck in running across things for which you weren't looking.

I love to travel, but I hate package tours. I have ten times the fun and excitement when I just take off to another country and let serendipity be my guide. Once you let those delightful adventures seek you out, the exciting things that happen around you will astonish you.

Often it's "the road less traveled," as Robert Frost put it, that will fascinate you the most, for at the end of that road lies adventure.

Incidentally, Frost had a delightful sense of humor and a Power Performer's belief in not taking himself too seriously. He made his fame and fortune by writing poems about the wonders of nature in New England, where he'd made his home. Once, after a dinner party, he and several other guests went out onto the verandah to watch the sun go down. "Oh, Mr. Frost, isn't it a lovely sunset?" exclaimed a young woman. Frost put his arm around her and smiled, "I never discuss business after dinner."

Let me give you a couple of examples of serendipity at work. In 1977 a group of friends and I planned a trip to the base camp on Mount Everest. I'll tell you more about that trip later. Four of us were from California and one was from Arizona, but we decided to fly separately to Nepal and meet up there for the trek into the Himalayas. On my way to Katmandu, the capital of Nepal, I'd arranged stopovers in London, where I visited my favorite uncle who was close to death in a cancer ward, and in New Delhi, the capital of India. I'd been in India before, but never to this city, so

I was very curious about life there. I could have had my travel agent fill my three-day stay with bus tours and group activities, but I saw everything—and enjoyed it so much more—with serendipity. So many people who travel are afraid of missing anything because they may never be back. I always assume that I will return one day and would much rather spend my time seeing what I want to see rather than frantically racing from one place to another. My rule when traveling is to never let the fear of missing something stop you from experiencing the joy of the unexpected.

Early the first morning I left my hotel and wandered over to one of the huge traffic circles near the main government buildings. I sat down on the grass and waited for serendipity—for a happy accident. After a while a snake charmer and his young assistant made their way over and began talking to me. "Was this it?" I wondered, as they set down their woven-reed basket and the charmer began to play his flute. It intrigued me because I knew it wasn't the sound of the flute that aroused the snake but the tapping of the owner's foot next to the basket. Slowly, the lid of the basket moved and the python swayed up in the air. I gave the snake charmer a few rupees and he moved on. That wasn't the fortunate accident I was waiting for.

> *Never let the fear of missing something stop you from experiencing the joy of the unexpected.*

I propped my head on my knapsack and watched the incredible assortment of traffic as it passed by. Motor scooters with the women in their saris riding sidesaddle, horse-drawn buggies, tiny open buses holding six to eight people, and peddle-driven rickshaws.

I thought about Gandhi, who was once asked what he thought about Western Civilization. "I think it would be a very good idea," he dryly replied. My favorite story about this great leader concerned his insistence that he always travel with the common man, over the protests of Lord Mountbatten, who worried about Gandhi's safety. If Gandhi determined to travel on a train with the untouchables, Mountbatten, without Gandhi's knowledge, would have them all especially selected and security screened.

Mountbatten once remarked, "He has no idea how much it costs to keep him in poverty!"

A half hour went by and then an elderly Indian approached me. He spoke well and dressed neatly, although his clothes were obviously very old. He told me that his name was Nelson, like the naval hero from the Battle of Trafalgar. He had learned English as an orderly for a British officer when he was a young man. We chatted until I began to feel comfortable with him, and then I asked him if he would like to show me around the city. He suggested a small fee, about $5 per day.

Nelson stayed with me for the next three days and kept his promise to show me New Delhi as an Indian would see it. We rode in every form of transportation and ate in all the local restaurants. He showed me Gandhi's tomb and spoke lovingly about how he was the last Indian leader who truly understood the soul of the people. That night we went to the sound and light show at the old fort, and I learned from him how the invasions of the Mongols, the Muslims, and later the English traders had changed the culture of his country forever. I learned more about India in those three days than I would have in a month of bus tours. I asked Nelson to meet me again when I finished my trip to Mount Everest and returned to New Delhi.

When I got back to the city a month later, there was a mixup in my hotel reservation and I had to move to a different hotel. Concerned that I would miss Nelson, because they would not let this old man who looked like a beggar into the hotel without me, I tipped the doorman to look out for him. Later in the day Nelson found me, although he looked as though he hadn't bathed in the month that I'd been gone. I lent him my shaver and told him to go soak in my bathtub for as long as he wanted.

The next day we rode a bus out to the fabulous Taj Mahal. Instead of taking me straight to it, he took me first to a fort around the bend of the River Yamuna. He could have pointed out the Taj Mahal, but instead he chose to let me discover it for myself. I was standing on the balcony of the fort when I glanced along the river and there was the Taj Mahal, shimmering in the heat and rising out of the weak mist that was rising from the river.

Very seldom does something as familiar to you in pictures as the Taj Mahal stun your senses when you first see it. When you first see the Eiffel Tower in Paris or the Tower Bridge in London, for example, they look so much like all the pictures you have seen that they are almost a disappointment. The Taj Mahal is different. However many thousands of pictures you've seen of it, nothing prepares you for the real thing. It was built as a monument to, and a sarcophagus for the wife of Mogul emperor Shah Jahan, who had been his constant companion for 19 years. Twenty thousand workers toiled for 22 years to complete the world famous structure. Every square inch of the building is a masterpiece of artistry. The marble mosaics that cover the building are so beautiful that any part of it would be displayed proudly in an art museum.

When finally I prepared to return to California, we ate together at one of the finest restaurants in New Delhi, where Nelson took on food as a camel takes on water. It would evidently be a long time before he would eat that well again. At our parting, there were tears on both sides as we knew we'd never meet again.

Perhaps I would have seen more if I had let my travel agent arrange a tour for me, but the sweet memory of my days with Nelson still lingers. A penniless man who slept under a bridge had enriched my life. What wonderful experiences we can have if we're willing to explore Robert Frost's "road less traveled"!

Opportunities for adventure await us at every turn of life's road, but will appear only once we've learned to drive fear of the unknown from our minds. We must be courageous and open-minded enough to move beyond what is comfortable to us. "A hundred thousand miracles are happening every day, and those who say they don't agree, are those who neither hear nor see."*

Power Performers understand that if you act as if exciting things will happen to you, they will. As a Power Performer, many new and exhilarating opportunities will come your way. Don't let the fear of the unknown conquer your desire to expand your world. Use serendipity to make your life an exciting adventure.

THE KEY TO MAKING YOUR LIFE AN ADVENTURE

You may be thinking this is all too much like Pollyanna for you. You may be thinking, "Roger, it's been too long since you had a real

---

*Oscar Hammerstein, *Flower Drum Song.*

job. I can't be taking off for trips around the world. I'm having a big enough struggle just getting by from one day to the next. I have a sick husband and a child who's flunking high school to worry about." To which I would reply, "I got to you just in time."

People who are obsessed with what's going on in their life are making a fundamental philosophical error. It's a very easy trap in which to fall, and I did it for years before I finally figured out the misery it was causing me. If you want to be an adventurer, if you want to be someone who's getting the most from life, you have to stop thinking that good and bad things happen to you. Good things don't happen to you. Bad things don't happen to you. Life is what happens to you. The more you examine the events in your life and categorize them into good things and bad things, the more messed up you're going to become.

> *Some mornings it just doesn't seem worth it to gnaw through the leather straps.*
>
> EMO PHILIPS

I no longer believe that you should try to avoid having bad experiences. A mother says to her daughter, "Don't get too involved with him, dear. He'll only break your heart." What's wrong with a broken heart? Having your heart broken is one of the most exquisite experiences that life has to offer. Look how much fun and excitement her daughter is going to miss if she decides to tiptoe through life trying to avoid having her heart broken.

Recently, S. L. Potter bungee-jumped from a 210-foot tower in California. That's unusual only because he was 100 years old. His children, who are 68 and 74, were there to watch him. He said, "I told them, 'If I die, I die.' I told everybody to bring a shovel and a mop, just in case." That's the spirit, Mr. Potter!

You'll really miss a lot from life if you cocoon yourself from the so-called "bad" things of life. As Gustave Flaubert once remarked, "That man has missed something who has never stumbled out of a brothel at sunrise feeling like throwing himself in the river out of pure disgust."

The point is that your world exists anyway only through your perception. When I was young a Buddhist monk in Sri Lanka recited a little verse to me. I have long forgotten the words he used, but the message has affected my life. He said, "I used to curse the flies in my little jar of ointment. Then I met Buddha [by which he meant discovered the truth]. Now I bless the ointment in my little jar of flies."

Once I went scuba diving in St. Thomas. I was on what I thought was one of the most beautiful beaches in the world. It was picture-postcard perfect with a line of palm trees that followed the crescent shaped beach out to the headland. The sand was soft, the water was blue, and I planned to dive around the coral reef at the entrance to the bay. I started talking to an attractive woman who was also in our diving group. "How are you doing?" I smiled at her.

"I'm having a miserable time," she told me.

"I'm sorry I asked. What's the problem?"

"I came here on a cruise ship, and it was the most miserable experience I've ever had in my life. The food was awful, my cabin's a broom closet, and the people are boring. I'm thinking of flying back."

"That's a shame," I told her. "You should have been on my cruise ship. The food's great and everybody is having the time of their lives."

She perked up, and said, "That sounds great. Which ship are you on?"

"The *Carnival*."

Then she got angry because she thought I was making fun of her. "I'm on the *Carnival* too," she spat out.

We swam out to the reef, and the incredible variety of tropical fish fascinated me. Our guide gave us plastic bags of dog food and we fed them by hand to the fish. It was a marvelous experience. Suddenly the woman who was so miserable started thrashing around and pushed up to the surface. I followed her to see what the problem was. "I've burst my eardrums," she was screaming.

"We were only ten feet below the surface," I told her. "You can't damage your ears at that depth."

"Well I did, and I'm going to find a doctor. I can't wait to get out of this miserable place." As I said, paradise is only a perception anyway. She reminded me of something that I once saw scrawled on a wall: "Fifty thousand lemmings can't be wrong."

Remember I was telling you about the children visiting Disneyland for the first time? Just as not everything is life is pleasant or the way we want it to be, so there were unpleasant things for them to cope with—the scary rides, the rain, the lines at the attractions. However, they took it all in as a wonderful experience. But what if you took them back to Disneyland every day for a week? How would they react? Probably they would do what we all tend to do. They would develop a list of likes and dislikes. They would have favorite rides and rides that wouldn't interest them anymore. In that way they would gradually drain away their excitement for the experience, and by the following week the thrill would be gone. Don't do that with your life. Quit evaluating every experience that happens to you and thinking, "I like this," or "I hated that." Good things don't happen to you. Bad things don't happen to you. *Life is what happens to you.* The more you examine the events in your life and categorize them into good things and bad things, the more messed up you're going to become.

Grow up and realize that so-called "bad things" are going to happen to you. Only rarely have I met people who told me that nothing really bad had ever happened to him or her, and I'm skeptical about them. Just about everybody, once you get to know them well enough, has had to face some awful things. Sixty percent of the people in this country are close to someone with serious mental illness, for example. Twenty-five percent of all women were sexually abused when they were girls, usually by their father or stepfather. Everybody has had their heart broken by a lover or a child. The majority of people will go through at least one divorce. Almost all people have to face the death of their parents. These things happen to everybody. They have happened and will happen to you. The good news is that you get to choose your reaction to them. You can let them devastate you, or you can react like an adventurer and say, "Isn't that fascinating? I didn't know it was possible to feel so much pain. Now I feel as though I've been punched in the stomach, even though I know it's only my emotions that are hurting. And I feel so depressed! I wonder how long that will last?"

The next time something "bad" happens to you, try relishing the experience. Don't ignore it—that would be foolish. Instead realize that you will see the "bad" things that happen to you as some of the most exquisite events in your life experience. Because only your reaction makes things good or bad. Good things don't happen to you. Bad things don't happen to you. *Life is what happens to you.* The more you examine the events in your life and categorize them into good things and bad things, the more messed up you're going to become.

When you believe that, it leads to a remarkable state of mind. You come to understand that joy is not the opposite of sadness, and triumph is not the opposite of defeat, and success is not the opposite of failure. They are really contained within each other, like a pearl hidden inside an oyster.

> *Joy is conceived of sadness.*
>
> *Triumph is born of defeat.*
>
> *Success is a child of failure.*

ADVENTURERS ARE NOT CRUSADERS

Where do Power Performers get all that energy they have to do all these exciting things? One big reason they have high energy is that they don't waste it complaining about the way things are. You won't find them walking picket lines or rallying to protest the acts of a remote foreign government. People with a sense of adventure have no constituency—they have no desire to convert others to their way of life. Nor are they great social reformers, for the simple reason that they see little wrong with the world.

So you'll find Power Performers in the yacht harbors of Tahiti and New Zealand, not just in corporate boardrooms. These people know the importance of taking a break from the power and glory of corporate life to realize the unique satisfaction of a dream come true. They approach whatever they're doing with the same gusto, the same drive to succeed.

Above all, they have an incredible fascination for, curiosity about, and love of the life God gave them. They see themselves as citizens of the world, who can enjoy the company of other people from all political, religious, and philosophical backgrounds without feeling any obligation to persuade them to change. They live in a world of fascination and understanding. They have a zest for living that transcends the ordinary lifestyle, and they derive an uncommon joy from the privilege of being alive.

◆◆◆

The First Secret of Power Performers is:
They have learned to make life an adventure

◆◆◆

2

POWER PERFORMERS TAKE CHARGE OF THEIR LIVES

We are ourselves responsible for the good and the ill that is said of us.

— Phillip II of Macedonia
to his son Alexander the Great

The price of greatness is responsibility.

— Winston Churchill

The buck stops here.

— Harry Truman

Beware of the three impostors who claim to control your life.

— Roger Dawson

The Second Secret of Power Performers, is that they have taken charge of their lives. You release an incredible amount of energy when you accept that you are the only person responsible for your success. Low achievers always think that external forces are controlling their lives. They are always looking for a savior or looking for an excuse. The same life forces batter Power Performers but they know that nothing out there can stop them from getting where they want to go.

THE THREE IMPOSTERS

There are three impostors who eventually show up in your life and claim that they control your future. Be aware of each of them, wait for them to show up, and then expose them for what they are— harmless impostors who have no right to influence you.

Let's take a look at each of these impostors separately:

IMPOSTOR NUMBER ONE: CIRCUMSTANCES

First realize that you can't reach your full potential if you think circumstances control your life. Some people spend their entire lives thinking that they are where they are because of circumstances. You are not where you are because of where you were born or who your parents were. As George Bernard Shaw wrote in his play *Mrs. Warren's Profession,* "The people who get on in this world are the people who get up and look for the circumstances they want, and, if they can't find them, make them."

The low performer says, "I was born in the ghetto. Down there it's an achievement just to stay alive and out of jail." The Power Performer says, "Yes, I was born in the ghetto, but I don't have to let that control my life. The street outside leads to a highway, and the highway can take me out of the ghetto. Even if I have to crawl every inch of the way, I'm leaving, and I'm never coming back."

The low performer says, "My parents are Mexican farm laborers who can't even read and write. When I was young we moved from ranch to ranch looking for work. Because they kept me out of school I can't speak or write English well. You can't expect me to accomplish much." The Power Performer says, "All of that is true, but I will not let my past control my future. I will have to work harder than anyone I've ever met, but I can catch up on my education. I can be somebody."

The low performer says, "I have never been very smart. I got behind in grade school and never caught up. In high school I smoked pot and was lucky even to graduate. With a start like that you can't expect much." The Power Performer says, "Maybe I'm not so smart, but I'll make up for it by working harder and trying harder. Then if I need brains I'll be able to hire people to do the thinking for me."

So Power Performers develop a stubborn refusal to let their circumstances affect their future. As Robert Schuller, the pastor at the Crystal Cathedral in Garden Grove, California, says in his *Possibility Thinkers Creed*: "When faced with a mountain, I will not quit! I will keep on striving until I climb over, find a pass through, tunnel underneath or simply stay and turn the mountain into a gold mine, with God's help."

During my childhood in England, one of the most popular books around was *The Jungle Is Neutral,* by Fred Spencer. Spencer was a soldier in World War II, stationed in a small garrison on the island of Singapore, just off the tip of the Malay Peninsula. There, facing the crossroads of world shipping at the junction of the Indian Ocean and the South China Sea, lay the outpost's only defense.

The defense of this garrison was virtually one-sided, as the British were sure that no army could pass through the impenetrable jungles to the north and that any attack on Singapore would have to come from the sea. It was a peculiar fact of the war that Winston Churchill did not know this. He attempted to stop the Japanese as they advanced down the peninsula but always assumed that if they failed to stop them in the jungles the island of Singapore could hold out for months. It was not until January 19, 1942, that he learned that, apart from destroying the causeway onto the island, there was little his troops could do to stop the Japanese. As he wrote in his memoirs, "I ought to have known. My advisers ought to have known and I ought to have been told, and I ought to have asked. The reason I had not asked about this matter, amid the thousands of questions I put, was that the possibility of Singapore having no landward defenses no more entered into my mind than that of a battleship being launched without a bottom."

> *I never got indigestion eating my own words.*
>
>   WINSTON CHURCHILL

On February 15, less than a month after Churchill found that they could not defend the island, the Japanese reached Singapore. By that time the British had only a few days' food, less than a day's water, and very little ammunition. The Japanese demanded and received an unconditional surrender. Singapore fell without a fight.

Spencer escaped and spent nine months in the jungle before he was able to rejoin his countrymen. In the garrison, living on the edge of the jungle, the only things Spencer had learned about the jungle were the rumors he'd heard from others, and they were conflicting reports.

He'd heard the jungle was a horrible place filled with snakes and insects, fruit so poisonous that one bite would kill, and brutal wild animals. So any man lost in the jungle would die very quickly. The other story they told Spencer was that the jungle was a lush, tropical paradise with plenty of fresh water and edible fruit—in other words it was a place where anyone could live with relative ease.

The truth Spencer discovered during his nine months in the jungle and used as the title of his book was that *The Jungle Is Neutral*. Spencer found the jungle was neither attempting to destroy him, nor was the jungle going to support him. He learned that his survival in the jungle depended directly and proportionately on the amount of effort he put forth to survive. For Fred Spencer, the jungle was neutral. Spencer was able to make of his environment whatever he chose.

I'm not saying life is a jungle—far from it. However, the parallel is obvious. Life itself is neither out to destroy you nor to support you. Life is neutral, so it will return its joys and rewards to you in proportion to the effort you put forth.

So first we learn that circumstances don't affect our performance. Our environment is neutral, neither working for nor against us.

THE SECOND IMPOSTOR: OTHER PEOPLE

The second great impostor is the thought that you are where you are because of what other people have done to you. You can't become a Power Performer without the help of other people—you can't go it alone. However, if you think that other people are responsible for your success or failure, you will never be a Power Performer.

The low performer says, "I have sick parents (or a sick child or spouse) for whom I must care. I don't have the options that other people have." The Power Performer says, "I can give that person the care they need without becoming so obsessive about it that it ruins my life."

The low performer says, "My boss thinks I'm an idiot, so there's no way I'm going to get ahead in this company." The Power Performer thinks, "Bosses come and go. Some of them like me and some of them don't. I'm not going to let that affect my performance. Anyway, if I can't make it here, this isn't the only ball game in town so I'll find a place where they will let me develop my skills. It's what you can do that gets you to the top, not who likes you."

The low performer says, "I'm trapped in a marriage that only torments me. How can I think about performance when negative emotions are draining away all my energy?" The Power Performer thinks, "The price I'm paying to be in this marriage is far too high. Whatever it takes, I will find a way out of it."

There is a line in the musical *Annie* that always gets a round of applause. The plot revolves around a ruthless billionaire (modeled after Bernard Baruch) who owns the world but has no love in his life. He invites an orphan to spend Christmas with him, as an overt public relations gesture. She stays to melt his heart and teach him that love is the most important thing in life. The line comes before the point when Orphan Annie teaches Daddy Warbucks that he must care about people. Daddy Warbucks says, "I never saw any reason to be nice to the people on the way up, because I have no intention of going back down." The audience always appreciates the audacity of the line, but it's not smart thinking. You do need other people. However, Power Performers know that you can't reach your full potential if you let other people control your life. Instead, Power Performers accept that they must learn the skills needed to be able to control the other people. I teach those skills in my cassette-tape program *Secrets of Power Negotiating* (Nightingale-Conant) and my book *Secrets of Power Persuasion* (Prentice Hall, 1992). With those people skills you don't have to worry about people stopping you from getting what you want. You'll also know how to convert them to your way of thinking, regardless of the circumstances.

Let me briefly cover the eight things that give you power over other people:

1. *Legitimate power.* Titles influence people. If you have a title, use it. Get it on your business card, your letters, and the name plate on your desk. When I was president of a large real estate company, I would let anybody who was "farming" an area put "Area Manager" on their business cards. (Farming means that they have staked out an area of 500 homes, and they are calling on those home owners consistently to establish themselves as an expert in that area.) They told me that it was amazing how the response of the homeowners changed once they saw a title on the business card.

Professional designations are another form of legitimate power. If you can put letters after your name it helps. So if you don't have any professional designations, go get some.

Another form of title power is positioning in the marketplace. If you can claim that you are the biggest, the oldest, the best, or simply that you try harder (as Avis rental cars did), do so, because this type of legitimate power influences people.

Use title power but don't be intimidated by it. Some of these titles don't mean a thing. My daughter used to be a stockbroker in Beverly Hills, in an office that had 35 vice-presidents. A. L. Williams is the founder of the A. L. Williams life insurance company, a multilevel operation that encourages people to convert their whole-life insurance to term insurance. He proudly brags in his book *All You Can Do Is All You Can Do* that he appoints 100 vice presidents a month. If he made it a policy just to shake hands with every new vice president, that alone would be a full-time job.

Be particularly wary of title power when you're dealing with bankers. Bankers love titles. You can be talking to a vice president of a bank and he or she may have the power only to say no to you, not yes.

2. *Reward power.* You have power over people if you can reward them. Instead of thinking of things that you want them to give you, look for things that you can give them because when you give people what they want, they'll give you what you want. That's why it's so important to talk benefits rather than features, when you're trying to persuade someone. Don't assume that the person understands how the feature will reward them. "This car has dual air bags" describes a feature. "The passenger's air bag could save the life of a loved one in the event of a crash," is the benefit. "This coffee pot is pure silver," is a feature. "It will keep coffee warmer, and your friends will admire your good taste," are benefits.

Conversely, don't be intimidated because you think the other person can reward you. If you think of your customers as rewarding you because they decide to do business with you, you have given them the power to intimidate you. You should be thinking that your product or service is so right for them that you will be rewarding them by making it available to them.

3. *Coercive power.* If they think you can punish them, you can influence them. Subtly make them believe that unless they team up with you, they'll be losing out. That's where legitimate power comes in. If you have convinced them that you are the biggest, the best, the oldest, the most experienced, or simply have the best solution for their problem, their going with your competition would end up punishing them. So many salespeople lose out because they don't include coercive power in their presentation. They tell the customer all the good things that will happen to them if they make a decision today. They don't tell them the bad things. What happens if they don't say yes today? Will they still be able to get the same deal tomorrow, next week, or next month?

4. *Reverent power.* If people look up to you, you can persuade them, and it's the strongest influencing factor of all. People look up to you if they see you as having a consistent set of values—then they want you to lead them. The easiest way to see this is to look

at past U.S. Presidents, because their performance is so familiar to us. John F. Kennedy had reverent power. When he talked about the mantle of power passing to a new generation born in this century, and when he described his presidency as the new frontier, he was projecting an idealistic set of values. Jimmy Carter did not do it well. He was one of the hardest working Presidents we have ever had, and certainly one of the most intelligent—he majored in nuclear physics. He lost the ability to influence people, however, because he appeared to vacillate. You never quite knew if he felt strongly enough about something to hang in if the going got tough. Take his handling of the visa for the shah of Iran, who was in exile in Acapulco and wanted to come to New York for medical treatment. He needed the courtesy of a visa to get into the country but at first Carter balked because he knew the problems it would cause in Iran, which was hostile enough toward Americans as it was. However, the Shah persisted and Carter issued the visa. All hell broke loose in Iran when they heard about it. They took the hostages in the embassy and Carter's nightmare began. He immediately changed his mind again about the Shah being in the country, and asked him to move to Panama to take the pressure off the situation. I don't think Ronald Reagan would have done that. He would have made a decision one way or the other and would have stuck with it because he understood the power of a consistent set of values. Contrast Carter's handling of the Shah's visa with Reagan's handling of the Yasser Arafat visa. The United Nations invited the head of the PLO to address the General Assembly in New York. All he needed was the courtesy of a visa to get into the country. Reagan said, "Sorry, we've not issuing visas to terrorists this year." The General Assembly decided by a vote of 150 to 2 to move their meeting to Geneva to circumvent this decision, with the only two dissenting votes being Israel and the United States. Wouldn't you think if you got voted down 150 to 2 you would think that perhaps you went too far and would back off? No! You make a decision and stick with it, because that projects reverent power.

5. *Charismatic power.* If people like you, you can influence them. In *Secrets of Power Persuasion*, I tell you how to develop a sense of humor and how to remember names. Also I teach you that charisma is a matter of expanding your sense of self to embrace all the people with whom you come in contact.

6. *Expertise power.* If they see you as having an expertise they don't have, it will draw them to you. Attorneys develop a whole new language to convince you that they know something you don't. Surgeons can persuade you to have an operation if they can convince you they know more about it than you do. This can, however, also be very intimidating when it's used on you.

7. *Situation power.* Think of the clerks at the post office. They may be powerless in any other area of their life, but if they can accept or reject your package, they have power over you. It's the people at the building department who have to stamp your plans before you can go and build a new house. While they have the stamp in their hands they have power over you, and don't they love to use it.

8. *Information power.* The human race has an incredible desire to know what's going on—we can't stand a mystery. You can put a cow in a field and it will stay in that field all its life and never wonder what's on the other side of the hill. We will spend a billion and a half dollars to put a Hubbell telescope up in space, because we just have to know what's going on. Once you understand how powerful this need is, you'll understand why you can control other people by knowing something that they don't.

That's just the barest primer on what influences other people. All I'm doing here is making the point that there's no need to let other people influence you unless you choose to, because you have the power to influence them.

Every unsuccessful person I've met has been blaming other people for their circumstances. Quit blaming other people for what's going on in your life and start taking responsibility. I believe that it doesn't matter how many times you fail, you are never a failure until you start to blame other people. Blaming other people is an escape mechanism. Under pressure, some people escape with alcohol, others become workaholics, and others escape the problem by making the excuse of blaming it on somebody else. George Washington Carver made an interesting point about this when he said, "Ninety-nine percent of the failures come from people who have the habit of making excuses." It makes you wonder which comes first, the failure or the excuse. It's true that failures are always making excuses, but isn't it also true that people who know they can make excuses are far more likely to fail?

> *Responsibility is the thing people dread most of all.*
> *Yet it is the one thing in the world that develops*
> *us, that gives us fiber .*
>
> FRANK CRANE

I once counseled a young man who had worked at 35 different jobs in the eight years since he'd left high school. I had him list each of the jobs and the reason he left. In 32 cases he left because the boss was an idiot. Isn't that a remarkable coincidence? There are probably only about 40 complete idiots running businesses in the country, and he'd already worked for 32 of them. I told him that the price he must pay for the things he wanted out of life was that he must accept responsibility for what happens and quit blaming other people.

THE THIRD IMPOSTOR: WHAT HAPPENS TO US

The third great impostor tries to tell you that events control your future. You can't reach your full potential if you think what happens to you controls your life. Power Performers know it's not what happens to you that affects performance. How you react to what happens to you is the only thing that makes a difference. As the great World War II admiral William F. Halsey said, "There aren't any great men. There are just great challenges that ordinary men like you and me are forced by circumstances to meet." So accept that events—the things that happen to you—don't control your achievements either.

The low performer says, "The company that I've worked for since I left college went bankrupt and I was out of a job. I don't have the skills that I need to get another good job in today's high-technology world. What am I going to do?" The Power Performer says, "I was a fool to think that the company was giving me a job. I should have realized that they were buying my skills. Now I'm going to develop skills that I can market to a hundred different companies if I have to."

The low performer says, "I'm on disability. Nobody's going to hire me with my poor health. I'll just cash my checks and muddle through." The Power Performer says, "Franklin Roosevelt was disabled, and so was Helen Keller. If they could make something of their lives, so can I."

The low performer says, "My father was killed in an automobile accident, and I had to drop out of college to take care of my family. Now I'll never get a top job." The Power Performer thinks, "Sure it changed my plans, but many people are successful without a college education. It's not going to stop me."

As Winston Churchill said, "Responsibility is the price of greatness."

That's why Power Performers are able to bounce back so quickly from misfortune. In July 1978 Lee Iacocca was on top of the world. From his huge presidential suite in Dearborn, Michigan, he had just led Ford through two record years during which the company had earned over three and a half billion dollars. He had been president for eight years and a Ford employee for 32 years, ever since he left college. One day Henry Ford called him to his office and fired him. When Iacocca pressed him to tell him why he was doing this when the company was doing so well, Ford only managed to mumble, "Well, sometimes you just don't like someone." The next day Iacocca was working out of a tiny transition office in a warehouse. Lee Iacocca didn't stay defeated very long by the ruthless way Henry Ford fired him. He understood that neither Ford, nor anybody else, was running his life. Within two weeks he got control of Chrysler and turned his greatest misfortune into his greatest opportunity.

> *Success isn't permanent, and failure isn't fatal.*
>
> MIKE DITKA

Art Linkletter had everything going for him, wealth in the hundreds of millions of dollars and he was as popular as anybody could be when his daughter Diane died while under the influence of drugs. It entitled him to spend the rest of his life bemoaning that tragic event, but instead he used it as a catalyst to make an impact on the drug problem in this country.

Or take the case of two young actors by the name of Burt Reynolds and Clint Eastwood. In the 1950s they were both fired on the same day by Universal Studios, which told them they couldn't act. Besides that, nobody would want to watch Clint Eastwood because his Adam's apple was too big. They thought Burt Reynolds was so ugly that they wouldn't let him play the romantic lead. In his first two movie roles he was cast as a rapist. The final blow came when the two actors walked out to their cars to leave the lot for the last time and the studio had already painted over the names on their parking spaces. All three television networks canceled Burt Reynolds: NBC sank *Riverboat*; ABC shot down *Hawk*; and CBS axed *Dan August*. However, they both kept on doing what they were doing—because they knew it's not what happens to you that makes the difference in your performance, it's how you react to what happens to you.

THE THREE GREAT IMPOSTORS
WHO CLAIM THEY CONTROL YOUR FUTURE:

Circumstances.

Other people.

Events.

Develop the stubborn refusal of the Power Performers to believe these three impostors. Know that circumstances, other people, or even what happens to you does not affect your level of achievement. Look at the great people who have triumphed because of this attitude:

◆ *Helen Keller* Suffered a severe illness that took away her sight and hearing when she was nineteen months old. Because of this she grew up unable to speak intelligibly. When she was six, her parents turned in desperation to Alexander Graham Bell, who helped to provide a tutor, Anne Sullivan—the *Miracle Worker*, as she became known when a Broadway play of that name made her famous. Sullivan was 20 years old and partially recovered from being blinded herself. She taught Helen the names of objects by pressing the manual alphabet into the palm of her hand. She taught Helen to speak by pressing Helen's fingers into her larynx so that she could "hear" the vibrations. She taught her to read and write in Braille and to excel in normal school work.

Seventeen years later Helen Keller graduated cum laude from Radcliffe College in Cambridge, Massachusetts. She went on to devote her life to touring the world giving speeches (using a translator, because it was still hard to understand her), promoting the idea that deaf and blind people can triumph over adversity. Her insight was far more than that of a handicapped person sharing her experience, far more than that she was sharing her insights and her intellect, for example: "Security is mostly a superstition. It does not exist in nature, nor do the children of men as a whole experience it. Avoiding danger is no safer in the long run than outright exposure. Life is either a daring adventure, or nothing." She became an inspiration for millions by demonstrating that triumph lay within the despair of her handicap.

◆ *Franklin Roosevelt* was born to a very wealthy family but became a lifelong champion of the poor. A shy young man, he was encouraged to pursue a career in politics by his admiration for his distant cousin Teddy Roosevelt, whose niece, Eleanor Roosevelt, he married. After a brilliant term as a New York state senator, he came down with typhoid fever and was unable to campaign for a second term, but won without making a single campaign appearance. After completing the second term, Woodrow Wilson rewarded his support with an appointment to assistant secretary of the navy. In 1920 Roosevelt was the Democratic vice-presidential candidate, but lost in the Warren Harding landslide. The following year, while vacationing at Campobello Island in Canada, polio struck him down and for a long time almost completely paralyzed him. His wealthy mother urged him to retire to Hyde Park, but his wife, with advice such as, "Nobody can make you feel inferior without your consent," urged him to stay in politics. She thought it would be good for his morale. It turned out to be good for the morale of the world.

When he ran for governor of New York in 1928 his opponents said he wasn't strong enough to serve because he couldn't walk without braces and assistance. He countered that by waging the most vigorous and tireless campaign the voters had ever seen. He won, even though the Democratic presidential candidate, Al

Smith, the former governor of New York, didn't even carry his own state. Roosevelt inspired countless future generations by overcoming his handicap to become one of our most effective Presidents.

◆ *Abraham Lincoln* has an incredible trail of misfortunes leading up to his eventual election to the presidency. He has inspired every politician since. His succession of failures included being fired from his job, having his business go broke, and being defeated for the legislature, for state speaker, for Congress, for reelection to Congress, for the Senate, for vice-president, and for the senate again. His baby brother died, his sweetheart died and caused his nervous breakdown, three of his four sons died, and his assassination caused his wife to go insane. (And you think you have insurmountable problems?)

◆ *Winston Churchill* is dear to the hearts of the English, not only because of his remarkable role in World War II but also because of his ability to come back from misfortune. He was born into the aristocracy of England and could have spent his life as a rich playboy, but he loved life too much for that. Everything should have been easy for him, but instead he ran into problems every inch of the way. His failures gave birth to his greatness. He attended Harrow Prep School near London and had to repeat the eighth grade three years in a row because he couldn't grasp English. He said later, "By being so long in the lowest form, I gained an immense advantage over the cleverer boys.... I got into my bones the essential structure of the normal British sentence."

His superb grasp of the English language led to a job as a correspondent for the London *Times*. When he was a journalist in the Boer War the enemy captured him, but he escaped. The story of his unfortunate capture made him so popular in England that he could run for and win a seat in the House of Commons.

As First Lord of the Admiralty during World War I, his first major offensive, the Dardanelles Campaign, was a disaster. Thousands of British troops died, and he resigned. However, he saw this misfortune only as a learning experience and went on to become a masterful war strategist. When Churchill finally got the opportunity to lead his country, it was during a wartime government and the King appointed him, instead of the people electing him as he'd have preferred. Within weeks of his taking on the defense of the British Empire, he was faced with the disaster of Dunkirk. The Germans had Blitzkrieged their way down through Holland and Belgium, then routed the French army. The British Army came close to being destroyed on the beach at Dunkirk. Only the miracle of a mirrorlike calm sea that enabled thousands of small pleasure craft to evacuate the troops avoided a total disaster. Churchill's reaction was to tell his cabinet: "Gentlemen, quite frankly, I find it exhilarating: with France falling to the Germans, we stand alone."

September 15, 1940, was the turning point in the war. "A Sunday," he recalled in his memoirs, "like the battle of Waterloo. The odds were great; our margins small; the stake infinite. I drove over to Uxbridge, and was taken down to the bomb-proof Operations Room, 50 feet under the ground. Red bulbs under the huge wall map told me that all of our squadrons were already in the air. I became conscious of the anxiety of the commander Air Vice-Marshall Park. 'What other reserves have we?' I asked him. 'There are none,' he told me."

Thousands of the Luftwaffe were in the air, softening up the country for the imminent invasion of the German Army across the 25-mile wide English Channel. And every British plane that could get off the ground, and every pilot who could fly was already up in the air.

However, even in the face of this disastrous situation, Churchill still refused to believe that circumstances were out of his control. For this was the man who had assured his people, "If the British Empire shall last for a thousand years, men will still say: 'This was their finest hour!'"

In October 1941, at the height of the war, Harrow School invited him to return and speak to the young students. How eager they must have been as they waited with pencils poised. The greatest Englishman of all time was to talk to them and share the wisdom he'd gathered over an extraordinary lifetime. Until that time, almost every other prime minister of the country had attended Harrow, on his way to Oxford or Cambridge universities. Churchill knew now that the British Empire would not last for a thousand years, but he must surely have felt the future of the nation would one day be in the hands of one of these young men, so he must have chosen his words carefully.

He stood up and looked out at the boys for a long, long time before he finally spoke. He must have been searching through the decades of memories to find just the right words for these future leaders. Finally he gave his entire speech in just a few words, "Never give in, never give in, *never, never, never, never*—in nothing, great or small, large or petty—never give in except to convictions of honor and good sense." Then he sat down.

England never gave in, and by 1945 the war was over and Churchill, the triumphant warrior, ran for prime minister. With all he'd done for the British people, it should have been a virtual coronation, but Clement Atlee and the Socialist Party beat him soundly. Although Churchill was now in his seventies, he refused to see this as a defeat. Six years later he led the Tory party to victory, finally becoming the elected prime minister.

The common thread in all of his experiences, was the belief that within each setback was contained the seed of triumph.

The next time you're in London, be sure you go to the underground war museum that was Churchill's headquarters throughout the war years. It's only a few hundred yards from the Houses of Parliament and an unbelievably fascinating place, left just the way it was over 40 years ago. I asked the curator why they didn't open it to the public until 1984. With classic English understatement he told me, "To tell you the truth, Sir, we didn't think anyone would be that interested!"

> *I am ready to meet my maker, but whether my maker is prepared for the great ordeal of meeting me is another matter.*
>
> WINSTON CHURCHILL

When we look at these heroes and their incredible tenacity, their almost unbelievable ability to plow through misfortune, it's easy to assume they must have an almost masochistic ability to survive unpleasant experiences. However, Power Performers don't see it that way. Power Performers see it as a stubborn refusal to believe any of the three impostors. Nothing shakes their belief that they, and not fate or circumstance or anyone else, are in control of their lives.

Accept that you are totally, absolutely, 100 percent, responsible for what's going on in your life—for where you've been, for where you are, and for where you're going.

Look out for the three great impostors who show up on your doorstep and proudly brag that they control your future. They are lying to you! None of them affects your performance! Only *you* control what happens to you.

1. Circumstances do not affect your performance.
2. Other people cannot affect your performance.
3. Events do not affect your performance.

◆◆◆

The Second Secret of Power Performers is:

They take charge of their lives.

◆◆◆

In the next chapter I'll teach you the most important word in the English language, and why it's so critical to Power Performers.

3

POWER PERFORMERS KNOW THAT THEY ALWAYS HAVE CHOICES

When you have to make a choice and don't make it, that in itself is a choice.

— *William James*

Nothing is really work unless you would rather be doing something else.

— *James Matthew Barrie*

Destiny is no matter of chance. It is a matter of choice: It is not a thing to be waited for, it is a thing to be achieved.

— *William Jennings Bryan*

The key to Power Performance is not working hard but loving what you do so much you'd rather be doing it than doing anything else.

— *Roger Dawson*

There is one word that is the cornerstone of Power Performance. I think it's the most important word in the English language. That word is *choice.*

I'm sure you've seen bumper stickers or license-plate frames that say, "I'd rather be skiing," "I'd rather be sailing," or "I'd rather be fishing," haven't you? What's your reaction when you see something like that on the back of the car ahead of you? Here's mine: "If you'd rather be fishing, then I wish you'd just go do it. I'd get where I'm going a lot faster, and I wouldn't be faced with your frustrations."

Of course, those little sayings aren't true. Power Performers understand the person who loves to ski, for example, but hates her work and especially her morning commute, has nonetheless made a conscious decision that she'd rather be on that crowded freeway than somewhere up in the mountains skiing. The person who proudly proclaims that he'd "rather be fishing," may be a proud advocate of his sport, but the truth is that he would really rather be on that freeway. You cannot be anywhere other than where you choose to be. Wherever you are, whatever you're doing is what you prefer to be doing. It may take some time for me to convince you of that, but once you believe you will have enhanced your life forever.

YOU'RE ALREADY DOING WHAT YOU'D RATHER BE DOING

Wait a minute, you say, the consequences of that person taking time off to go skiing or fishing when he or she should be working might be too great to be acceptable. Well, let's take a worst case basis. Let's consider John, who is a hopeless ski bum. He wangled his way into the University of Colorado at Boulder to be close to the mountains. He dropped out in December of his sophomore year, however, and spent the next five years waiting on tables at the Crystal Palace restaurant in Aspen so that he could spend his days skiing. He enjoyed the fun atmosphere in the restaurant, and when they invited him to participate in the show that the waiters and waitresses put on for the customers, he eagerly agreed and poured a lot of energy into his performances. He even found that he had a reasonably good singing voice. For a while he wondered if he'd be good enough to make a living singing and took a few voice lessons from Susan, a retired Broadway singer who lived just out of town. Susan thought John had potential but doubted that he'd have enough dedication to stick with it. She warned John that there were thousands of people out there with good voices but who were never able to make their living performing. Susan told John that if he wanted to make it as a singer, he would have to dedicate himself 100 percent to the profession and work harder at it than he'd ever thought of working before. As Susan had expected, John quickly dropped the idea.

> *Consider the postage stamp, my son. It secures success through its ability to stick to one thing till it gets there.*
>
> JOSH BILLINGS

Then one night a group of young women took a table at the Crystal Palace and when John sang his big number, "Somewhere out there..." he made a point of singing it to them to the delight of the other customers. They were all well dressed and attractive, but one appealed to him more than any of the others. She was slim and had her long blond hair tied into a ponytail. As he finished his number all the girls gave him a standing ovation and playfully tucked dollar bills into his uniform. On his way home John stopped at the Embers for a drink and he ran into the girl with the ponytail as she hung up the telephone in the entryway. He asked her to have a drink with him and she invited him to join her friends at a table by the fireplace. Her name was Judy, her father owned an oil company in Houston, and she was spending the week at her family's Snowmass condominium with a group of her sorority sisters. That night he rode with her to Snowmass to see her home, even though it meant he would have to hitch a ride back. They skied together for the following three days, and John thought he had never seen anything so beautiful as Judy gracefully gliding down the slopes ahead of him with her ponytail flying in the breeze and her slim hips rhythmically moving from side to side. At the end of the week her girl friends left, but Judy told them she was going to stay another week and John quietly moved into her family's condo.

They fell in love, married, and had two children, and now he works at a plant in Denver that assembles computer components.

He's on his way to work, driving out highway 287, with his "I'd rather be skiing," sticker on the back of his Toyota, listening to the ski reports on the radio. Six inches of new snow have fallen in the mountains, and the skiing is the best it's been all year. John is aching to go skiing but he's played hooky from work so many times that if he does it one more time he'll get fired. With his work record, he'll be lucky to get a job bagging groceries in a supermarket. Judy, whose father has been begging her to dump the turkey ever since they first met, will call it the last straw and take the kids on the next plane back to Houston. John is broke. He could put the lift ticket on his over-limit MasterCard, but if he does the bank will probably pull his card and ruin his credit.

Are you ready for the question? Here it is. Should John go skiing, or should he go to work? Probably you answered "go to work," right? You're sure that it's the only sane choice for John to make. Under the circumstances he has to go to work, you're thinking.

No, he doesn't *have to* go to work. Nobody *has* to do anything. Suppose that John is an adventurer, someone who understands that life is a one-time occurrence, that every day should be full of passion and excitement, that any one day is just too valuable to spend doing something you don't want to do? Then should he go to work?

Yes! However, the difference is that he goes to work because he chooses to go to work, not because he has to. He's evaluated his possible alternatives and has made a decision. The decision is that, all things considered, he'd rather be on that freeway going to work than anywhere else in the world. If he would just accept that fact, then most of his frustration would go away. He would find new joy in his work, because it is what he has chosen to do, rather than something he has to do. James Matthew Barrie said, "Nothing is really work unless you would rather be doing something else." By making work what he has chosen to do, John blurs the line between work and play. That's why it's so hard to tell whether Power Performers are working or playing. Because they choose to work rather than feel they have to, work becomes fun. That's why they're able to give everything they have to everything they do.

YOU DON'T HAVE TO GRIND IT OUT

Most people think that to get anywhere in life you have to grind away. Ray Kroc, the founder of McDonald's, called his autobiography *Grinding It Out*. His philosophy was that you have to outwork the other guy. You have to keep grinding it out, even when you're drop-dead tired and bored to death with the monotony. Let me tell you something: as much as I admired what Kroc did for McDonald's, it doesn't work for everybody. Nobody worked harder than my father, who quit school and went to work at 14 as a plumber's mate. His father was a heavy drinker, and he wanted to do that to support his mother. He drove a London taxi for most of his life, and I remember spending a day with him when I was about seven years old. His work was a constant battle against the traffic, the terrible London weather and air pollution (in those days—they've cleaned it up since), and the heavy competition from the thousands of other cabs. In those days the taxi driver had a roof over his head and a windshield in front of him, but apart from that he was exposed to the elements. He maneuvered his stick-shift, no-power-anything taxi for 12 hours a day, through freezing cold, pouring rain, sticky heat in some of the worst traffic in the world. For 12 hours a day! While I loved him dearly, all that hard work didn't give him any financial success.

> *I like work. It fascinates me. I can sit and look at it for hours.*
>
> JEROME K. JEROME

The key to Power Performers is not working hard but loving what you do so much you'd rather be doing it than doing anything else. That's what releases the energy that makes you a Power Performer.

Learning to love what you do starts with understanding that you have choices, that you're doing what you're doing because you choose to do it, not because you have to. *You don't have to do anything.* How excited could you get about life, how much internal energy could you release, if you knew you'd never again have to do anything that you didn't choose to do?

> *The key to Power Performance is not working hard but loving what you do so much you'd rather be doing it than anything else.*

WHERE WOULD YOU RATHER BE?

At my *13 Secrets of Power Performance* seminars, I ask my audience how many of them, instead of listening to me that evening, would rather be somewhere else. Then I pick a really great place, such as at a restaurant in the Piazza Navona in Rome—that happens to be one of my favorite places in the whole world. It's a beautiful plaza in the heart of that great city, surrounded by picturesque buildings. Down the center are some of the finest fountains in the city, including Bernini's famous Fountain of the Four Rivers. In ancient times the Piazza Navona was the Stadium of Domitium, where the Romans held chariot races. Around the piazza are many fine restaurants and sidewalk cafes.

"How many of you," I ask my audience, "would rather be at the Three Steps restaurant in the Piazza Navona? The sun is shining, and you're enjoying one of those incredible five-course Italian lunches?"

After I assure them that it won't offend me, hands begin springing up all over the room. Most of them agree that they'd rather be enjoying Rome than attending my seminar.

"That's just not so," I tell them. "The truth is you'd rather be here, listening to me, than anywhere else in the world. You've proven it to me. The proof is, you're here, not there." This usually produces a rather stunned silence from the audience as "yes, buts" race through their minds

"I'd rather be in Rome," someone will finally say from the audience, "but I've used up all my vacation time."

"You could have quit your job, but you chose not to."

"I don't have the money to pay for a plane ticket and the hotel."

"You could have put in on your charge card, or written the travel agent a bad check, or stolen the money, or sold your house or car—but you chose not to do that."

"I run my own business, and there's nobody else to take over for me."

"Oh, but you could have let your business go under, but you chose not to do that."

After a while, they all get the idea. Each of us is where we are because of the conscious decisions we've made. It's impossible to be doing anything other than what you choose to do.

Do I still hear a "yes, but" or two? What about the store owner who's being held up at gunpoint? Surely he has no option but to hand over the money. I agree with you he can't choose from two attractive alternatives, but it's still choice, isn't it? He still chooses between handing over the money and accepting the consequences of not handing it over.

If you want to take this thought further, you could also come to the conclusion that the store owner has chosen to decide that he is being robbed. Nothing really exists except that which we perceive to exist. Doesn't that sound crazy? Not really. In this case a man has walked into his store, pulled a gun out of his belt, pointed it at the store owner, and demanded money. The store owner calls it a robbery, but is it really? Consider this: Every year the Internal Revenue Service, the state tax collector, the county assessor, and the people at city hall all demand money of him and threaten him if he chooses not to hand it over. He doesn't call that a robbery. He calls it paying taxes. Either way he's handing over money under threat of punishment, but he chooses to interpret one as paying taxes and the other as being robbed. Events exist in your life only if you choose to interpret them as existing.

A brush fire starts to rage in a canyon and races toward a community of expensive homes. Flames destroy two homes that stand side by side. One homeowner sees it as the biggest tragedy that has ever happened to him. His neighbor sees it as a blessing because now she can take the insurance money and rebuild her home the way she really wants it to be. Events exist in your life only if you choose to interpret them as existing.

Two people lie dying in a hospice center. One chooses to struggle against death as it envelops her. The other sees it as a joyous event as he makes the transition to spending eternity with Jesus in heaven. Events exist in your life only if you choose to interpret them as existing.

THE CONCEPT THAT CHANGES YOUR LIFE FOREVER

Well, where are we with this thought? Is it just so much semantic game playing, or can it really have a bearing on whether we become Power Performers?

It's one of the most important concepts you must grasp to enjoy life fully, and in doing so release the power within you.

Let me tell you about the day when I finally bought the concept that you can never be doing anything other than what you choose to do. For the past several years, since the success of my cassette tape program, Secrets of Power Negotiating. (Nightingale-Conant), I have been a full-time speaker giving seminars about Power Negotiating, Power Persuasion, Confident Decision Making, and the 13 Secret of Power Performers to corporations and associations around the country. Of course, it's a great opportunity to travel and see this country and the other English-speaking countries of the world, but sometimes when you've been away from home for weeks on end you wish you could just go home and stay there for a while.

I remember being in Denver airport once, changing planes on a journey from Seattle to Amarillo, Texas. As I passed one of the concourse gates they were announcing the departure of a flight to Ontario, California, which is my local airport. I stopped to watch the passengers boarding. How I ached to join them! I thought of my beautiful home in an orange grove in the hills of Southern California and could smell the sweet springtime scent of the blossoms. I could almost hear the click of the golf balls from the country club at the end of my driveway. I thought of my children and the golfing buddies with whom I could go play.

Much as I wanted to go back to California, however, I couldn't, because I'd signed a contract to speak in Amarillo. If there's one thing I've learned about the speaking circuit, it's that you'd better show up. Meeting planners would rather you showed up and bombed than have you not show up at all. If you fail to show the word gets around, and you're out of the business.

Having to do things you don't want to do is the antidote to Power Performance. I believe, however, that we always have choices. So for a moment I wondered whether I should forget about going to Amarillo, even though I knew I wouldn't. Once I understood I really didn't have to go to Amarillo, I could choose to go back to California if I wished, I still went to Amarillo—I would never break a commitment—but I went with a different attitude. Instead of going grudgingly, because I "had to," I went willingly because it was what I chose to do.

Jim says, "I'd love to quit my job with the county, but I can't. I have only eight years left before retirement."

Did he say only eight years—*eight years?* You can accomplish anything in eight years. He should stop playing the role of a victim trapped in a situation he doesn't like. Jim should be saying, "I'm in control of my life, and I'm perfectly capable of changing my lifestyle if I choose. However, I've considered all my options, and I've decided to stay with my current job for eight more years."

Harry says, "I'd have invested in real estate years ago, but my wife wouldn't let me." Nonsense, Harry. Quit playing the loser. *You* decided not to invest in real estate, because nobody can control your life but you.

Mary says, "I've always dreamed of moving to Alaska, but I can't. I have this sick husband, and you just don't have many alternatives when you have someone else to look after." Baloney, Mary. You have all kinds of alternatives. I'm not saying you should leave your husband and move to Alaska, but I'm telling you to stop being a martyr and to accept that you're doing what you're doing because that is what you have chosen to do.

THERE IS NO OTHER FORCE CONTROLLING YOUR LIFE

There are occasions when we all sense that there's some other force in control of our lives, a force we don't understand. Circumstances, responsibilities, and obligations are tugging us back and forth. They are using up all our time, draining all our energy, and in that way are controlling our lives. If those thoughts get out of hand we call you mentally ill. The most self-destructive thought that any person can have is thinking that he or she is not in total control of his or her life. That's when, "Why me?" becomes a theme song.

While I believe in a Life Force that we can tap for the enrichment and betterment of our lives, I'm equally convinced there's no such force working against us. We all have a tendency at times to believe that somewhere out there there's some malignant power just waiting to throw problems our way and ruin our best prospects just when it looks as though we're ready to succeed. Sorry if you disagree, but I don't believe in the devil, not in the religious sense of the word. The only devil I know is the one inside us that keeps telling us that we can't make choices.

In this great country we prize freedom of choice, don't we? We insist on the freedom to worship and the rights of a free press. We defend our freedom to bear arms in spite of the remarkable number of deaths attributed to the easy availability of weapons. In 1989 the Supreme Court said we even have the freedom to burn the very symbol of our freedom, the America flag. Can you believe that?

> *The only devil I know is the one inside us that keeps telling us we can't make choices.*

We value our freedom above all things, and yet all too often we fabricate a world for ourselves that deprives us of many of our personal freedoms.

Let me give you an example: In the preface of this book I encouraged you to take a day out of your life and go somewhere where you can be totally alone, to assess your life and its direction. It's amazing to me how many people tell me they can't do that. They would like to, but they can't.

"How could I explain it to my wife?" they say.

"My boss would never give me the day off."

"My kids might need me to drive them somewhere."

How can we expect your life to be an adventure, full of excitement and romance, to release the Power Performer within us, if we've constructed such a limiting environment in which to live?

So many people live with the misconception that life somehow exists as an entity apart from us, that we're placed in it, must adapt to it, and somehow pummel our lives into a form that matches our circumstances.

We are our lives. When our lives stop, our world stops. It's all over—for us. Our world exists only through our perception of it. Change our perception of our world and we change the world—for us.

WHY NOT WRITE YOUR OWN HOROSCOPE?

How sad it is that so many people fall into the weird belief that life is preordained and that we can't direct it, only experience it. How sad it is that nearly every paper in the country carries a horoscope column, where millions of people search each day to learn what will happen to them, not realizing their day and their life is totally self-directed.

I first met Rick Keppler when he was the marketing director for The Catalyst Group, a company in Burbank that places products in movies. It's owned by two beautiful and talented women, Gisela Kovach and Dabney Day. They maintain a wonderfully close relationship with the studios that enables them to get the products of their clients on screen. If you see a scene in a movie where the star is playing basketball and it's a Spalding basketball, chances are that The Catalyst Group was responsible for placing it in the movie. If you see your favorite star wearing Armani sunglasses in a movie or smoothing on Hawaiian Tropic suntan lotion, it was probably because The Catalyst Group made the arrangements. One day Gisela and Rick invited me to join them for lunch in the executive dining room at Warner Brothers Studios. When we met I asked Rick how his day had been. "Terrific!" he told me, "I had a wonderful morning that turned out just the way my horoscope said it would." (Rick, who is from Germany, sounds just like Arnold Schwarzenegger, and when he met the star on a movie set once, Arnold's face lit up in surprise and he said, "Whoa—you sound just like me!")

"Your horoscope was right on?" I asked him.

"Yes. It said I would close a deal first thing this morning and I did, at a breakfast meeting. Then it said that an important new client would call me before lunch and want to sign up with us and they did."

I said, "Wow, that's a really specific horoscope. What paper was it in?"

"It wasn't in a paper," he told me. "I wrote it myself."

"You write your own horoscope?"

"Yes, every night I sit down and write out my own horoscope. It's amazing how often it turns out to be true."

Rick is someone who is living a self-directed life and refuses to let any outside sources dictate to him what will happen in his life, much less a horoscope written by someone who has never met him.

Frustration with life comes from the feeling that we're not in control, that things are happening to us that we haven't planned. Looking at horoscopes in the paper and thinking that they in some way predict what will happen to you is surrendering to the notion that you are not in control of your life. If this fixation gets out of hand, we call you neurotic.

> *Depend on the rabbit's foot if you will, but remember it didn't work for the rabbit.*
>
> R. E. Shay

"Who, me?" you say. "I don't have a trace of neurosis. I'm always in control of my life." Oh, really? Have you ever found yourself driving down the street, ten minutes late for an appointment, and having to stop at every red light? So you're thinking, "Why do the lights always turn against me when I'm late? It never happens when I'm early, only when I'm late. Why me?" Instead of thinking that, why don't you accept that you have a bad habit of being late that you need to correct.

Have you ever been fumbling for a key in the dark, thinking, "Why is it the last key on the ring, especially in the dark? It doesn't happen to other people. Why me?" Instead of that, why don't you accept that you failed to solve the problem by filing a notch in the key so that you could find it in the dark?

Have you found yourself standing by an empty water cooler wondering why it's always you who has to change the bottle? Instead of thinking that, why don't you accept that you wouldn't have this problem if you set up a system for who should be responsible for changing the water bottle?

Do you remember how to tell the difference between a psychotic and a neurotic? Ask them to add two and two. The psychotic is likely to say the first thing that pops into his head, even if it doesn't make any sense. So the answer might be 72, 149, or 3,211. The neurotic knows the answer is four, but hates it. "Why is it always four? That's so boring! I'm sure that other people don't have this problem. I bet it's not always four for them. Why does the world have to be this way?"

THE THREE THIEVES OF FREE CHOICE

To be a Power Performer we must continually be aware of how important free choice is to us. Constant vigilance is needed because there are three thieves of free choice that are constantly patrolling our world, looking for us to let down our guard.

Let's take a look at three major things we permit to steal away our freedom of free choice:

1. Peer group influence.
2. The promise of reward.
3. The fear of punishment.

THE FIRST THIEF OF FREEDOM OF CHOICE: PEER-GROUP INFLUENCE

Peer group pressure is a big one—and really terrifying when we examine it. In the Kew Gardens section of Queens, New York, in March 1964, a young lady in her late twenties who was on her way home from work late at night was stabbed to death. Catherine Genovese escaped her attacker three times, and it took him 35 minutes to kill her. The homicide detectives discovered that 38 people had watched the killing from their windows, and not one of them had called the police. Newspapers would not have widely publicized the murder if it had not been for a chance event. A. M. Rosenthal, the metropolitan editor for *The New York Times* was having lunch with the police commissioner a few days later. Rosenthal asked him about a murder in Queens, and the commissioner, who had been pondering the Genovese murder, wrongly assumed that Rosenthal was asking him about that one. The commissioner expressed his outrage that Ms. Genovese had not been quietly stabbed down some back alley but had been publicly killed as 38 of her neighbors watched. Why had not one of them picked up the phone to call the police?

Rosenthal had a reporter write an exposé that highlighted the indifference of the people in Queens. It appeared on the front page a week later. It said in part:

> Assistant Chief Inspector Frederick M. Lussen, in charge of the borough's detectives and a veteran of twenty-five years of homicide investigations, is still shocked.
>
> He can give a matter-of-fact recitation of many murders. But the Kew Gardens slaying baffles him—not because it is a murder, but because "good people" failed to call the police.

The national press took up the cry, deploring the apathy of big-city dwellers. Reporters interviewed the people who watched the murder and found them unable to say why they had not called the police. A few said that they didn't want to get involved, but when reporters asked them why they didn't at least make an anonymous call, they couldn't answer. The reporters came to the conclusion that the problem was the incredible insensitivity of our society. Commentators across the country picked up the Genovese case and told the story as an illustration of a major change in people's attitudes, people who had now become hardened to the crime all around them. We had become a nation of people too hardened to our plight to care about others. For a while, the entire nation played, "Ain't it Awful?"

However, two psychology professors from New York, Bibb Latane and John Darley, suspected apathy wasn't the problem at all and started an extensive investigation. They finally concluded, after interviewing most of the onlookers, that Catherine Genovese did not die *in spite* of the thirty-eight spectators, but *because* of them.

> *New York now leads the world's great cities in the number of people around whom you shouldn't make a sudden move.*
>
> DAVID LETTERMAN

The incident had happened at night. Every witness could see the other people watching from their windows. As long as no one else was calling the police, the others felt they shouldn't either.

Scary, isn't it? The two professors subsequently staged other apparent emergencies and found that the percentage of people who will offer to help in an emergency goes down dramatically when others are present. If the professors coached the bystanders to respond with indifference, the random passers by would respond only 10 percent of the time. Studies by other researchers have backed this up: People who would do the right thing if they were alone will violate their personal standards if enough other people are doing it.

Once I was driving late at night on highway 395, which runs the entire length of the Eastern Sierras, from Reno to Los Angeles. I had been skiing with my children at Mammoth Mountain, and we were on our way home. Suddenly the right front tire blew out. I hung onto the steering wheel and swerved the car over to the shoulder of the road. We climbed out into the silent mountain air. In the moonlight we could see the deserted road stretching over the horizon in both directions. No cars or buildings for 20 miles. "Don't worry," I told my children. "I'll have the spare tire on in a few minutes."

"The spare tire is flat," my youngest son, John, calmly told me. He was eight at the time. Don't you admire the purity of thought that children display at that age? He had known for days that the spare was flat, but he saw no reason to clutter up my mind with this piece of information until I really needed to know.

> *Before I was married I had three theories about raising children. Now I have three children and no theories.*
>
> JOHN WILMOT,
> SEVENTEENTH CENTURY EARL OF ROCHESTER

It was beginning to look as though we were in serious trouble. After 15 minutes of trying to come up with a solution we saw headlights coming over the horizon. They slowly wound their way toward us and came to a stop. A friendly voice said, "Need some help?" This kind man drove us back 10 miles to a gas station, waited until we'd bought a new tire (that was very reasonably priced), drove us back to our car, and helped me put the tire on. He wouldn't take any money for his trouble or the extra gas he'd used. Try that on a busy freeway. Thousands of cars will pour past you before you'll be able to get one to stop and help. You're much more likely to get help with a stalled car on a deserted road from a lone good Samaritan than you are by the side of a crowded freeway. Surrounded by others who are ignoring your plight, the situation will license even the most helpful people to ignore you because of peer-group influence.

We could learn to solve any of our nation's problems if we learned to harness peer-group pressure. When I first did a speaking tour of Australia, for example, it struck me how few people smoke in a seminar, or at a party, or in a restaurant. I found out that it wasn't because of any laws. It was because it's no longer acceptable to smoke in public in Australia.

In this country we rarely hear comedians telling drunk jokes any more, whereas a few years ago they were very popular; and we adored Foster Brooks and Dean Martin for their "drunk" acts. Now the Mothers Against Drunk Drivers have done such a good job of teaching us that people who drink too much are dangerous and pathetic characters that we no longer think it's funny. It's unfortunate the name of their group creates the acronym MADD. If there's ever a group that suffers from a bad press, it's the mentally ill of the world. They are really no more violent or likely to commit any crime, than the population at large—but you sure can't tell it from watching television or reading a newspaper, can you?

So a primary consideration for Power Performers would be to what extent am I *making choices* about my activities, my values, and my attitude toward my life, rather than being affected and thus controlled by my peers? If we let peer group influence us too much, we become conformists—the antithesis of the High Achiever. You'll never become a Power Performer if you insist on behaving just like everyone else.

It's hard to imagine Ken Kragen, the organizer of *Hands Across America* and *U.S.A. for Africa*, a Power Performer emeritus, backing down because some people didn't agree with what he was trying to do.

The extent to which other people affect us varies tremendously from one person to another. Some people are very "field dependent," as psychologists put it—the moods, attitudes, and opinions of those around them influence them a great deal. If they're in a room full of happy cheerful people, they're happy, and cheerful too. They make a great audience for a speaker because they get swept up in crowd enthusiasm. Others are field independent people—they could walk through Times Square at midnight on New Year's Eve and still not get caught up in the excitement.

> *Men who never get carried away, should be.*
>
> MALCOLM FORBES

THE SECOND THIEF OF FREEDOM OF CHOICE: THE NEED TO BE REWARDED

The next big influence in our lives is the need for others to reward us. In transactional analysis terms this is very much in the child state. In his book *Games People Play* Canadian-born Eric Berne, a Carmel psychiatrist, wrote about the parent, child, and adult ways of thinking. We all have within us three ego states, and in differing circumstances different ego states will dominate our behavior. The parent ego state is the controller, the one that makes us want to take command of a situation and dominate it and is something we absorbed from our parents when we were very young. The child is the part of the ego that wants to be told what to do and is a carry-over from our own childhood. The adult part of the ego is the one we develop when we have developed mature reactions and is the ego state that causes us to reason out a situation and act logically.

Eric Berne probably adapted his theory from Sigmund Freud, who described the three ego states as the superego (parent), the id (child), and the ego (adult).

◆ *The superego.* Freud described the superego (the parent in transactional analysis) as that part of the ego that restrains the other two. We absorb this part of our personality from our parents. Human beings rely on the guidance of their parents for a remarkably long time compared to other species, so this part of the thought process can be deeply ingrained.

Freud further broke down the superego into two parts: the ego-ideal and the conscience. The ego-ideal contains ingrained thoughts of what our parents told us was good (tidiness, politeness, eating all of our food, keeping our clothes on, etc.); and the conscience contains what we have learned from our parents is bad (stealing, shouting, lying, touching our genitals, etc.). From this we develop an internal system of reward and punishment. Fifty years later our ego-ideal may be telling us that we deserve a vacation because we have worked hard, or we deserve sexual gratification because we have been a faithful partner. On the other side of the coin, our conscience tells us that we should be punished if we are bad. So if we feel guilty because we were greedy or manipulative, we tend to get depressed, suffer from an upset stomach, or may even involuntarily punish ourselves with a psycho-somatic illness.

Power Performers have somehow grown out of the state where their superego dominates. They do not feel that they have to *earn* the good things of life. For example, they don't feel that they have to work hard for a lifetime to deserve that trip around the world. They feel deserving simply because they exist. Neither do they feel they have to suffer because things went wrong and they made mistakes. They forgive themselves, pledge that it won't happen again, and promptly get on with living their lives.

◆ *The id.* Freud described the id (the child in transactional analysis) as the part of the ego that seeks immediate gratification (particularly regarding sexuality and aggression). Freud referred to this as the pleasure principle, the purpose of which is to relieve tension (aligned with pain or discomfort) by moving us toward pleasure. An infant feels pain and discomfort and reacts to it without realizing that it has the power to be proactive rather than reactive—that it can choose how it responds. So the infant feels the discomfort of a full bladder and immediately releases it. It feels the discomfort of a wet diaper and screams for help. Later when it feels hungry it cries until it gets the pleasure of being fed. As we grow older we should learn that it's no longer appropriate to let the id dominate, that we must learn to temper our response to discomfort. Some people never make the transition and turn into the gang member who guns down someone who laughs at him or her, or the rapist who cannot react without aggression to a woman rejecting him.

◆ The ego. The ego (the adult in transactional analysis) is what Freud described as the part of the personality that most closely aligns with our perceived selves. It functions by reconciling the forces of the id (Let's do it!) and the superego (You can't do that!) by reasoning through the situation (Why should I? Why shouldn't I?). Freud referred to this as the reality principle, because the ego deals better with what's really going on in the world than the superego or the id. The ego enables us to tolerate the pain and discomfort of tension until we develop an appropriate strategy to handle it.

Freud	Berne	Description
Superego	Parent	Restrains the other two parts of the ego
Id	Child	Seeks immediate gratification
Ego	Adult	Uses reason to make sense of a situation

Eric Berne developed dozens of games that these three ego states tend to play with each other. He gave these games fanciful names such as: "Ain't It Awful?" "How Do You Get Out of Here?" "I'm Only Trying to Help You," And "I'll Show Them." Those games gave him the title for his book *Games People Play*.

Psychiatry is the care of the id by the odd.

So in the parent state (when our superego dominates) we tend to think that we can and should direct the actions of others because we have an exaggerated sense of what's right and wrong. A store owner being held up at gunpoint might respond in the parent state, "You can't do this to me!" Of course the gunman can shoot him if he chooses, so what the storekeeper is really saying is that in the perfect world that his mother and father trained him to expect, the gunman wouldn't be allowed to rob him or shoot him.

If the storekeeper were in the child state (when his id dominates), he would say to the gunman, "Please don't do this to me." As a child he learned to look to others for rewards, and if he never outgrew it, transactional analysts would say that he's in the child state. People in the child state are reverting to their kindergarten days, when it was natural to look to others for direction. Freud would say that he's simply taking the shortest course he sees to relieve the tension and return to a pleasurable state.

Power Performers live in the adult state, where logical thinking prevails and the ego, in the Freudian sense of the word, dominates. We'd think, "This suckers got a gun. It might be loaded. He might pull the trigger. Later on I might get angry or upset. Right now it would make sense to stay calm and give him the money."

That's why you won't find a Power Performer complaining to his boss that he never gets any appreciation. The employee who does this is letting his id (Freudian) or child (transactional analysis) dominate and is looking for immediate gratification of the distress of feeling unwanted. Power Performers think in the adult, logical state of mind; they understand that satisfaction with themselves must come from within.

Similarly Power Performers don't sail oceans for financial reward alone, or for public adulation; they do it for the feeling of fulfillment that comes from the accomplishment of an objective that is important to them. And Power Performers who work for corporations work hard for their own reward, not for promotions or raises in pay. Promotions and pay increases come, of course, but only as a by-product of the activity.

> *Power Performers think that fame, fortune, or pleasing someone else are three lousy reasons for doing anything.*

DON'T WORK FOR MONEY—THE MONEY WILL FOLLOW

Remember the story of Chuck Yeager breaking the sound barrier for the first time in 1947? Attempting to break the sound barrier had killed other pilots, and many people thought that the physics of the universe prevented anything from flying faster than sound. Yeager was also a believer in the theory. The speed of sound at sea level is 760 mph, but at 40,000 feet it is only 660 mph. When he'd gone into steep dives pursuing German pilots during World War II he had exceeded 700 mph in his Mustang, but never at a high enough altitude to break through the sound barrier. However, he had felt what approaching the barrier had done to his plane as the shock barriers broke over his wings and buffeted his ailerons and stabilizer. The plane began to shake violently and felt for all the world as though it would break up.

> *Flying is hours and hours of boredom sprinkled with a few seconds of sheer terror.*
>
> GREGORY "PAPPY" BOYINGTON,
> WHO SHOT DOWN 24 JAPANESE PLANES (PRESUMABLY DURING THE WAR)

Geoffrey De Havilland, Jr., the famous British test pilot, lost his life at .94 Mach when his tailless experimental aircraft *The Swallow* disintegrated. It was enough to cause the British to abandon their entire supersonic program.

Bell Laboratories had asked their test pilot Slick Goodlin to fly the experimental X-1 plane beyond Mach One and offered to pay him $150,000—an incredible amount of money in those days. He refused the assignment as being too dangerous. The plane was little more than a cockpit strapped onto four huge liquid oxygen- and alcohol-powered rockets, and the chance of the pilot surviving an accident was virtually zero. At that point the Air Corps got impatient with Bell Laboratories and demanded to take over the X-1 program. They had programs that were waiting in line once the sound barrier had been broken, including an aircraft designed to fly at Mach 6, an atomic-reactor-powered bomber, and eventually a program to put men into space. However, everything was stalled until they could find a pilot with the courage to prove that the sound barrier could be broken. When General Boyd of the Air Corps asked Chuck Yeager to make the first flight, money had nothing to do with his decision—he was perfectly content with his $200-a-month Air Corps pay.

> *The purpose of life is a life of purpose.*
>
> ROBERT BYRNE*

---

*Robert Byrne is the author of my favorite quote book *The 637 Best Things That Anybody Said* and three similarly name sequels. I highly recommend them.

THE IMPORTANCE OF LOVING WHAT YOU DO

On top of a silk cottonwood tree in the mountains of Guyana, South America, nature photographer Neil Rettig peers through his viewfinder at a Harpy eagle feeding its baby. He shudders at the thought that the eagle may object to his being so close to her nest and attack him, for this is the most predatory bird in the world. With its six-foot wingspan and talons the size of bear claws it could easily rip his chest open if it were not for the bullet proof vest that he wears. Many years before he had photographed such an eagle as it swooped down at over 50 mph to pluck a large monkey from a tree and carry it off.

It has taken Rettig weeks to locate the eagle's nest and another week to construct the blind where he has positioned his camera. He got there by shooting a crossbow with a fishing line attached to the top of the huge silk cottonwood tree that is 200 feet high and has immense branches that make it as wide as it is tall. He attached a string to the fishing line and pulled it up and then tied a rope to the string. Then he pulled himself up using mountain climber's clamps called ascenders. Working only one hour a day, so as not to disturb the eagle, he has built a small camouflaged camera platform on another branch of the same tree as the eagle's nest. He will spend ten hours a day, seven days a week for the next six months, perched in his tiny blind. Every evening when the light fails he will lower himself down a rope and walk 30 minutes through the dense jungle to his crude camp. At daybreak he will pull himself back up the rope to repeat his lonely vigil. The jungle is so damp that his clothes will never dry and mold will grow on his skin. His reason for doing this? He wants to photograph the first flight of the baby eagle. What great things could you accomplish if you loved your work as much as Neil Rettig loves his? Meanwhile, back in the city, schoolteachers have walked out of their classrooms and onto the picket lines to protest the school board's offer of only a 5 percent raise.

Does Frank Sinatra continue to pour his talent and his heart into songs because he needs the money, or the recognition? Of course not. He does it for the sheer joy of doing it. Does Bob Hope continue to maintain a hard driving schedule well into his eighties because he needs the money? He's reported to be worth over $400 million dollars now. He could have retired 20 years ago to every accolade civilian life has to offer. He continues for the sheer joy of doing it.

> *I had promised to perform on my 100th birthday at the London Palladium, but Caesar's Palace made me a better deal.*
>
> GEORGE BURNS (THIS IS A NEWS ITEM, NOT A JOKE!)

Okay, you say, "As soon as I'm rich, I'll be able to do things I love doing too. Right now I just have to keep on plugging away at what I don't like to do." Hey, wait a minute, wouldn't it be a lot simpler to find something you love to do and then figure out a way to make money doing it? Power Performers never do things they don't like to do for the rewards, they look for rewarding things they like to do. They know that the money will follow them when they adopt that attitude.

THE THIRD THIEF OF FREEDOM OF CHOICE: FEAR OF PUNISHMENT

The opposite side to promise of reward is the fear of punishment—something we learn early in life and should outgrow. Unfortunately it's all too often the product of a hostile childhood environment. Children whose parents raise them with love grow up self-confident and emotionally strong. Children whose parents raise them with criticism and fear grow up lacking self-confidence. Then they either turn into emotional wimps dominated for the rest of their lives by girl friends, wives, and bosses; or they rebel from this and turn out sullen, resentful, and hostile.

If you "have a friend" who suffers from lack of self confidence, you can't give him or her any better advice than to join one of the thousands of Toastmaster clubs around the country and around the world. There the person learns to develop self-confidence by learning how to talk in front of a group of people. Ralph Smedley, the founder of this fine organization, understood that if we can get over our fear of speaking in front of a group, we can also learn to be more self-confident in one-on-one conversations. The audience is small at Toastmaster meetings, typically about 15 members, and the atmosphere is very supportive. Because critiques by other members are a regular part of the program, members also learn to accept criticism gracefully. I've never heard a bad word about this fine nonprofit organization. If you'd like more information, write to Toastmasters International World Headquarters, 2200 N. Grand Avenue, Santa Ana, California 92711. If you try to call them be careful because the Toastmaster Appliance company is also in Santa Ana and you may get the wrong number from the information operator.

I don't think it's possible to become a Power Performer unless you've overcome the fear of dealing with others. I devoted my book *Secrets of Power Persuasion* (Prentice Hall, 1992) to teaching you personal power in dealing with others.

So Power Performers understand that we create our lives by a series of choices we make, not by fate, chance or circumstance. We mustn't let the three thieves of freedom of choice steal them from us.

Keep an eye out for the three bandits of choice:

1. *Peer group influence.*
2. *The promise of reward.*
3. *The fear of punishment.*

CHOICES ARE WHAT WILL CONTROL YOUR FUTURE

The choices you have made controlled your past and control your present. Now let's see how much you feel they control your future.

To what extent do you feel you control your own future? One hundred percent? Seventy-five percent, maybe? Fifty percent? Twenty-five percent? Or not at all?

When I was a student in London in the 1950s, the Soviet Union had just invaded Hungary, the Arabs and the Israelis were at each other's throats, and we all had a pervasive feeling that global destruction was inevitable. Some dropped out of college because they believed they had no control at all of their lives and whatever was going to happen would happen. The same feeling of futility overwhelmed a whole generation in this country, during the Vietnam War.

David Lean demonstrated this way of thinking beautifully in his motion picture *Lawrence of Arabia*. Do you remember when Lawrence was traveling with the Arabs across the desert through a sandstorm? T. E. Lawrence had hired a servant whose name was Gasim, who turned out to be a surly, disreputable fellow whom Lawrence planned to fire when they got to the next town. Suddenly they located Gasim's camel still loaded with his rifle, his food, and his saddlebags, but Gasim was missing. Lawrence knew that the desert heat would kill a man by the second day, but without water thirst would turn him into a stumbling, babbling maniac in an hour or two. He debated asking another native to return to look for Gasim—he could certainly claim that an Arab would suit the task better than an Englishman. Lawrence neither wanted to risk his life nor jeopardize his mission for this pathetic man, but he accepted that Gasim was his servant and he was responsible for him. The Arabs tried to dissuade him from the search by telling him destiny had ordained that the man should lose his life in the desert and told Lawrence that he shouldn't tamper with destiny.

Nevertheless, Lawrence went back into the desert on his own, to save the man's life. Eventually Lawrence found the lost Arab and at great peril carried the man back to the rest of the group. He eloquently described finding him in his classic book *The Seven Pillars of Wisdom*:

> I had ridden about an hour and half, easily, for the following breeze had let me wipe the crust from my red eyes and look forward almost without pain; when I saw a figure, or large bush, or at least something black ahead of me. The shifting mirage disguised height or distance; but this thing seemed moving, a little east of our course. On chance I turned my camel's head that way, and in a few minutes saw that it was Gasim. When I called he stood confusedly; I rode up and saw that he was nearly blinded and silly, standing there with his arms held out to me, and his black mouth gaping. The Ageyl had put our last water in my skin, and this he spilled madly over his face and breast, in haste to drink. He stopped babbling, and began to wail out his sorrows.

The next day, however, the Arabs caught Gasim stealing and condemned him to death. After they had executed him, the other Arabs said to Lawrence, "You see! Fate decreed he should die. Regardless of how you tried to stop it, Fate was in control." (Lawrence did not mention Gasim's execution in his 660 page account of his adventures in Arabia. Rather than accuse screen writer Robert Bolt of inventing a story for the sake of emphasis, let's just consider it an oversight on Lawrence's part. The scene that showed Lawrence coming out of the sandstorm, appearing first as a mere dot on the huge 70-mm screen and then growing to become two men on a camel, was the highlight of the movie because it enabled us to experience the vastness and the harshness of the desert. True or not, the execution episode that followed it made a great impact and was certainly consistent with Arab beliefs.)

> *For some people life is like the weather. It's something that happens to them.*

To Power Performers, the extent to which they feel they control their future is a measure of how much they're getting out of life. To some people, life is like the weather—it just happens to them, and they have no control. For Power Performers, life is a majestic journey, An exciting adventure that they totally orchestrate and direct, by the hundreds of choices they make every day.

There's a homework assignment attached to this chapter. I hope you'll *choose* to do it. I want you to pick a day this week and tally the number of choices you make. On the selected day, wake up and choose whether to get up. When a motorist tailgates you on the way to work, choose whether to get irritated or not. If you're late to work, choose whether to feel guilty or not. The accounting department calls and needs your help right away, so choose whether to go. Your boss calls you into his or her office and lectures you. Choose to stay and listen, or walk out. All day long, tally the choices you make. Be aware of the influences affecting your decisions, for example, "I choose not to walk out on my boss, because I fear punishment." That's Okay as long as you let they choices remain influences that affect decisions, not controlling factors. You'll come away from this experience with a true under-standing of the control you really have on your life.

Understand that you create your life from a series of choices you make, and you can never be doing anything unless you've cho-sen to do it. The quality of your life is the result of choices you make.

Don't let the three thieves of freedom of choice steal your ability to make choices. The three bandits to watch for are peer group influence, promise of reward, and fear of punishment. Understand that by controlling your choices, you control your future.

◆◆◆

The Third Secret of Power Performers is:

They know that they always have choices.

◆◆◆

In the next chapter, we'll learn that to Power Performers there's something far more important than reaching their objec-tives in life. Doesn't that seem hard to believe?

4

POWER PERFORMERS KNOW THAT THE JOURNEY'S THE THING

Who cares about great marks left behind? We have one life. Just one. Our life. We have nothing else.

— *Ugo Betti*

Measurement of life should be proportioned rather to the intensity of the experience than to its actual length.

— *Thomas Hardy*

Being there deflates you. Getting there energizes you.

— *Roger Dawson*

Imagine being one of life's truly great Power Performers. You're Reinhold Messner, the only man who has climbed all 14 of the world's highest mountains. That means that you've climbed every summit over 8,000 meters (26,240 feet). Again you're approaching the summit of Mount Everest, but this time you're attempting a history-making solo attempt.

Two years before, along with Peter Habeler, you had become the first person to climb the mountain without oxygen. Just as many experts warned Chuck Yeager that nothing could fly faster than sound, many experts had warned you that it was impossible to climb to 29,000 without oxygen. (When Edmund Hillary became the first man to stand on the summit of Everest in 1953 he removed his mask for ten minutes to take pictures. It was the first proof that man would not immediately become unconscious at that altitude without it.) When you first announced your campaign to raise money for the climb, shock waves rippled through the world's mountain-climbing community. Experts appeared on television shows and at press conferences to state unequivocally that it was impossible, and even if you could reach the summit you would kill yourself trying to descend, or at best you would come back as a mental vegetable. At first this mental battle with outside critics caused you to doubt your own sanity, and then it served to strengthen your resolve. You were convinced that the only way to reach the top was to do the last two days climbing in one, to minimize the time you would spend above 8,000 meters. That meant an eight hour ascent and an agonizing descent suffering from snow blindness caused by removing your goggles to operate the movie camera.

What happened after the climb astounded you. The mountaineering experts who had insisted your feat was impossible now refuse to believe that you did it. The film proved nothing to them, because they say that you could have hidden the oxygen from the camera. Even your climbing companion is challenging your version of what happened on the climb. Your status as one of the world's great mountain climbers is crumbling. However, you are a Power Performer who does not climb mountains to win the acclaim of others but simply because it enriches your life.

Now you're back on Everest spending your own money for the expedition and determined to vindicate yourself by climbing the mountain solo. You're been alone for two and a half days now, ever since you left your only companion, Canadian journalist Nena Holguin, at 21,000 feet. You set off alone, without radio contact or oxygen, to be the first person ever to make a solo conquest of Mount Everest. On the first day after you left your companion, a snow bridge collapsed and you'd tumbled into a seemingly bottomless crevasse, to be miraculously saved by a tiny ledge of ice.

For the last two days and nights your only companions have been hallucinations, brought on by the lack of oxygen at this high altitude.

Finally, on August 20, 1980, you're alone on the 29,028 foot summit. Later you will write about the final few meters: "That last section of the summit ridge seemed to go on for ever. My tempo had become so slow that I despaired of ever making it. I could not manage the last few meters—I crawled on hands and knees. It was continual agony; I have never in my whole life been so tired as on the summit of Mount Everest that day."

You want to take back proof, so you sit in the snow and point your camera at your feet and at the tripod left behind by a Chinese expedition five years before. From your vantage point at the top of the world, endless chains of snow-capped peaks stretch off for hundreds of miles in every direction.

What do you feel at this history-making moment? Exhilaration? Self-exaltation? A feeling of self satisfaction that will last a lifetime? "I sat there like a stone. I was empty of feeling," the explorer said of the triumph.

Reinhold Messner had discovered what all Power Performers must learn—that after the momentary euphoria of accomplishment, you quickly learn that true joy in life comes from the thrill of the journey, not in being at your destination.

WHY A NATIONAL HERO CALLED IT QUITS

Think of Australian John Bertrand, who skippered the *Australia Two* to victory in the America's cup, beating the American team for the first time in 132 years. Losing three of four races in the best of seven series, he had pulled off a miraculous victory by winning all three of the remaining races. It's hard to imagine that there's ever been a greater national hero than John Bertrand in September of 1983. As he said in his book *Born to Win*: "It wasn't possible to buy a bottle of champagne in all of Australia. There was none left. The same applied to gold and green ribbons. Australians decked out the whole country in the colors of Australia Two. They festooned the entire continent—from Perth to Brisbane, from Adelaide to Darwin. The government had declared a national holiday. Down at the Newport, Rhode Island, dock, in our little office, the teleprinters hadn't stopped for one second, day or night, for nearly two weeks. Headlines in the *Sydney Morning Herald read The Biggest Thing Since Peace in 1945—Triumph Unites Nation.* Because the last tie breaking race showed on TV in the middle of the night down under, nearly all of her 16 million people stayed up all night to watch it. The next day the normally jam-packed Sydney Bridge was without any traffic, and the Prime Minister, Bob Hawke, got on television and just about forbade any employer from firing someone for missing work. Sydney airport was paralyzed, with neither pilots or passengers willing to leave their radios or televisions to go on board."

Weeks later when John Bertrand showed up as a casual spectator at the Melbourne Marathon, the race came to a halt as all the runners stopped to shake his hand.

> *I have to feed off my own ambitions. I must broaden my horizons and set new goals for myself.*

So why did John Bertrand decline to defend the Cup in Perth in 1987? "As the America's Cup ended, I knew that I wouldn't be doing it again," he said. "All through my career, I've always progressed to a different boat, or taken up a different challenge. I have to feed off my own ambitions, I have to feel that fanatical determination to win that has characterized all of my racing over the years. I must broaden my horizons now and set new goals for myself."

John Bertrand understands that the joy is in the journey to an objective, not in the accomplishment.

WHY A PIZZA MAN WOULDN'T STOP GROWING

Tom Monaghan is another example. He was born in 1937 in Ann Arbor, where his corporate headquarters in still located. His father was a long-distance truck driver who died of bleeding ulcers when Tom was four. For the next year German foster parents took care of him although they spoke no English and he understood no German. For the next seven years he was raised in a very strict

Catholic orphanage, and then he suddenly returned to his mother, who was a night nurse in Traverse City and was very permissive. This got him into trouble and he spent the next year at a farm orphanage. Pursuing a childhood dream to become a priest, he entered seminary school in Grand Rapids but was kicked out the following spring. His mother didn't feel she could handle him so she called the police and had him sent to a detention home for delinquent children. Upon release he finally developed a taste for schooling and got good enough grades to spend a year in Ferris State College, paying his own way by working as a ditch-digger and a construction worker. Unable to earn enough money to pay for the sophomore year's tuition, he enlisted in the Marine Corps, where he saved $2,000 to continue his education but got cheated out of it and had to hitchhike back to Ann Arbor.

Monaghan's brother suggested they buy a pizza parlor called Dominick's in Ypsilanti, so he borrowed $500 for his share and became an entrepreneur. It would have made a great story to say that from then on his troubles were all behind him, but it wasn't so, and problems would continue to plague him for many years to come. After a year his brother lost interest and Tom bought him out by giving him a used Volkswagen. He took in a new partner who embezzled from the company and left him broke and deep in debt. Forced to change the name of his company when he dissolved their partnership, he selected Domino's. His original store burned, and he hadn't paid for fire insurance. Finally he was big enough to go public, but the systems and overhead that the investment company insisted upon again put the company deep in debt and Tom lost control. The bank imposed manager only made things worse. Tom pleaded with the bank to give him back control which they only did when the business was a financial basketcase. However, he was able to dance around their creditors and finally, inspired by the work that Ray Kroc was doing at McDonald's, he got the chain up to 100 stores. Then Amstar Corporation, which owned Domino's sugar, sued him for infringing on their name. It took five years, $1.5 million, and a fight all the way to the Supreme Court for him to be able to retain his company name. He went on to make a personal fortune of $400 million.

One of his big ambitions was to meet Ray Kroc, the man who had inspired him by his example. For years he would call Kroc's

office every month to get an appointment, but was never successful. Then he heard that Kroc, who was by then 78 years old, was
in failing health. So Monaghan flew to San Diego, determined to
stay until he could meet his idol. His persistence paid off and
Kroc's assistants finally granted him a 15 minute audience that
turned into a two-and-a-half-hour mutual-appreciation meeting.
Kroc peppered him with questions about his operation and
impressed Monaghan with how quickly he caught on. "In no time
at all he understood Domino's as well as anyone except me," Tom
said.

> *Business is a good game. Lots of competition and a*
> *minimum of rules. You keep score with money.*
>
> ATARI FOUNDER NOLAN BUSHNELL

Suddenly Ray Kroc leaned forward in his chair and said, "I'm
going to give you some advice. You have it made now. You can do
anything you want; make all the money you can possibly spend.
So what I think you should do now is slow down. Take it easy.
Open a few stores every year, but be very careful. Don't make any
new deals that could get you into trouble. Play it safe."

This astounded Monaghan because conservatism was the last
thing he expected to hear from his hero. He finally blurted out,
"But that wouldn't be any fun!"

Kroc paused and looked hurt. Finally he broke into a huge
grin and started pumping Tom's hand. "That's just what I hoped
you'd say!"

Wouldn't you think that someone who had struggled that hard
would be glad that the struggle was over and would want to take
Kroc's advice and luxuriate in his wealth? Far from it. Monaghan
says, "I got to the point where material things didn't mean a darn
thing to me anymore. They did to me when I was young. Now I
have just about anything I've ever dreamed about, and the great
lesson of that is, it's not that big a deal. I just don't have the same
interest in making money. Accumulating and accumulating, that's
all I've done for the last 30 years, and what the heck for?" In 1989
he announced that he'd spend the rest of his life seeing if he could

give all his money away. Tom Monaghan knows that being there means nothing—it's getting there that gives you all the fun and satisfaction.

WHAT AN ENGLISHMAN LEARNED SAILING SOLO AROUND THE WORLD

On May 28, 1966 Francis Chichester, who was 65 years old, became the first man to sail around the world alone. In a specially built 53-foot sailing yacht *The Gypsy Moth IV,* named after the plane in which he made the first solo flight from England to Sydney as a young man, he astounded the world with his remarkable feat. The first leg of the trip, from Plymouth, England, to Sydney, Australia, was just over 14,000 miles without a stop, and took him 105 days and 20 hours. This was only five days more than the giant tea clippers had taken in previous centuries. He carried all the food and water that he needed on board and slept by attaching the tiller to a self-guiding auto pilot that he had invented.

After a seven-week layover in Sydney to repair and restock the yacht, he set off for the journey across the South Pacific, around the southern tip of Argentina, and up the Atlantic to England. This was to become the longest nonstop sail of any small boat in history: a journey of 15,517 miles that took him 119 days.

As he sailed back into Plymouth harbor over nine months after he left, he knew that Queen Elizabeth was waiting to knight him with the same sword that Queen Elizabeth I had knighted Francis Drake. Half a million people crowded the hills around the harbor to cheer him home.

His wife, Sheila, came aboard and was the first to congratulate him. Francis Chichester looked out at the masses of cheering people and turned to Sheila and said, "It's strange, but I don't feel anything at all."

It's the journey that matters, never the destination.

The following year, spurred on by a rash challenge from a London newspaper, nine sailors left on the first round-the-world solo race. Although Sir Francis Chichester was the honorary chairman of the race, he wasn't able to lay down strict entry requirements that would have prevented several ill-prepared adventurers from taking part. By the time Italian skipper Carozzo had reached Portugal he surrendered to duodenal ulcers from the pressure. Before the first boat rounded the Cape of Good Hope in South Africa, four more of the yachts had sunk, and Donald Crowhurst appeared to be missing at sea.

The remaining three boats made it around Cape Horn, with Frenchman Bernard Moitessier far ahead of Robin Knox Johnston and Nigel Tetley. Then Englishman Donald Crowhurst suddenly reappeared and called in positions that would indicate he was a strong contender. Nigel Tetley overreacted to this new challenge, raised too much sail to catch up, and sank his trimaran off the Azores. Then Donald Crowhurst mysteriously disappeared again. When rescuers finally found his boat it carried two sets of log books, which revealed that he had been planning to cheat in the race and return to England to claim the prize, without having gone around the world. Investigators assumed that he had killed himself.

Now only two remained: Frenchman Bernard Moitessier and Robin Knox Johnston. Moitessier was far ahead. All he had to do was finish the easy sail up the Atlantic to claim the prize—a golden globe and a large sum of cash—and become world famous for his feat. When he saw that victory was his, however, he suddenly turned and sailed back around the Cape of Good Hope to spend the rest of his life on a South Pacific island. Sir Francis Chichester understood exactly how he felt.

It's the journey that matters, never the destination.

THE REAL MEANING OF SUCCESS

Of course you don't have to solo Mount Everest, win the America's Cup, make hundreds of millions, or sail around the world to be a Power Performer. It's not how much money you make or how many awards you win that makes you a success. It's the amount of personal satisfaction you get from accomplishing what's important to you in your own way that makes you a success. That's what releases the internal energy that Power Performers relish.

The lesson we learn from Reinhold Messner, John Bertrand, and Tom Monaghan is clear. Don't set objectives where the only reward comes from the accomplishment, because being there is going to be a terrible disappointment. It's getting there that thrills and inspires us.

> *Being there deflates you.*
>
> *Getting there energizes you.*

GETTING CAUGHT IN A CORPORATE TRAP

In my twenties and early thirties, I made the mistake of spending 13 years of my life trying to climb the ladder at a nationwide department-store chain. I started as a management trainee in Napa, California, and after 18 months the company sent me to Stockton for a six-month advanced-training course. Then I spent three years in Auburn, two years in Yakima, Washington, and three years in Bakersfield before being transferred to the Los Angeles metropolitan area. My daughter Julia was born in Napa, my son Dwight in Stockton, and John was born in Yakima, Washington.

Apart from the two years in Yakima where I had the good fortune to work for an outstanding store manager, Don Rainwater, I can't think of any assignments I enjoyed. However, the challenge of the next promotion continually lured me on. The pay was awful, and the demands they made bordered on inhumanity—particularly their policy of constantly transferring me from one town to another. Just as I came to like the Gold Rush foothill community of Auburn they shipped me to Yakima. I said, "Isn't the weather awful in Washington?" They said, "It rains on the coast but Yakima is in the middle of the state. It doesn't get much rain and the climate is like the Mediterranean." So we bundled up our two young children in our compact car and drove there in time for the worst winter in 50 years. I remember looking out the window in December after the first snowfall and seeing all the neighbors furiously shoveling snow from their driveways. Not having lived in snow before I thought, "What fools. Working so hard when the snow will have melted away by this afternoon." The joke was on me when the snow was still on the ground at the end of April and I had been slithering in and out of my driveway for over four months. A white Christmas is a big thrill, but a white Easter I can do without.

> *Shoveling the walk before it stops snowing is like cleaning your house while your kids are still growing.*
>
> PHYLLIS DILLER

The first winter was tough, but then we started to like the Northwest. I took up skiing and mountain climbing, and we fell in love with the gentle, friendly people who lived there.

Then the call came. "We need you to report to Bakersfield, a week from Monday. This is a great promotion, and you'll be getting a $1,000 more a year."

Never mind my strong suspicion that Bakersfield was the armpit of the nation. I said, "Doesn't it get hot in Bakersfield?" They said, "Yes, but it's a dry heat. You'll get used to it quickly."

Bakersfield was at least a hundred miles from a mountain worth skiing on or climbing, and it certainly didn't match my newly acquired lifestyle (what little lifestyle I could afford on the money they paid me), but to turn down a promotion meant that they would never offer me another. So we loaded up the three children in our non air-conditioned compact car and drove through Central California to Bakersfield. The first 30 days we were there it was over 100 degrees every day. Sometimes it would still be 90 degrees at midnight. When it's that hot, it really doesn't matter much if it's a dry heat; it's simply miserable.

After three years in Bakersfield, I'd begun to like it—almost. My family and I had become part of the community, and we had made new friends. Then the call would come for me to move again. After six such promotions, I really began to wonder when all this was going to start paying off and started to take a closer look at the people up the corporate ladder from me. To my amazement it didn't look as though they were enjoying their careers at the company either. I could understand that my store manager wasn't happy, because he was always hoping for a good promotion. The district manager always seemed to be under a great deal of pressure too, but I could understand that. He was pushing hard to become regional vice-president. It was when I realized that the regional vice-president was miserable too that I started to wonder where I was going with the company. These people were all living in the future, all thinking that satisfaction and contentment lay on the next rung of the corporate ladder. That wasn't how I wanted to spend the rest of my life. I wanted to get fun and satisfaction from my career now, not just hope that I'd be happy when I finally reached the corporate office. With this awareness I suddenly realized how important it is that the journey to the objective be the reward, not arriving at the destination.

WHY I BELIEVE THAT IT'S THE JOURNEY THAT COUNTS

Achieving all of life's objectives doesn't mean much. The value of objective setting in your life is for the joy of the journey, and not in reaching the destination. Does that sound like one of those platitudes that doesn't hold up well under scrutiny, such as "Money won't buy happiness" or "You are what you eat"? Let me tell you why I feel so strongly it's the journey and not the arrival that counts.

I love mountaineering. There's something about forcing my way to the summit of a snow-covered mountain that thrills and fascinates me. Nothing stimulates me more than being way above the tree line, where the sky turns a deep midnight blue and the cares and concerns of the people far below seem so insignificant.

I still experience the euphoria I felt when I stood on the summit of Mount Rainier for the first time. It's not a challenging climb for professional mountaineers because the mountain is a relatively low 14,410 feet high. However, because it was my first big mountain, for me it was an immense challenge.

I had been in Yakima, Washington, for about nine months and was beginning to realize that if I was to be happy I should start taking part in some of the local activities. Three snowcapped mountains were clearly visible from the town: Mount Rainier, Mount Adams and Mount St. Helens, which blew its top off in a huge volcanic explosion years later and is no longer snowcapped in summer. For some reason snowcapped mountains have always appealed to me and fascinated me. A psychic once told me that it was because in a past life I was a sheep herder in Andorra, a tiny country in the Pyrenees between France and Spain. For whatever reason, these mountains kept saying, "Climb me." I was beginning to understand George Mallory when he was asked at a fund raiser in the Albert Hall in London why he wanted to climb Mount Everest, and he simply said, "Because it's there." (A line good enough for Edmund Hillary to purloin when reporters asked the same question as he returned to base camp after his successful climb.)

A mountain climbing club called the Cascadians sponsored an annual climb of Mount Adams every year so I signed up for it. I was 29 and I hadn't done anything athletic for years, so I enrolled in a morning YMCA exercise class that they held in the city park especially for people who wanted to join the mass climb. I couldn't believe the first class. We did a few stretches and then set off for a jog around the park. I did about 50 yards and heard this loud knocking noise. It was my heart pounding to get out. I had no idea I was in such bad shape. It took me three months of daily exercise to get in good enough physical condition to even think of attempting the climb.

On the evening of July 12, 424 of us along with a few hundred family members who wouldn't be climbing assembled at Timberline base camp. After trying to get a few hours sleep we set out at 1:00 A.M. for the climb to the 12,327-foot summit. Ten hours later 332 of us had made the summit, including a seven year old and a 73 year old. Mass climbs such as this are very controversial. Opponents claim rape of the wilderness by putting so many people on a mountain at one time. Proponents point out that it's the first chance many people get to be on a mountain and that it turns them into lifelong environmentalists. I know that the experience made me a lifelong lover of outdoor experiences.

With Mount Adams under my belt I turned to Mount Rainier, which is over 2,000 feet taller and a much tougher climb. I stayed in training for another year and arranged to join a guided climb the following June. The climb of Rainier began at Paradise Inn, which sits on the shoulder of the mountain at 5,557 feet. One of the most scenic spots in any National Park, it's a beautiful old lodge, probably built by the WPA. The huge snowcapped mountain towers above. As with the great mountains of Europe, there's a bank of high-powered telescopes where visitors can watch the climbers inching up the snow-clad mountain above them.

Just across the parking lot from the lodge is Lou Whittaker's mountain-climbing school and guide service. His brother Jim, an international known climber in his own right, was the first American to reach the top of Mount Everest in 1963. There's a full-size model of Jim approaching the summit in the visitor center next door.

Starting out from Paradise, we spent the first day climbing first over dirt and rocks and then up the huge Muir Snowfield that rises between the Nisqually and Paradise glaciers. We spent most of our time there in a damp swirling mist of clouds that depressed our spirits. Apart from not being able to see that we were making any progress up the mountain, we knew that the guides would abort the climb if the weather did not improve. Suddenly, about halfway up the snowfield, we walked out of the clouds into bright sunshine. The massive mountain towered directly above us, out-lined against a dark blue—almost black—sky. Far below the sum-mit we could see the rugged huts of Camp Muir, the mountain shel-ter where we would be spending the night. Our spirits soared. Now we could clearly see our objective, and it was amazing how it transformed our attitude. However, we soon learned that at that altitude, the air is so clear that the shelter was much further away than it appeared to be. Much further. It was 4 P.M. before I dragged my exhausted body onto the narrow ridge by the side of the Cowlitz Glacier known as Camp Muir. The camp is at 10,068 feet so it had taken me seven hours to haul my body up 4,511 vertical feet. The following day I would have to do almost that again to reach the summit, at much higher altitude, and then descend the full 9,000 feet. I was beginning to wonder what I was getting myself into.

Camp Muir consists of a few rough huts with bunks in them where we could grab a few hours of very restless sleep. At midnight we left for the summit. During the night the snow is cold and firm, making the climb much safer because the spiked crampons strapped to our boots could grip the snow. Once the snow became soft in the sunshine, it would be much harder to climb, and the avalanche danger would be much greater. Roped together, we made our way down and out onto the Cowlitz Glacier. With helmet lights illuminating our way we must have looked like the monks descending to the village in *Lost Horizons*. On the far side of the glacier our guides led us to a narrow trail that climbed over Cathedral Rocks and then safely under huge cliffs of ice that would become treacherous later in the day. Way above the clouds now, the bright moonlight showed us the way. After several hours we reached the Ingraham Glacier, and the sun was beginning to come up behind us as we had now moved around to the east side of the mountain. We could look down onto Little Tahoma peak, which is a dramatic appendage to the main mountain. Above us we could see the huge crevasses that we would have to skirt on our way to the top.

We reached the summit at about ten in the morning, but until I put my foot on the rim of the volcano, I still wasn't sure I would make it. Nothing in my life had ever challenged me this much physically. My guide Persumba, a sherpa from Nepal, kept yelling encouragement. Even when I was only 50 feet from the top, I still was thinking, "I may not make this after all." The top of Rainier is a giant volcanic depression. Like Mount St. Helens, the top had blown off, although this had happened millions of years ago. Before the explosion the mountain was probably 2,000 feet taller than it is today. Lou Whittaker was at the summit leading a team of climbers on a training session, and he invited me to go with him into the steam caves that run through the bowl. If caught in a storm you can take refuge in the caves and stay warm from the steam sent out by the volcano. The climb had so exhausted me that I declined but I did accept his invitation to get some sleep in his tent. Later I made the pilgrimage around the rim of the volcano to the true summit on the west side.

Beginning mountain climbers always tend to exhaust all of their efforts on reaching the summit and forget the enormous effort that getting down again will take. Mountain-climbing lore says that far more people die descending mountains than ascending them. George Mallory may well have reached the summit of Everest, but he was never heard from again, and it doesn't count unless you make it back to tell the tale. In the early afternoon we headed back down, all elated by our triumph and not realizing how much hard work still lay ahead. By the time I got back to Paradise that evening, I could hardly stand.

Once I'd recovered from the climb a new objective started to form. If I could climb Mount Rainier, why couldn't I climb to 20,000 feet? There's something mystical about reaching 20,000 feet. It's the dream of most American mountaineers, but you can't do it in the continental United States, because the highest mountain in the lower 48 states is Mount Whitney at 14,494 feet. To reach 20,000 feet, a mountaineer must go to Alaska (Mount McKinley is 20,320) or to South America or Asia.

In subsequent years I kept pushing on to higher mountains. Fifteen thousand feet on Mont Blanc. Eighteen thousand feet on Mount Everest and Mount Kilimanjaro. But my dream was always to reach 20,000 feet. It wasn't until almost 20 years later that I made it that high, on Mount Chimborazo in Ecuador. After five days trapped in our tents during a savage snowstorm we had retreated and then made one last dash for the summit. A huge cornice of snow blocked our way to the top, but I insisted that we keep going until I reached 20,000 feet, over the protests of my daughter Julia who was accusing me of trying to get us all killed. Finally I reached the objective of which I'd dreamed for almost 20 years. How did I react? I sat there in the snow for a few minutes, and then started thinking, "Now what am I going to have as an objective?"

Many climbers become obsessed with the objective of reaching 20,000 feet—even more so because it's rarely accomplished by someone over 50 years old. I was 48 when I did it. This yearning becomes almost a symptom of midlife crisis for mountaineers. Their rallying cry is, "Once before I die! I'll risk my life to prove I can still do it." Many climbers have risked their lives and had their toes amputated because of frostbite, or even suffered brain damage from altitude sickness. Some have died, just to reach the amateur mountaineer's dream of reaching 20,000 feet.

Here's the fascinating thing about this. Twenty thousand feet on a mountain doesn't mean a thing. It doesn't have any impact on anyone else in the world, other than a small handful of Americans, because everywhere else in the world mountain climbers measure mountains in meters, not feet. America is one of the few remaining countries that still measures anything in feet, and 20,000 feet to us is 6,096 meters to the rest of the world. Does it make any sense to risk your life to reach 6,096 meters? Of course not!

Your attitude determines your altitude!

I remember when my son John and I spent a month in South America. The highlight of the trip was hiring a guide and porters and trekking to the lost city of the Incas, Machu Picchu. This incredible archeological site is one of the world's great things to see. Cuzco was the capital of the huge Inca empire when the Spanish invaded almost 500 years ago. They mistreated the Inca rulers so badly that one night the Incas took all of their gold and escaped into the jungle. On the top of a hill, where nobody could see them from below, they built a new city that housed thousands of people. Everyone knew that the city existed, but nobody could find it. It became known as the lost city of the Incas. It wasn't until 1918 that Hawaiian archeologist Hiram Bingham finally found it.

For four days my son John and I hiked through the beautiful Peruvian Andes, following the trail that the ancient Incas took as they smuggled their gold away from their Spanish conquerors. One evening we were sitting around the campfire when I asked our guide if any of the surrounding mountains was over 20,000 feet. He had heard of feet of course, but wasn't sure how to translate it into meters. We debated it and finally agreed that there are 3.28 feet in a meter. He did some calculating, and then exclaimed, "That explains it!" He told me that the previous year he had been guiding some American climbers up one of the highest mountains in the area. The weather turned bad, and he told them they must abort the climb. Climbing tradition dictates that as the leader it was his prerogative to do so, although when rich climbers are paying destitute local guides, the line of authority blurs a little. These climbers refused to turn back, insisting that they go a little further. Frustrated, he continued, wondering how he could get them to do the right thing and turn back. He noticed that every 15 minutes, they would stop and peer at their altimeter. "They must want to reach 6,000 meters," he thought. "We can do that and then turn back." They reached 6,000 though, and still insisted on pushing on. An hour later, when he was getting desperate for their safety, they suddenly said, "Okay, this is far enough, let's go back down." Until that moment he'd never understood what they were doing.

Now he knew that they were just trying to reach 20,000 feet, or 6,096 meters.

WHY GOALS ARE AN ILLUSION

The point is that an objective of 20,000 feet is an illusion. It doesn't mean anything, because it's just a number that we've assigned so that we can make comparisons. If reaching 20,000 feet, or any other objective, is a meaningful activity to you, that's fine. Just don't feel that having done it has any value. Don't try to impress other people with the fact that you've done it, because it may not mean anything to them.

In many other ways, the objectives that Power Performers have in their lives are meaningful only to them, not to others. Hard to believe that Neil Rettig would sit on top of a silk cottonwood tree in Guyana for six months, isn't it? Only he could tell you why getting that picture of the Harpy eagle chick making its first flight was so important to him.

Hard for us to understand why Chuck Yeager, who was very much in love with his wife Glennis, and his two young children, would be willing to strap himself onto four huge tanks of liquid oxygen and take the enormous risk of trying to crash the sound barrier when so many experts told him it was impossible. But it was important enough to him to risk everything.

Almost impossible for us to understand why Reinhold Messner would risk his life to try to vindicate himself with the mountain-climbing community by climbing Mount Everest alone and without oxygen. But to him it meant more than anything else.

If you make objectives in your life to impress others, you'll end up disillusioned. I remember how foolish I felt when I met a group of climbers on the Eiger mountain in Switzerland and tried to impress them by telling them that I'd been to 20,000 feet. They looked at me with blank stares because it didn't mean a thing to them. One of the key things that separates Power Performers from ordinary people is that trying to impress anyone else simply doesn't appeal to them.

Let's say you decide your definition of Power Performance is to become a millionaire. You're sure that if you had a million dollars in net worth you'd then be financially independent and could do whatever you wanted with your life. So for five years of your life you devote every waking effort to achieving this objective. You put everything else on the back burner while you work for this. And you make it! Five years later, you truly do have a net worth of one million dollars. I can promise you—you'll suffer a great period of depression. It won't make the change in your life you'd expected. You'll be wandering around repeating the words of the Peggy Lee song, saying: "Is that all there is?"

> *I don't know much about being a millionaire, but I'll bet I'd be darling at it.*
>
> DOROTHY PARKER

Why? Because the objective of having a million dollars is completely subjective. One million dollars is 130 million Japanese yen, or 1,725 million Italian liras. Can you imagine trying to explain to an Italian that you had lost five years of your life trying to accumulate 1,725 million Italian liras? The idea is ridiculous. So once you realize that this objective for which you gave up five years of your life is an illusion, you'll slip into depression. You'll probably stay there for about a year, until you set a new, more meaningful objective and start living your life again.

HOW TO INVENTORY YOUR ENERGY

Let's play a game to take inventory of the areas of your life where you're devoting your energies. On the next page is a chart listing several categories of your life where you're probably devoting time and effort. I want you to put an *X* in the box that corresponds to the amount of energy you're expending in that particular area. Go ahead and mark up the book because I'll want you to go back through the list a second time before you can draw any conclusions.

For example, the first category is career. If you don't have an occupation outside your family responsibilities—you're a housewife or house-husband—you'd put your *X* in the one column. If you're a hard-driving, 6- or 7-days a week, 12-hours-a-day, career person, you'd give it a 10. If you go to a job 40 hours a week, but it's become a routine for you and doesn't really present a challenge, then you'd give it a 5. Do you have the idea? Good. So go ahead and rate career, remembering it has nothing to do with how much success you're having, only the amount of effort you're putting forth. If you're unemployed (I prefer to think of you as being on a consulting basis), but are devoting all of your energy to finding a job, give it a 10.

Now rate politics. How involved are you in studying the political scene and supporting or opposing various political candidates or causes? Can you name your state and federal congressional representatives? When did you last write to them or call them?

Community. How much of your life do you spend attending local council and planning meetings? Are you a mover and shaker in your community or do you take the attitude that you can't fight city hall?

> *In the first place, God made idiots. That was for practice. Then he made school boards.*
>
> Mark Twain

Charity is next. How much of your effort do you channel into helping others? Apart from mailing in the occasional check are you actively involved in fund raising for your favorite charity?

Spectator sports. Are you an avid baseball, football, or basketball fan? Do you know who won every game last weekend and can you beat the best of them when you rattle off statistics?

Hobbies—including activity sports such as golf or tennis. Remember we're ranking not just the time you spend but the energy you expend in this area. How intensely you involve yourself would affect the rating.

Now let's move into personal areas of your life and have you rate marriage. If you're unmarried but devote a great deal of effort finding someone to marry, you can still give yourself a high rating.

Children. How much time do you spend with your children? How involved are you in their education? Do you religiously sup-

port them if they play sports at school? Again you could give this
a high rating even if you don't have any children, if getting some is
a high priority.

> *If the kids are still alive when my husband gets*
> *home from his job, then hey, I've done my job.*
>
> ROSEANNE ARNOLD

Then rate self-development. How much of your energy do you
devote to building a better you? Are you constantly listening to
audio tapes in your car? Do you keep current on all the latest skill-
and attitude-building books?

Physical fitness. If you spend a couple of hours a day down at
the gym and run marathons, give yourself a 10. If your idea of
exercise is bringing your TV recliner upright so you can go get
another beer, give yourself a 1.

Social life is the next category. Rate the amount of energy you
put into developing and maintaining a group of friends. Do you
find yourself at a party or social gathering at least once a week, or
does the office Christmas party do it for you?

Sexual activities. Remember it's not necessarily how much
luck you're having, but how much effort you're putting forth.

How much energy do you devote to worrying? This may seem
like a strange category to you, but some people can consume their
lives with this activity, and I suppose all of us have faced a period
of our lives when this was a major concern. If you worry a lot, give
yourself a high number. If you can take most problems in your
stride, give yourself a low number.

Then finally rate how much of your time you simply waste. If
you pride yourself on time efficiency, give yourself a 1. If you have
a tendency to lend new meaning to the word procrastination, then
give yourself a 10.

Now we're ready to make some sense of this. I want you to go
back down the chart and put a circle in the square that corresponds to the amount of energy you'd *like* to be expending in that
area. Sometimes your circle will go around your cross.

LIFE ENERGY GRID

	1	2	3	4	5	6	7	8	9	10
Career										
Politics										
Community										
Charity										
Sports										
Hobbies										
Marriage										
Children										
Self-Development										
Physical Fitness										
Social life										
Sexual										
Worrying										
Wasting Time										

For example, you may have given yourself a 10 in the career area, but you're really not comfortable working that hard. It may be affecting your marriage or your relationship with your children, or your golf game, or whatever. The amount of energy you'd like to be expending may be closer to a 6.

To give another example you may have marked a 3 as the amount of energy you're spending on your children. However, you wish you had more time for them and mark the amount of energy you'd like to be expending as an 8.

Go on down the list and assign a second number to each category. When you finish you'll have two columns of numbers.

Finally, go back down the list and check off in the right hand margin any of the 14 categories where your cross and your circle are three or more squares apart. So if your first number was a 4 and your second number in that category was a 7, that's three apart and you check it off.

The point of this is that Power Performers know it's not what you're doing with your life that makes the difference, it's whether you're doing *what you want to be doing* with your life that releases internal energy.

Look at the areas of your life you circled as having a spread of three or more squares between the energy you're expending and the amount of energy you'd like to be expending. These are the areas where you need to be making some changes in your lifestyle. The objective is not to have you at a 10 in each of these areas, or a 1, or a 5, or whatever the national average might be. The objective for a Power Performer is to be devoting your energy to the area of your life that you really and truly value.

I retake this exercise every three months, only looking at the previous sheets after I've completed it. It's a valid and valuable test of lifestyle assessment. Please have all the members of your family take it also.

The other thing this exercise does is clarify how much of your life is self-directed, or to what extent outside influences have manipulated it. For example, when I first rated community activities, I was a 1 looking for a 0. I can't ever recall attending a council meeting, a planning meeting, or a political rally unless I had an ulterior motive, such as something to do with my real estate investments. Quite frankly, I've always felt guilty about that. Society tells us to get involved. However, when I rated my *desire* to spend energy in this area, I was also a 1 looking for a 0. So now I know better where I stand. It doesn't interest me, and as long as things in my community keep jogging along as well as they have, I don't intend to spend any of my life's adventure feeling guilty about it. (I live in the tiny community of La Habra Heights in Southern California. It's a city of about 1,800 homes that we formed 15 years ago to preserve the rural environment, a phrase that a cynic would translate as "keep the developers out." So not much happens here. We've never had anybody run for City Council on any other plank than preserve the environment, so we don't have what you could even remotely call a political opposition to get excited about.)

> *I am strongly in favor of common sense, common honesty and common decency. This makes me forever ineligible for any public office.*
>
> H. L. Mencken

Please don't think Power Performers are remiss in setting objectives for our lives. Of course we're competitive, but we always clearly understand that the fun comes from devoting our lives to things that are satisfying now, not wasting our lives in the hope of some future reward. That's what releases the energy that takes Power Performers to the top.

The difference between daydreams and objectives

You take another key step toward Power Performance when you learn the difference between objectives and daydreams. Many people go through life thinking they have objectives when they have only filled their minds with grandiose daydreams.

The D'Arcy, Masius Benton and Bowles advertising agency once took a fascinating survey. *USA Today* reported on it in a front-page headline story, under the banner "We Daydream About One Life, But Lead Another." They found that most of us fantasize about becoming an instant hero—76 percent fantasize about saving a life, 35 percent about finding a cancer cure, and 33 percent about winning an Olympic gold medal.

They also asked what we would do if we could do anything we wanted. Women chose to gamble at Monte Carlo or dine at the White House. Men chose to go on a safari, closely followed by a desire for hot-air ballooning and white water rafting.

The most interesting thing was the tremendous gap between what the people surveyed would like to be doing with their lives and what they were really doing.

Sixty-eight percent said that their greatest pleasure was watching television. Can you believe that?

So let's spend some time clarifying the difference between objectives and daydreams.

If you had asked me ten years ago about my objectives, I would probably have mentioned three things:

1. I wanted to make a million dollars.
2. I wanted to climb to 20,000 feet.
3. I wanted to drive down to Buenos Aires.

So far I have accomplished the first two: I became a millionaire through investment in real estate, and I did reach 20,000 feet on Mount Chimborazo in Ecuador. However, the third one still eludes me.

For years now, I've described driving down to Buenos Aires as an objective. I have always thought it would be great fun to take a year off and get together with a group of friends, buy a Land Rover or a minibus, and drive through Central America, and all the way down to Buenos Aires. We would learn the language as we went, see all the fascinating sights of South America as we moved south, and thrill to all the exciting adventures that we would encounter on the road. This was my objective.

Or so I thought. Then I realized that this wasn't an objective at all—this was merely a pleasant daydream. Until I had a written plan, until it was in focus, it wasn't an objective, it was only a daydream. I needed to decide when I would leave, with whom I would go, how much money I would need, and my exact route. Until I had put all the details together, I was daydreaming. The closest I have come to my objective so far is to buy a four wheel drive and take a month long test run as far as Honduras and El Salvador. Apart from that I've never really taken the time or made the effort to make that daydream of driving to Buenos Aires into a solid objective.

Unfortunately most people never take the time to turn their daydreams into objectives. They have what they think is an objective, a target—such as becoming wealthy or being named the president of a big corporation. In reality those hopes are only flimsy daydreams because people never laid down a firm plan to make it happen.

Let's compare the difference between objectives and daydreams.

◆ With objectives you make things happen to you; with day-dreams things just happen.

◆ Objectives require a great deal of planning and effort, while daydreams require no effort on your part. One morning you wake up to find a long-lost rich uncle has died and left you a million dollars, or that your lottery number was a winner.

◆ Objectives take time, maybe even a lifetime (although I personally feel it's very self-limiting to make an objective for any longer than five years). However, daydreams can come thick and fast—they require only one giant leap into fantasy. When a daydream does come true, it happens overnight.

◆ Objectives are a vision—a mental picture that can work for you, even when you're not aware of it. Daydreams are nothing more than illusion, because often we don't believe they will ever really come true. Dreams don't provide the motivating images, they don't provide the vivid prompting of an objective because they lack the solid backing of plans and efforts. These illusions can be so deceiving that most of the time they work against you as your subconscious mind understands (even if you don't) that you're fantasizing and that these things will never really happen.

◆ Objectives are always written down, while daydreams are merely floating around in the imagination. This is the major difference between the two: *objectives are in writing and daydreams are not.*

Some of the highest achievers of all time didn't reach what others might see as "the objective." Frank Wells didn't climb all seven summits, but look at what it meant to his life. Sir John Hunt, leader of the first successful ascent of Mount Everest, never stood on the summit. Moses never reached the promised land. Columbus never reached India. It's not the achievement of an objective that releases the energy to become a Power Performer, it's the satisfaction and joy you get from the journey to that objective.

While Power Performers thrive on stretching for and reaching stimulating objectives, they never fall into the trap of sacrificing the enjoyment of life to the attainment of an objective. There is nothing more tragic than a person who achieves wealth, fame, power, or prestige only to find he's lost the love of his family and friends, the respect of his colleagues, and above all has lost the ability to appreciate life for its own sake.

If the journey to your objective isn't fun and exciting, if it's filled only with sacrifice and hard work, you'll probably become discouraged and quit. You might never reach your objective anyway, and what a waste that would be! Even if you did achieve what you wanted, you would have lost more than you could possibly gain.

So only set objectives that will give you an exciting, rewarding journey, for the destination itself is bound to disappoint you.

◆◆◆

The Fourth Secret of Power Performers is:

They know that the journey's the thing.

◆◆◆

In the next chapter I'll teach you how you can apply Harold Geneen's philosophy of building a corporation to the challenge of building a new life for yourself.

5

POWER PERFORMERS EXPERIENCE SUCCESS LONG BEFORE THEY ACHIEVE IT

Life consists in what a man is thinking of all day.

— Emerson

Our life is what our thoughts make it.

— Marcus Aurelius

If you don't know what you want to become, your objective is to be a nobody.

— Roger Dawson

In this chapter I'm going to teach you how to condition your mind so that it becomes the vehicle that will take you from where you are now to where you are capable of being in the future.

Harold Geneen, the former head of ITT and now head of his own investment company, is a remarkably successful business-man—an authentic Power Performer. When he started with International Telephone and Telegraph Company it specialized in international telephone services and was doing $800 million in sales. During the seventeen years that he ran ITT, he took his company to over $22 billion in sales, and annual profits soared from $29 million to $562 million. By then ITT was the eleventh largest company in the United States, and one of the world's largest conglomerates, owning 250 other companies. Employees at his company revered him so much that they would teasingly ask if they should pronounce his name with a soft "G" as in Jesus, or a hard one as in God, and proclaimed that their favorite prayer was, "Harold be thy name . . . " according to his (unofficial) biographer Robert Schoenberg.

Harold Geneen was arguably the most successful businessman in the world during the 1960s and 1970s, and even today professors at business schools around the country talk about his accomplishments with reverence. Yet he sums up his entire business philosophy in three sentences: "You read a book from the beginning to the end, but you run a business the opposite way. You start with the end, and then you do everything you must to reach it."

Power Performers really relate to that. They understand that the energy and the drive to be super-successful come from clearly creating the destination in their minds. In many ways they are like heat-seeking missiles: Once they lock onto the target, they can zoom toward it. Remember how my attitude changed on Mount Rainier, once I climbed out of the clouds and could see the summit outlined against the navy blue sky? Clearly seeing your objective energizes you. Low performers spend their lives in the fog of unfocused effort. Power Performers see the objective clearly and stride out boldly toward it. They know that once they lock the objective clearly into their subconscious mind and reinforce it with positive self-imagery they can then focus all their internal energy on achieving the objective.

So in this chapter I'm going to teach you how to condition your mind the way Power Performers do. However, don't forget what I told you in Chapter Four: Your objective in life shouldn't be just to acquire something, such as a million dollars or a Rolls-Royce; nor to become something, such as president of your company or mayor of your city. You must also get joy and satisfaction from the journey if you're to release all your internal energy.

YOU ARE ALREADY MOVING TOWARD AN OBJECTIVE

The first thing to learn about conditioning your mind is this: You are already moving toward an objective whether you realize it or not. Just because you may be thinking, "I haven't really figured out what I want out of life yet," doesn't mean that you're not focused. You are already moving in a specific direction, even if you haven't consciously set an objective. As we climbed the mountain through the clouds we relied on an experienced guide to keep us moving toward our objective. Without his help we would still have been moving toward an objective, but probably the wrong objective. If you don't know what you want to become, your objective is to be a nobody. If you don't know what you want to get, your objective is to get nothing.

Think of a sailboat out in the ocean. If the person at the helm doesn't set a course, it doesn't mean that the boat isn't going anywhere. The winds and the currents will still take it to a destination, but it will end up somewhere other than where the helmsman wanted it to go. If we don't set objectives, we human beings drift like that sailboat. You can never be without purpose and direction. Since you're always moving toward a destination, you can only be moving toward an objective that you didn't set. This is because of the way our sub-conscious mind works.

> *If you don't know what you want to become, your objective is to be a nobody.*
>
> *If you don't know what you want to get, your objective is to get nothing.*

WHAT WE KNOW ABOUT HOW THE SUBCONSCIOUS MIND WORKS

Let's look at the history of psychology to see what researchers have learned so far about how the subconscious mind works. Sigmund Freud was the first person to prove scientifically the existence of the subconscious mind. As a researcher in Austria at the end of the nineteenth century, he discovered that the subconscious mind is dynamic and a powerful motivator of human behavior. He taught that problems in the way the subconscious mind thinks can not only cause dysfunctional thinking, it can also cause serious physical problems. He showed us that a minor event in childhood could grow into a major neurosis in later life. Like a pearl that begins as a minuscule grain of sand to be coated and recoated until it becomes large, so these neuroses begin with microscopic thoughts in the subconscious mind. Freud felt if he could reach into the subconscious mind and expose the nucleus, he would be able to cure the patient.

What Freud needed was a method of reaching and influencing the subconscious mind. He studied with French hypnotist Jean Charot in Paris for a year and back in Vienna worked with hypnosis for several years. From physician Joseph Brueuer he learned the cathartic form of inquiry that in layman's terms means, "Let the patient talk." Then he realized that he could uncover what was in people's subconscious minds by using free association. He was a trained scientist so he had a very organized approach to solving problems, and with extraordinary zeal he began to probe deeper and deeper into his patient's subconscious minds. He soon realized that there were dynamic forces at work in the patient's mind of which the patient was not aware. Gradually he began to realize that the conscious mind could not perceive most of the dynamic forces of our mind, and he developed his theory of the subconscious mind.

> *After a year in therapy, my psychiatrist said to me, "Maybe life isn't for everyone."*
>
> LARRY BROWN

What happened in Freud's tiny office in Vienna was a remarkable leap forward in the march of mankind. Almost by accident a highly talented and brilliant scientist was exposed to a new theory and decided to spend the rest of his life pursuing it to see where it would lead him. His office became his laboratory, his only scientific data were the rambling comments of his patients, and his only piece of equipment was his couch.

Free association worked best when the patient was lying down and could not see the analyst, who would sit behind him. (For decades Freud's disciples exactly duplicated this arrangement, thinking that there was some deep scientific reason for Freud's position in relationship to the patient. When Freud finally heard about it, he said, "Oh for heaven's sake! Don't they know I sat that way because I'm hard of hearing in one ear?" Sometimes a cigar is just a cigar!) He encouraged his patients to express any thought that occurred to them. If they thought it, they should say it, even if it was obscene, insulting to Freud, or simply appeared to be an idiotic or irrelevant notion. Freud discovered that this was an ideal condition for his patients to discover resistance or conflict between what was in the unconscious mind and in the conscious mind. If a thought popped out in free association that caused the patient discomfort, Freud would pursue it to find the cause of the discomfort, something that the patient may have suppressed since childhood.

From Freud's early beginnings with free association, he developed the system we call psychoanalysis. In analysis, a trained psychologist talks to the patient about his childhood and early years, and in this way leads the subject within his subconscious to find the nucleus of the problem. The objective is to strengthen the ego, or adult in transactional analysis terms—that part of the personality that thinks logically and is not a victim to the immature id or the controlling superego.

FOUR MEN WHO HAVE CHANGED WESTERN THOUGHT

I have always thought of Sigmund Freud as one of the few people who have substantially affected the way Western people think. Ever since Alvin Toffler wrote *Future Shock* a new fear has entered society's consciousness, that one day the dramatic changes that our world forces us to undergo will be too much for us, and the collective intelligence of humankind will blow a fuse. Although it's true that we must live with more uncertainty than former generations, most of the rapid changes we've seen are in the area of communications. Our access to information has multiplied so rapidly that unless we learn how to manage it better, it will deluge us so much that we will no longer be able to make any sense of it at all.

However, that's largely in our hands. We need to decide what is important for us to know and what isn't. For example, I no longer read newspaper stories about the information highway and how our televisions, computers, and telephones will all merge into one. It's interesting stuff, but since what I read today will be obsolete by next week, it hardly seems worth my time.

So, although we appear to be living in a society changing so fast we can hardly keep up with it, changes that substantially affect the basic thinking patterns of our society are very rare. I can think of only four people who have caused genuine shifts in our culture, and Freud is one of them.

Of the other three, I must first include Jesus Christ. His life was Western people's first real clue to the existence of a universal life-force from which we derive our internal energy. There really is a flow of psychic energy in the universe, and we have either aligned ourselves with that flow or we haven't. Power Performers align themselves perfectly to this energy flow, and it's the key to their seemingly effortless top performance. Conversely, I'm sure you know people who haven't aligned themselves to this force. They work hard, they try hard, and they often achieve a lot. However, they seemed dogged by bad luck—eventually they come crashing down.

The second person on my list is the world's first space explorer, Italian Galilei Galileo. A musician's son, he was born in Pisa in 1564 and went on to study medicine at the university there. It was during his first year at the University of Pisa that a chance happening changed his life. He was daydreaming and found himself watching a large lamp swing in the breeze. It occurred to him that the lamp took the same time to swing from side to side, no matter how far it swung. (Later he used this observation to invent the pendulum as means of regulating clocks.) From this observation he developed a fascination for mathematics, changed his major, and went on to a chair of mathematics at Padua University.

When he was visiting Venice at the age of 45 another chance encounter changed his life. He heard of a new-fangled gadget called a telescope and rushed home to build one, starting with a 3× magnification and then improving that to a 32× magnification. His telescopes were so good that they were the first ones star gazers could use for astronomy, and they were soon in great demand all over Europe. With such a great technological advantage, he made many discoveries, including that the surface of Mars was irregular, not smooth; that the Milky Way was really a collection of stars; and he also discovered the satellites of Jupiter and the rings of Saturn.

His promotion of Copernicus's theory that the Earth was not the center of the universe shocked civilization. The Catholic church accused him of heresy in 1633 and held him under house arrest. He caused the furor with his book *Dialogue on the Two Chief Systems of the World,* published in 1632 (the two systems referred to were Ptolemy's, who believed that the Earth was the center of the universe; and Copernicus's, who believed that the Earth revolved around the Sun). Before Galileo published this book, few men questioned that the heavens revolved around the Earth. It was a courageous thing to do, because Cardinal Bellarmine had warned him 16 years before what would happen to him if he pursued his ideas beyond saying that they were only a mathematical theory. The pope ordered him arrested, he was convicted at trial in Rome, and he spent the last eight years of his life under house arrest. The Vatican did not admit they'd made a mistake until 1984, although even then they declined to overturn the charges. Galileo had proved that the Earth was only a speck in an immense universe and was certainly not the center of it. As with Christ, Galileo gave Western people a new way of looking at themselves and the world.

Next on my list is Charles Darwin, who was a highly unlikely candidate to become someone who would change the way we think. He was a very poor student whose father told him that he would disgrace himself and all his family. After Darwin failed in medicine at Edinburgh University, his father sent him to Cambridge to study for the ministry. He was failing at this when a friendly botany professor interceded and recommended him for a position of naturalist on board the H.M.S. *Beagle,* which was leaving for a five-year voyage to the South Pacific. Since Darwin had no qualifications for the job, we can only assume that his friend thought that he would be better off to have some adventures until he grew up and decided what he wanted to do with his life. His father certainly saw it as goofing off and objected at first, but gave up in frustration. So at the age of twenty-two, young Darwin set sail on his big adventure.

> *All modern men are descended from a worm-like creature, but it shows more on some people.*
>
> WILL CUPPY

All of Darwin's later scientific observation and theories derived from his observations on that voyage and from his subsequent examination of the thousands of samples he collected.

It was a good thing that he didn't have any scientific training because if he had he probably never would have developed his theory of evolution. Scientists in those days were extremely scrupulous about studying scientific evidence and conducting experiments without any preconceived notions. Darwin was not schooled in this and preferred to come up with a fanciful theory and see if he could find evidence to support it. The theory of evolution was not new, and even his grandfather Eramus, who was a philosopher and inventor, had advanced it, along with several French philosophers. The problem was that organized religion would strongly oppose such a speculative theory so they had to have hard evidence to support it, and nobody had come up with any.

In 1838 Darwin read Malthus's *Essay on the Principle of Population,* in which he tried to point out that selective evolution must exist because the world's population was increasing geometrically while the world's food supply was increasing only arithmetically. Darwin immediately saw the "Yes, but . . ." in this theory. Whatever the ratios, humankind did increase its food supply to meet its need, which avoided forced partial eradication of the species. However, it also immediately occurred to him that this didn't apply to birds and animals. Because they could not increase their food supply it followed that there *must be a forced eradication of the part of the species.* A scientist would have stopped to prove these theories stage by stage, but Darwin's mind was leaping ahead, and he intuitively developed his Survival of the Fittest theory of evolution. Suddenly he knew why the birds and animals of the Galápagos Islands were different on each island, although the physical conditions on the islands were identical. Suddenly he knew why the South American rhea, for example, could so closely resemble the African ostrich.

Charles Darwin knew how controversial his theory would be, so he determined to keep it to himself until he could finish exhaustive research to support his theory. Exhaustive turned out to be a major understatement. As he said, "It is a cursed evil to any man to become as absorbed in any subject as I am in mine." Twenty years later, when he was still not ready to publish, he got a letter from Alfred Wallace, a naturalist working in the Malay Archipelago, that outlined a complete statement of Darwin's own theories on evolution and natural selection. Devastated that he was about to get scooped after 20 years of work, Darwin quickly developed an abstract of his work that he called *Origin of the Species* and rushed it into publication. It became an instant best-seller, and never again would the public permit him to be the reclusive naturalist puttering through his accumulation of samples. He spent the rest of his life in a maelstrom of controversy and died 23 years later of a heart attack triggered by a disease he had picked up on his H.M.S. *Beagle* voyage.

So Darwin's theory of evolution gave us one more reason to rush home to our teddy bears by raising the possibility that huumans might have been a biological accident instead of the result of divine creation. Again people's ideas of themselves had changed.

Finally Sigmund Freud, the father of psychology. Until Freud, Western people felt that they alone controlled their thoughts, but he proved us wrong.

For many years, we considered Freud's methods of psycho-analysis an excellent way to deal with neurosis, in spite of its disadvantages. It's a very expensive process that may take as many as five visits to the psychologist a week for as long as five years. Recently many psychologists have abandoned their belief in Freudian analysis, feeling that spending up to five years lying on a couch rehashing a problem can make you sicker than when you went in. Albert Ellis, the brilliant founder of the rational-emotive school of therapy, dismissed the whole movement by saying: "Insight will help you very little. [You think that] your knowledge of how you got disturbed will make you less neurotic? Drivel! It will often make you nuttier!"

> *A wonderful discovery—psychoanalysis. Makes*
> *quite simple people feel they're complex*
>
> SAMUEL N. BEHRMAN

THE PSYCHOLOGICAL THEORY
THAT EVERYONE SUPPORTS

There is one area of psychological study, however, that nobody disputes, and that's Carl Rogers's belief in self-image psychology. Rogers, like Darwin, studied in a seminary but decided it wasn't for him. He switched to psychology, got his Ph.D. from Columbia University, and went to work in a community guidance center in Rochester, New York. He came to the conclusion that therapists guided their patients too much, so he moved his chair around to face them so that they would feel more like the center of attention. He also started calling them clients rather than patients so as not to reinforce the feeling that they were sick and needed the therapist to cure them. Before explaining Rogers' work any further, I'd like to give you a test that will show you what Rogers found out about his clients. It's similar to the one you took in the last chapter, but it covers personal characteristics rather than activities.

Put an *X* in the column that you feel most accurately describes your reaction to the statement in the left-hand column. Number 1 would mean that you don't agree with the statement at all. Number 10 would mean that you agree with the statement. Don't be afraid to mark a 1 or a 10 even though this may seem that you're taking an extreme position.

When you have completed the first run-through and marked an *X* on each of the lines, go back down and mark a circle to indicate how true you would like that statement to be.

For example, when you considered the first line "I feel liked," you thought, "Well, I'm not the life and soul of every party, but my family likes me, my coworkers seem to like me, and I have a group of affectionate friends." So you put an *X* in column 8. When you considered how much you'd like other people to like you, you thought, "I feel good about where I am on this one. I can see that some people might want to be a 10, but I'm happy with an 8." So you mark your circle around your *X*.

When you considered how powerful you felt it was a different story. You thought, "I really don't feel that I have much influence over what's going on in my life. My spouse consults with me but usually has his (or her) way. I sure don't have any power at work. I'll give that a 3." Then when you think about how powerful you'd like to be you think, "You know that's one area of my life I'd really like to change. There's a fire inside me that tells me that I should be running things more. I don't want to be a dictator but I'd like more control." So on this one you put your circle in the column 8.

You should find this a very revealing exercise. It's not the same one that Carl Rogers gave his clients, but the flavor is the

SELF-ESTEEM GRID

	1	2	3	4	5	6	7	8	9	10
I feel liked										
I feel powerful										
I feel loved										
I feel submissive										
I work hard										
I am intelligent										
I am artistic										
I'm a good parent										
I'm a good lover										
I am attractive										
I am charismatic										
I feel respected										
I love my life										
I care about people										

same. After he'd given it to a few clients, he really began to feel that he was on to something. So he set up an experimental group, half of whom were people who had sought therapy for personality problems. The other half had never sought therapy and so presumably didn't think they needed it.

With remarkable conformity the people who had sought therapy saw large discrepancies between how they thought of themselves and how they would like people to think of them. The people who had not sought therapy saw themselves much as they would like to be.

From this he developed a strong belief in self-image psychology and came to the conclusion that nearly all psychological problems were revealed not only by a discrepancy between who we thought we were and who we would like to be, but were probably also caused by that discrepancy.

How did you do on the test? Were there some areas where you saw a big difference between how you saw yourself and how you'd like to be? Go back down the chart and check off at the side all the lines where your X and your circle were 3 or more squares apart. So if your first number was a 4 and your second number in that category was a 7, that's 3 apart and you check it off.

Problems of maladjustment come in when we're not able to integrate our reactions to events with our self-image. For example, a traffic cop pulls you over and gives you a ticket for not wearing your seatbelt. You blow your stack at the cop and suggest that he spend more time trying to stop drive-by shootings and less time harassing good law-abiding citizens who are just trying to get to work so that they can earn some money and pay their taxes. For good measure you throw in a lecture about who is working for whom in this relationship. The cop has heard that lecture 15 times already today and doesn't think it's very helpful. He mentions that you were also going 11 miles over the speed limit and he wasn't going to mention it but since you're so law abiding you'd probably want him to write you up for that too. That really gets your goat, and your next tirade gets you a fix-it ticket for a broken tail light. You snatch the tickets out of his hand and squeal off, something that gets you another ticket a mile down the road for making a lane change without signaling and again exceeding the speed limit.

As this experience sinks into a bank of millions of other experiences you have two choices in terms of how you will integrate this experience with your self-image:

1. *The healthy reaction* would be to realize that in most instances you are a law-abiding citizen. You broke the traffic laws in this instance but that's not a reason for society to condemn you or for you to lower your image of yourself. Also you see yourself as a person who can typically deal well with frustration but have lost it on this occasion. No reason for everyone to go around fearing your reactions or for you to develop a new self-image over it.

2. *The unhealthy reaction* would be to deny your reactions to the experience or to see them in a distorted way. You're sure that the cop was picking on you because you drive an expensive car and that the system is unfair because he has a quota to meet. (Of course cops have quotas to meet! How else is their supervisor going to know if they're doing their job or just goofing off? The quota for a highway patrol officer may be as high as 150 tickets a month. The quota for a local sheriff or police officer may be as few as 15 a month.) Then you start feeling rotten about yourself because you've set up dissonance between your self-image and your reaction to your experiences.

So Carl Rogers divined that all people form images of themselves in their subconscious minds. He went on to establish that that self-image in turn sets the limit of each person's development. A person can't grow beyond the self-concept he or she has established in the subconscious mind. Remember the story of the farmer who found a jar in a pumpkin field? To see if the pumpkin would be strong enough to grow and break the jar, he poked a growing seedling inside it and left it there. When he went back to harvest the grown pumpkins he found that this one had not been able to break the jar. It had merely grown to mold itself to the size and shape of the jar and then had stopped growing. Our self-image puts the same kind of limit on what we can accomplish. If we can expand our self-image we can expand our potential. I believe that it's a prerequisite: We cannot expand our potential unless we first learn how to expand our self-image.

All this points to the same truth: If you want to become a Power Performer, you must begin by learning to change your own self-image.

THE GREAT-GRANDDADDY OF ALL SELF-HELP BOOKS

A great book about self-image psychology is *Think and Grow Rich* by Napoleon Hill. This is probably the great-granddaddy of all self-help books. Napoleon Hill was a newspaper editor and later a speech writer for President Franklin Delano Roosevelt. It was Hill who wrote the famous sentence: "Let me assert my firm belief that the only thing we have to fear is fear itself—nameless, unreasoning, unjustified terror which paralyzes needed efforts to convert retreat to advance." He probably adapted it from a line that Henry David Thoreau wrote: "Nothing is so much to be feared as fear."

The book came about because industrialist Andrew Carnegie hired Hill to write a book about his success principles. Carnegie had come to the United States penniless from Scotland and had worked as a telegraph operator for the Pennsylvania Railroad for 12 years. He became the richest man in the world because he saw the potential of steel beams for railway-bridge construction, rather than wood trestles. This simple insight led to his starting the Carnegie Steel Company, which he sold to U.S. Steel for $250 million in 1901.

It's fascinating that we human beings tend to forget the difficulties of accomplishment once we've reached our objective. Once we've done something, we tend to look at others and think, "Why are you having so much trouble? It's not that hard." We do that regardless of the difficulty we may have had when we first tried it. Carnegie felt that way about making money.

I remember I felt that way about climbing Mount Rainier. I told you earlier what a challenge that was for me, and how much agony I was in afterward. For a week following the climb, my legs were so stiff, I couldn't lift my feet up onto sidewalk curbs and I'd have to reach down and pick my legs up by my knees.

Just as mothers quickly forget the pain of childbirth when they first hold their baby, so we soon put behind us the pain of attacking and conquering life's objectives. Only two weeks later, when people would say to me, "How tough was it? Do you think I could do it?" I'd cheerfully respond, "Go for it; anyone can do it. It's not that hard."

Power Performer Andrew Carnegie felt the same way about making money. During his rise to power I'm sure he faced incredible difficulties, but after his success he couldn't understand the poverty that he saw all around him. It astounded him that so many people were having trouble surviving in a country that had given him a fortune.

He wanted to endow the world with his secrets of success. A high-school dropout, he lacked the education to write a book so he hired Napoleon Hill to write it for him.

Hill says in the preface:

> In every chapter of this book, mention has been made of the money-making secret which has made fortunes for hundreds of exceedingly wealthy men whom I have carefully analyzed over a long period of years.
>
> The secret was brought to my attention by Andrew Carnegie, more than half a century ago. The canny lovable old Scotsman carelessly tossed it into my mind, when I was but a boy. Then he sat back in his chair, with a merry twinkle in his eyes, and watched carefully to see if I had brains enough to understand the full significance of what he had said to me.
>
> When he saw that I had grasped the idea, he asked if I would be willing to spend twenty years or more preparing myself to take it to the world, to men and women who, without the secret, might go through life as failures. I said I would, and with Mr. Carnegie's cooperation, I have kept my promise.

Hill followed Carnegie around for many years, watching everything the billionaire did. From this experience he wrote *Think and Grow Rich.* If you haven't already, I urge you to read it or to listen to Earl Nightingale's brilliant audio condensation. It amazes me that everyone doesn't read and covet this book, which is available for a few dollars in every bookstore. At my seminars, when I ask for a show of hands typically only 10 percent of the audience has read it. The book will make an incredible difference in your perspective. As Earl Nightingale says, "The hand that puts this book down after finishing it, is a different hand." The book fascinates me because Hill never spells out Carnegie's success secret.

In the preface of the book he assures you that by reading it, you'll learn the secret of accumulating wealth. "The secret to which I refer has been mentioned no fewer than a hundred times throughout this book. It has not been directly named . . . if you are ready to put it use, you will recognize this secret at least once in every chapter." So you can't turn to a page and find the secret carefully outlined in a little box. Nevertheless, you'll understand the secret as soon as you've finished the book because you will have planted it in your subconscious mind. This was consistent with Andrew Carnegie's feelings that you have to make people work for their own success. As he said, "There is no use whatever trying to help people who do not help themselves. You cannot push anyone up a ladder unless he is willing to climb himself." Although it may be cheating, I'm going to tell you the message that's buried in that book.

In his day, Carnegie had an opportunity to rub shoulders with hundreds of self-made millionaires. As he got to know them, he realized that there was a common denominator amongst all of them. What they all shared was that even in the earliest days of their careers these millionaires knew what they wanted and what it would be like to be successful. They experienced their success long before they achieved it.

They could create a visual image of their success. They could experience the feeling of stepping into their Rolls-Royce and sinking into the fine leather seats. They knew what it would be like to wear the world's finest clothes and have dozens of servants at their disposal. They knew how it would feel to walk into the boardroom of a corporation they owned and have everyone present rise in respect. They knew what it would be like to enter a ballroom filled with people who would turn and be awed by their approach.

Hill called this ability to experience the future "imagizing." These high achievers were able to imagine—to create in their mind—the feel of success. When Carnegie first looked at a wooden trestle railway bridge and visualized how steel beams could replace all that wood, he didn't see himself as a steel salesman. He saw himself owning a great steel mill.

Napoleon Hill taught us that to become successful we must first change our subconscious thoughts. Power Performers must first imagize—project onto the subconscious mind—the experience of great success.

As Harold Geneen said, "First you start with the end, and then you do everything you must to reach it."

The Cadillac Motor Company once did a commercial that illustrated what I'm telling you. It began in black and white and showed a young man, dressed in the golfing attire of the 1930s, caddying at an exclusive country club. He was loading golf clubs into the trunk of an early model Cadillac. As it drove off down the driveway, the young man watched after it wistfully. The voice-over said, "Even way back then, you knew that someday you'd be driving a Cadillac." Then the commercial burst into color and we saw the young man, all grown up, driving out of the same country club in his own shiny new Cadillac.

> *Can you hold in your mind the image of yourself as a Power Performer? When every day is an exciting adventure?*

Can you really visualize and hold in your mind the image of yourself as a Power Performer? Can you experience your success before you achieve it? Can you imagize the day when petty fears and worries no longer influence you, and when every day is an exciting adventure?

CHANGING THE LIFE OF THOSE AROUND YOU

You can use imagizing not only to change your life, but also to change the life of those around you. I think one of the great joys of being an employer is the gift it brings of being able to expand the self-image of your employees. Power Performers love to see someone start at the bottom in their company, as a receptionist, for example, or in the shipping department. They can see that they're good people, honest and loyal and willing to put in a day's work and then some. However, they've always worked in the past for someone who has wanted to control and dominate them, instead of helping them grow. So the Power Performer gives them the training they need and gradually lets them take on more and more responsibility. Suddenly their self-image expands dramatically. Instead of thinking of "getting by," and "hanging on" to their job, they're thinking about ways to fulfill their potential.

Many times I've seen people who worked for me develop beyond the opportunity I could offer them, or I could see that they wanted to grow in a different direction. I always encouraged them to move on to greater opportunity and never stood in their way.

Once a key department head talked to me about a dream she'd had for most of her life. As a youngster she'd wanted to go into nursing, but had failed the training course. She never forgot her dream of becoming a nurse, however. She asked me, "Do you think I'm too old to try again?"

"Of course not," I told her. "Go for it." So she quit and signed up in nursing school and for many years after that she would send me the warmest notes, telling me how she was doing and how glad she was that she had recaptured her youthful dream.

Patty Carpenter started with my company as a part time secretary, then became our marketing director. However, she wanted to grow even further, so I helped her go into business for herself. Now she's president of her own company, Carpenter's Speakers Bureau, and I'm so proud of her.

I've always encouraged them to go, and grow, even when they were my key people. Because I've found when you run that kind of operation, word gets around, and there's never a shortage of good people to take their place.

As an author and speaker, I get to encourage hundreds, sometimes thousands, of people a week to follow their dreams. What a joy it is to hear from someone who tells me, "What you had to say came at just the right time in my life. Now I'm doing what I've always dreamed of doing, and I couldn't be happier." Usually I hear from them when they're just getting started, when they're not sure if they can be super successful, but they don't care about that. They really don't care if they make a million dollars or not. The important thing for them is that they're doing something their limited self-image stopped them from doing before.

Harry Belafonte used to wash dishes in a restaurant in Harlem. What a tragedy if a limiting self-image had stopped him from sharing his true talent with the world. What if you had that kind of talent within you and never explored it?

At the height of her career, Barbra Streisand risked everything to produce and direct the movie *Yentl.* "Why on earth would she do such a thing," her friends asked her. "It had nothing to do with the desire for fame and fortune," she said. "I had all that. I did it because one night I dreamt that I had died, and God revealed my true potential to me. He told me about all the things I could have done, but didn't because I was afraid. That was when I decided that I had to create *Yentl* even if it cost me everything I had."

For a really chilling story of a positive self-image lost and regained, listen to best-selling author Og Mandino tell the story of hitting rock-bottom one day in Cleveland. Thirty-five years old, he'd lost his family, his home, his job, and his self-respect. He stood in front of a pawn shop window in the rain, with his last $30 in his pocket, looking at a handgun for sale, thinking of ending his life. To this day he can't say why, but he was drawn instead to a library down the street. There a self-help book by W. Clement Stone captured his interest. The book was *Success Through a Positive Mental Attitude,* and reading it saved Mandino's life. He put his life back together, eventually went to work for Mr. Stone at his insurance company, and later became the editor of his magazine *Success Unlimited.* He went on to write *The Greatest Salesman in the World* and eventually sold over fifteen million self-help books.

YOU DID *WHAT* WITH YOUR LIFE?

I often wonder about some devotees of the Eastern religions who believe that existence is suffering and that we create our own pain by being attached to the world in which we live. They maintain that we remain on a treadmill of life after reincarnated life, until we achieve true "nirvana," which is nothingness. The path to nirvana, then, is to eliminate all concept of self. So they devote their lives attempting to create nothingness by removing all idea of self and environment. Wow! What if you came face to face with God and had to explain to Him that you'd taken the gift of life and devoted it to making it nothing? Now that would be a tough sell! I've had to talk myself out of some difficult situations during my life, but that would be a classic. God would probably look at me and say, "Would you give me that again? I gave you life on that beautiful planet, with green meadows full of butterflies, snow-capped mountains, sunsets, the joy of children's laughter, and the ability to love one another; and you devoted your entire life to creating nothing?"

> *You just gotta save Christianity, Richard! You just gotta!*
>
> Loretta Young to Richard the Lionhearted
> (in the 1935 movie *The Crusades*)

So imagizing Power Performance is the way to start changing your self-image. Learn to experience success before you achieve it.

The next step is to change your self-talk from negative fears to positive expectations. Eliminate "I can't do this," and "It'll never work," and "Other people are just lucky." Replace them with "I can do this," and "No problem, it'll work," and "I'm the lucky one." Soon you'll find your image of yourself changing—you'll see yourself as a different person, so you'll become a different person.

> *Eliminate "I can't do this," and "It'll never work," and "Other people are just lucky."*
>
> *Replace them with "I can do this," and "No problem, it'll work," and, "I'm the lucky one."*

LEARNING THE STRANGEST SECRET

Many people, beside Carl Rogers and Andrew Carnegie, have promoted the idea that if we are to change our lives we must first change our self-image. The best-selling talking record of all time is Earl Nightingale's *The Strangest Secret*. Earl was a successful radio personality on WGN in Chicago with his own daily commentary show. He did so well that he was able to achieve financial independence and retire at the age of 35. One of his investments was a life-insurance company, and he got in the habit of attending their sales meetings and giving the salespeople a motivation talk. When he was leaving for a vacation his sales manager begged him to record a message for him to play to the salespeople when he was away. Legend has it that Nightingale sat down and at one sitting recorded the message that was to sell over a million copies and win a gold record.

A friend of mine, Bob Elmquist, gave me the record over 20 years ago. I was walking by his office and saw it sitting on his desk. I picked it up and was reading the cover when he came in. "What's this?" I asked him.

"It's a motivational record."

I had never heard of such a thing. "What's a motivational record?"

"You listen to it and it's supposed to make you feel good."

"May I borrow it?"

"You can have it. I've listened to it already." So in such a casual way he handed me something that would turn my life around and make me many hundreds of thousands of dollars.

Unlike Napoleon Hill, who preferred to bury the secret of success in his book, Earl Nightingale revealed it in the first two paragraphs:

> Why do men with goals succeed in life . . .and men without them fail? Well, let me tell you something which, if you really understand it, will alter your life immediately. You'll suddenly find that you seem to attract good luck. The things you want just seem to fall in line. And from now on you won't have the problems, the worries, the gnawing lump of anxiety that perhaps you've experienced before. Doubt . . . fear . . . well, they'll be things of the past.
>
> Here's the key to success and the key to failure: We become what we think about. Let me tell you that again. We become what we think about.

Later Earl and I became friends and I got a chance to tell him how much his brief recorded message had changed my life. I spent the weekend with him when he lived in Naples, Florida, and he and his wife Diana came out to the airport to meet me. I knew that he'd had some very serious health problems so the first thing I asked him was how he was feeling. "I'm in wonderful health, Roger," he told me. "Far better than five years ago. I feel great. I've had both shoulder joints and hip joints replaced because of arthritis, but they work fine. Oh, yes, and I did have an aorta replaced in my heart that was giving me trouble. But I feel wonderful." Although he passed away in 1989 when he was only 67, his positive mental attitude and love of life kept him alive many years past when ordinary people would have given up.

His theory that we become what we think about has changed the life of millions. If a person thinks all day long about becoming rich, he or she will become rich one way or another. If a person is single and thinks all the time about being married, it won't be long before he or she will marry. Conversely, if a person with a negative self-image thinks constantly of nothing but becoming poorer, that will probably happen, too. In other words, a self-image is self-fulfilling.

A MORE SCIENTIFIC EXPLANATION FOR WHY YOU BECOME WHAT YOU THINK ABOUT

Maxwell Maltz wrote a great book called *Psycho-Cybernetics*, which explains in more scientific detail why this happens. The title itself is revealing—psycho means the mind, and the word cybernetics is a Greek word meaning a steersman who stands in the back of a boat. Maltz explained that the subconscious mind behaves just like an automatic, nonthinking, objective-seeking machine. He says that whenever you present the subconscious mind with a vision, it will perceive it as an objective and get the conscious mind to accomplish that objective whether the objective is positive or negative.

If you play golf I'm sure you understand this. Think about a hazard and you're more likely to hit it. Worry about the sand trap and it draws your ball like a magnet. Old golfing buddies often like to make the game more fun by turning it into a psychological battle. As one is teeing up to drive over water, the other will say, "Watch out for the water on this hole. It's tricky." The opponent's subconscious mind will "hear" water, but not know whether it's a good objective or a bad objective, and into the water the ball will go.

If you're playing golf and trying to avoid a tree, one of the worst things you can do is think about the tree, because the subconscious mind hears the idea of the tree as an objective, without interpreting the value of the objective.

> *If you are caught on a golf course during a storm and are afraid of lightning, hold up a 1-iron. Not even God can hit a 1-iron.*
>
> LEE TREVINO

Recently I was touring Ireland and called my friend Michael Crowe, who was on vacation with his family in Scotland. He was really excited because he had a tee-off time the following day on the Old Course at St. Andrews. This is the most famous golf course in the world because it's the home of the Royal and Ancient Golf Club, where the rules of golf were first laid out in 1754. "It's almost impossible to get a starting time on this course," he told me. "Why don't you come over and play with me. It may be the only chance you'll ever have." So I flew over and we scurried around to buy the equipment I'd need. "You do have a letter of introduction from your golf club, don't you, Roger?" he asked me. "They won't let you onto the course without it."

"Of course I don't have one," I told him. "I had no intention of playing golf on this trip." We racked our brains trying to come up with a solution until I finally had a brainstorm. "Is there a college or a university here?" I asked him.

"Yes, the University of Scotland has a campus in the middle of town."

So I raced down to borrow one of their computers and created a letter of introduction from my golf pro. Then I ran it through the copy machine several times, until it looked authentic. "That's brilliant," Michael told me when he saw it. "Wrinkle it up as though you've been carrying it your back pocket, and they'll never know."

"I hope we don't get caught," I told him. "These people take their golf so seriously that what I've done is probably worse than child molesting to them."

The next day we had a wonderful time playing this famous course. The starter could not have been more friendly and didn't ask to see any credentials. St. Andrews has the largest sand bunkers I've ever seen, and most of them have at least a six-foot peat wall on the side closest to the green. As we'd hit toward the green we'd play a psychological battle of wits with each other. "Don't even think about that bunker," Michael would tell me, knowing that I'd immediately start thinking about it.

I'd come back with, "Especially don't think about hitting your ball right at the base of that wall on the far side of the bunker. You'll never be able to play it from there." Sure enough, I have a picture of him standing in Hell's Bunker, with his ball lodged at the bottom of the wall of turf. That bunker is so deep that he couldn't even see out.

Maxwell Maltz was right. The subconscious mind behaves just like an automatic, nonthinking, objective-seeking machine. It hears an objective and goes for it, without stopping to think if it's a good objective or a bad one.

> *The subconscious mind is an automatic, nonthinking, objective-seeking machine that hears an objective and goes for it.*

At my talks I always like to stand in the doorway, greeting the people as they come in. You can tell a lot about the key concerns of an audience by their reaction when you first meet them. Also I confess that I can change the entire mood of the audience by doing this. Perhaps they've been out partying the night before and they're dragging a little bit. If you don't do something about it, it's hard to get them involved in your talk because they're all sitting there glassy-eyed. That makes it hard work. It's like going hunting and having to carry the dog. A cheerful word or two at the doorway, however, can change the atmosphere in the room and make the audience eager to hear what I have to tell them.

The fascinating thing is you can tell a lot about what's going on in a people's minds when you first greet them.

I say, "How are you this morning?"

They reply, "Oh, I'm not feeling so well." They're imagizing poor health, and that's what their subconscious mind will see as an objective.

"Good morning!"

"Oh, honey, when you get to be my age, every morning is good." She's imagizing old age, and that's what she'll get. We all become what we think about, whether it's good or bad.

Maxwell Maltz, the author of *Psycho-Cybernetics*, was a plastic surgeon, and he became interested in the power of self-imagery after repairing the face of a young woman disfigured in a car wreck. As he took off her bandages after cosmetic surgery, he thrilled with how well it turned out and proudly handed her a mirror.

"You look beautiful," he told her.

It astonished him when she said, "But, Doctor, I still feel ugly."

He knew then that what we see in a mirror is not nearly as powerful as what we see in our minds. He knew that reality doesn't always change the way people feel about themselves. Maltz's theory not only explains why beautiful people can feel ugly inside, it also explains why even some billionaires are never content with what they have and spend their lives trying to accumulate even more. Despite their actual success, inside they still feel poor.

It's amazing how our self-image can be so contrary to reality. In August 1989 I realized to my horror that my weight had gone completely out of control. I'd reached the "gross-out" point—the day when you look into the mirror and gross out and know that you have to take drastic action. I analyzed what I was eating and realized that I must be addicted to fat. The fat content of my diet was so high that I was addicted to fat just as much as an alcoholic is addicted to alcohol or a drug addict is addicted to cocaine.

I went on a low-fat diet of fruits and vegetables and in three months lost forty pounds. The difference in my appearance was so dramatic that, even a year later, I didn't recognize myself. A year later, I still thought of myself as fat, even though I was slim. I'd pass a mirror and not realize that the person I was seeing was me.

That's how strongly we implant our self-image into our minds.

WHY POWER PERFORMERS SEEM TO LIVE CHARMED LIVES

Every self-image psychologist agrees that before you can change your life dramatically, you must first change your self-image. You must train your mind to imagize the person you can become. Self-image psychology explains why the lives of Power Performers seem charmed. It seems they can do no wrong. Success washes over them in gigantic tidal waves. Good things happen to them much faster and in larger quantities than seems possible. Napoleon Hill put this beautifully in the first chapter of *Think and Grow Rich* when he said:

> We believe you are entitled to receive this important suggestion. When riches begin to come, they come so quickly and in such great abundance that one wonders where they have been hiding during all those lean years.

This is an astonishing statement, especially considering the popular belief that success comes only to those who work long and hard. As Henry David Thoreau said, "We must walk consciously only part way toward our goal, and then leap in the dark to our success."

Gamblers experience the same burst of success consciousness. They call it a winning streak. The following passage is a quote from *I Want to Quit Winners,* the autobiography by Harold Smith, the developer and for many years the owner of one of the largest gambling casinos in Reno. (The title of the book confused me at first. To quit winners is a gambler's expression that means to walk away from the table when you're winning. It doesn't mean to quit being a winner.)

Harold Smith wrote:

> Not long ago I stepped onto the sidewalk in front of Harold's Club for a breath of fresh air. It was late afternoon, and the Sierra's snows to the west were pale pink in the fading sunlight, as I stood a moment watching rosy neon blossom from the gambling clubs along North Virginia Street.
>
> It was precisely at that moment that I felt the hunch. It came on in a surge like a gust of wind off the desert, or the sudden chiming of bells: electric, keening, impelling. I suddenly felt strong, bold, confident. I wanted to gamble for big money. A true hunch hits like that. It flames in your consciousness like the crimson flare you come upon suddenly in a highway accident. Through the thickest fog of illness, preoccupation, or dulling medication, it blazes. Your senses are alerted, the next conscious move is yours.
>
> Unlike highway flares, though, a hunch fades swiftly. The deed must be done fast. Going for big money, moreover, is not child's play. It's for blood, thick blood. Yours or the other mans. When the hunch hits, there's no time for planning or debate, though you may come home later carrying your head in your hands. All this I knew.
>
> I strolled across the street and into the Horseshoe Club of my friend, Bernie Einstoss. The dice table nearest the door was empty, I noticed, save for two dealers idly clinking silver dollars. I gave the house my marker, and took $10,000 in chips. I laid $400 on the line and took the dice. Never have dice felt so right to me. In forty minutes I won $29,500.

One of the worst things that can happen in life is to win a bet . . . at an early age.

DANNY McGOORTY

It works this way for Harold Smith and for Power Performers such as you and I because the way you think controls your environment. As you enter a winning streak and think of nothing but succeeding, your mind begins to shape your destiny by not only influencing you, but also—in some mysterious manner that humankind has yet to define—by affecting the things and people around you. If you start to feel that you don't deserve your success, that tough times lie ahead and that all of this is too good to be true, here's what will happen. Like a roller coaster that tips over the crest of the hill, suddenly you'll find yourself descending into failure at an ever-increasing speed. You'll find yourself achieving all of your negative objectives at a rate that will only confirm your fears.

Power Performers know you can learn to change your whole life by changing the way you think about yourself.

Power Performers learn to experience success—to taste it and smell it—long before they've achieved it. Every step of the long journey to accomplishment, they carry an image of what they want to be. Power Perfomers change their own mental image of themselves, and in doing so make the rest of their lives a stage on which they act out a fascinating and fulfilling script. So concentrate on what you want to be, change your self-talk, and become a Power Performer. As Harold Geneen says, "You start with the end, and then you do everything you must to reach it."

So from this moment on, you must stop thinking of yourself as someone you *could* become a High Achiever. Think of yourself as already being a Power Performer. I don't care how little money you have in the bank, I don't care how much in debt you may be, I don't care how down and out you feel. You are already a Power Performer, and accumulating the wealth and influence are only the details that you'll put together later. Don't you feel better now?

◆◆◆

The Fifth Secret of Power Performers is:

They experience success long before they achieve it.

◆◆◆

In our next chapter, we'll talk about the one thing that can stop you from acquiring the wealth and influence that is due you.

POWER PERFORMERS DON'T LET OTHER PEOPLE DRAG THEM DOWN TO THEIR LEVEL

One who is fond of us isn't necessarily our friend.

— *Seneca*

God save me from my friends—I can protect myself from my enemies.

— *(Proverb)*

Change has its enemies.

— *Robert Kennedy*

The streets of America must be paved with gold.

— *Roger Dawson*

The most memorable day of my life was the day I caught my first glimpse of California. It took me all the way back to when I was a nine year old in school in England. I can vividly remember a geography class where a teacher showed us slides of California. It was just after the end of the war, and the schools had very little money

125

for equipment so it was a thrill when the teacher took us into a darkened classroom and started feeding large glass slides from a wooden box into an antique projector. This was long before I'd ever seen a color photograph so it didn't seem strange that the images on the wall were in black and white with only a sepia tinge to them. The teacher showed us a picture of the huge sequoia tree in Yosemite park with a car driving through it that astounded all of us (over 20 years later on a cross-country skiing trip I would ski through it). Then we saw pictures of the San Joaquin valley with its huge fields stretching to the horizon. Then some pictures of the Warner Brothers studio in Burbank and, saving the best for last, I thought, he showed us pictures of San Francisco and the Golden Gate Bridge. I remember him telling us (probably inaccurately) that it wasn't called the Golden Gate because of the color it was painted or because of the California gold rush. Instead it symbolized the agricultural wealth that poured under the bridge because of the richness of the soil in the San Joaquin Valley.

I never thought that I would ever see it for myself, because nobody in my family had ever been outside England (a country only half the size of Oregon), but 11 years later a strange sequence of events saw me standing on the deck of the P & O ocean liner S. S. *Orcades*, approaching the Golden Gate Bridge. I was the first photographer, hired for four-month voyages that took us one and a half times around the world.

Our voyages started at Tilbury docks outside London, and then took us through the Mediterranean and Suez Canal to India. This had traditionally been a major route for P & O Lines, and it was because of this route that ticket agents invented the word *posh*. In the early days the ships were not air conditioned, so the best cabins to India would be on the north side of the ship, which would be the port side on the outbound journey. Returning, it was cooler to be on the starboard side of the ship. Thus the best cabins were P.O.S.H.—Port Out, Starboard Home.

In India we would drop off diplomats, tourists, and returning natives and then continue with mainly English people who were emigrating to Australia. This was still before the days of jet travel,and people who traveled the world went by ship, not plane, so these were true voyages, not cruises. It was possible to travel from England to Australia by prop plane but it took several uncomfortable days with many stops for refueling. When the 747s came into vogue, traveling by ship almost vanished other than for pleasure cruises.

With stops at Freemantle, Adelaide, and Melbourne as we moved around the south coast of Australia, we would finish the first month of the voyage with a five-day stop in Sydney for restocking and any repairs that the crew couldn't handle at sea. Then we would start out again for the 11-day voyage to Manila in the Philippines, and on to Hong Kong. From there we would pass carefully between mainland China and Formosa (now Taiwan), which was a world crisis point because of the communist's threat to take over the island, before making two stops in Japan and heading out across the Pacific. Hawaii, reached over two weeks later, surprised me because it wasn't the expected isolated island with natives paddling out in canoes with baskets of fruit. It had just become the fiftieth state, something that appeared to thrill everyone, and the island economy was booming. Two more weeks and we were in Vancouver, British Columbia, and started down the West Coast for the long-awaited glimpse of San Francisco that was to become the highlight of my trip.

THE STREETS OF AMERICA ARE PAVED WITH GOLD

I stood on the deck, peering expectantly through the morning fog, until I finally saw a large gap appear in the coastal mountains ahead. At first I thought that we must be off course because it seemed that nobody could build a bridge across a gap that wide. However, as we sailed closer, I could see the thin spider web of the Golden Gate Bridge soaring gracefully from one peninsula to the other.

It was peaceful on the waters outside the bay, and from the sea I couldn't tell that we were only a few miles from one of the world's largest cities. We were almost under the bridge before I heard the roar of traffic crossing far above. We came in under it, curved to the right, and San Francisco exploded into view before us.

The sun was barely rising, lighting up the white clapboard sides of the houses of North Beach. Alcatraz, still a grim and foreboding federal prison in those days, rose from the bay to our left. The Bay Bridge soared over to Angel Island and then took off again for Oakland in the distance. The steep streets that climbed every hill slowly paraded before me. A tiny cable car tipped over the top of the hill between two tall hotels and plunged toward the wharf. It was a breathtaking, heart-stopping, beautiful sight that stays locked in my memory. Like a favorite old 45 RPM record, I take it out and play it often.

San Francisco enchanted me! As I roamed the hills of the city, I couldn't believe the wealth that I saw everywhere I looked. I peered up at the skyscrapers and the thousands of magnificent cars roaring off the Bay Bridge in the morning traffic and ogled the street cleaners smoking cigars. I'd come more than halfway around the world but I had never seen so much wealth in one place. It astounded me. I said to myself, "The streets of America must be paved with gold for anyone who wants to go out and work for it!"

After living more than 30 years in this country, I know I was right. I believe it more today than ever. The streets of America *are* paved with gold for anyone who has the courage, the initiative, and the persistence to work for it.

> *When I first arrived in this country I had only 15 cents in my pocket and a willingness to compromise.*
>
> WEBER CARTOON CAPTION

MEETING A MAN WHO HAD A GREAT INFLUENCE ON MY LIFE

Traveling back across the South Pacific, heading for my home in England, I met a man who greatly influenced my life. His name was Dr. Henry Catleen, and he dropped into my lap a real key to Power Performance. He was an English-born economist who now lived in Lausanne-Polly on the north shore of Lake Geneva. He'd had a brilliant career, helping Europe restructure its economy after the devastation of World War II. I was 21 at the time, and I would guess he was in his mid-sixties. One day he asked me, as older men often do when talking to a young man, "What do you plan to do with your life, Roger?"

"Well, I don't really know. I haven't given it much thought," I replied. "I enjoy being a ship's photographer. It gives me a chance to travel around the world and get paid for it, but I don't want to become addicted to this way of life. Some of the older crew members don't seem to know any other life, and that scares me. I wouldn't enjoy doing it for the rest of my life."

"Then let me give you a piece of advice," he said. He called for the steward to bring another round of drinks and then told me, "It really doesn't matter in which direction you head. A good person can find success in any direction. The key is to choose the course you'll enjoy most and then pursue it with all of your strength and vigor." The sun sparkled on the ocean as he paused to let these words sink in. "Let me help you make a plan," he continued. "What do you think you're best at? Pick something."

I told him that I'd always thought of myself as a good salesperson. Before I ran away to sea, I'd sold televisions, radios, and refrigerators in England. I'd enjoyed doing that and was successful at it. Dr. Catleen said, "So let's plan a career for you in sales, Okay? First, where would you like to work?"

"I live just outside Bognor Regis, on the south coast of England," I told him. "I could work there, or I could take the train to London and work in the city."

"No, no." He shook his head. "I asked you where you would like to work."

I didn't understand. "And I thought I told you. I could work in Bognor Regis, or take the train to London."

"No, Roger, don't think small. Think big. I'm asking you where *in the world* would you like to pursue this career in selling? You've traveled the world—pick a place."

No one had ever spoken to me like that before. No one had ever told me that I could go anywhere I wanted to go in the world and do anything I wanted to do.

As Ernest Holmes once said, "A moment's insight is sometimes worth a lifetime of experience."

I remembered how overwhelmed I was with San Francisco and told him with excitement, "If I could pick anywhere in the world, then I'd pick San Francisco. That's a fabulous city—I'd love to live there."

"Then do it! Do it! A year from now, you can be living in San Francisco, working there." He seemed to have all the confidence in the world.

"I just don't see how that's possible," I said. "When I get back to England I'll be broke. I won't have a visa to get to America, and I don't have any friends there. In fact, I don't know anyone there at all. How on earth could I do that?"

He had an answer for every one of my protests. "In the purser's office they have a telephone directory for every one of the cities where the ship docks. You simply need to look up the names of stores in the San Francisco area and write to them. Arrange for an interview the next time the ship docks in San Francisco."

THE SOLUTION TO A CHALLENGE IS USUALLY RIGHT WITHIN OUR REACH

He was teaching me a lesson that I would never forget: The solution to a challenge is usually right within our reach, but we fail to focus on it and then take action. Succeeding takes courage and initiative. It takes the willingness to ask the questions, to make the phone calls, to write the letters. All too often we can think of a possible answer to our dilemma, or a way to maximize an opportunity, but we shy away from it because we hesitate to make an investment, we fear rejection, or we simply think that the odds are too long.

Why hesitate to invest $20 in a long-distance phone call that could open a door to a new future? Because of the potential return on such a petty investment you could never consider it a gamble. If you don't have the $20 skip a few meals or walk to work for a week but don't give up on your dream for the future.

SO YOU SAY YOU WANT TO CHANGE YOUR LIFE?
You have to make the investment.
You have to ignore your fear of rejection.
You have to thumb your nose at the long odds.
You have to do something. You have to take action.

Why fear to write or call a person who could give you the advice you need, or connect you with the right person, simply because you fear his or her rejection? What if the person does slam the phone down, or refuses to return your call or respond to your letter, or even calls you an idiot? Anything that doesn't kill you strengthens you, so you have everything to gain and nothing to lose. (In my experience most successful people are happy to offer a few words of advice and encouragement, as long as they sense that you're willing to do the work and you're not expecting them to carry you where you want to go. And if they're not willing you give you advice and encouragement, you don't need them.)

Why shy away from a possible opportunity simply because the odds are too long? A good friend of mine was an actress before she realized that her talents lay in the business side of movies, rather than in being in front of the camera. She told me of the hundreds of auditions and casting calls that she'd been on where the chance of getting even the smallest role was 1 in 50. "How much would these roles pay if you got one?" I asked her. The answer astounded me. Most small acting roles pay only $400, which is the actor's union scale. Do the arithmetic. If you'll get only $400 for the work, and you'll get only 1 job in 50, you can't afford to spend more than $8 per audition before you start losing money. Isn't that discouraging? However look at the potential upside. Unless you are already an established stage actor or celebrity, it's the only way to get into a business that could pay off with fame and fortune and an incredible sense of fulfillment. Why risk losing all that because the odds seem so long to you?

> *The important thing in acting is to be able to laugh and cry. If I have to cry, I think of my sex life. If I have to laugh, I think of my sex life.*
>
> GLENDA JACKSON

If you have a dream, if you see a chance for a better life out there, you have to get past being unwilling to make a small investment. You have to get past your fear of rejection, and you have to quit being immobilized by long odds. You have to take action. You have to do something!

THE BEST ADVICE I EVER RECEIVED

So I did exactly what Dr. Catleen told me, and his plan moved me from dreaming to acting. I went up to the purser's office where, just as he'd told me, they had rows and rows of phone books covering every city the ship called at around the world. I borrowed a typewriter and wrote letters to six department stores in San Francisco. Two of them, the Emporium and J. C. Penney, responded, and I arranged to interview with them when the ship returned four months later. Both admired my initiative and were very encouraging but were unwilling to offer me a job unless I was already in the country with a work permit. So when I finally came, I didn't have a job waiting for me, but from the interviews I had learned that Americans are remarkably receptive to immigrants and that there was a good chance I could find work.

A few days later I ran into Dr. Catleen on deck and excitedly told him that the plan was in the action stage. He leaned back in his chair and listened to me intently as he digested what I'd done. Then he leaned toward me, and gave me another key to Power Performance: "Roger," he said, "there's only one thing that can stop you from reaching your dreams, and that's if you let other people drag you down to their level."

It shocked me, because it sounded so unkind, but later I grasped what he was telling me. He was saying that there are so many people in the world who aren't accomplishing very much with their lives, and often they'd prefer that nobody else did either, because it makes them feel bad.

> *There's only one thing that can stop you from reaching your dreams. That's if you let other people drag you down to their level.*

From that point on I started counting the number of people who told me not to emigrate to the United States. Before I finally landed in San Francisco a year later with $400 and everything I owned crammed into two suitcases and with no job waiting for me, 32 people had tried to talk me out of it.

The things people would tell me to keep me from going—

"Americans are so competitive!" they'd say. "You'll never stand a chance in America."

"You'll hate it. There's no way you can succeed."

Then the favorite excuse of people who aren't accomplishing much with their lives: "Your timing is all wrong." They talked about the poor economy in America at the time, and told me that if I'd made my move a couple of years before, or maybe even a couple of years in the future, it might work out, but not right now. Someone even tried to tell me that people in America were having to sell their refrigerators to buy food, because the economy was so bad. What nonsense!

It took me years to figure out that in analyzing this situation, I was making a fundamental mistake in judgment: I was asking the wrong people. Who were these people who were giving me all this negative advice? Who were these "friends" trying to stop me from doing something for which I had this great passion? They were all people who hadn't done what I was planning to do and who weren't prepared to make the sacrifices I was prepared to make. If I wanted to know if it was a good idea to move to California, to whom should I have listened? I should have been asking English people who lived in San Francisco, right? What would they have told me? "Come on over!" They'd have told me life in America was fantastic, that I should come right away, and that I'd love it there.

> *Isn't it nice that all the people who prefer London to San Francisco all live there?*
>
> HERB CAEN

We all have a tendency to find out what other people think of our objectives before we move on them. Often we try to get a second or even a third opinion on major ideas. However, to whom do we usually turn for advice? Often we turn to people who haven't done what we plan to do, or people who aren't willing to make the sacrifices we'd be willing to make.

Even when you're familiar with this principle, it's still very easy to fall into the trap. It's the reason I've never finished a novel that I started many years ago. One morning I was having breakfast at the Oriental Hotel in Bangkok, which is one of the grand old hotels in Asia, along with Raffles in Singapore and the Peninsular in Hong Kong. Just about every famous person in the first half of this century stayed at the Orient at one time or another, including many famous authors such as Somerset Maugham, Noel Coward, James Michener, and John Steinbeck.

> *Writing is easy. All you do is stare at a blank sheet of paper until drops of blood form on your forehead.*
>
> GENE FOWLER

As I sat there I started to dream up a theme for a novel in which the hero would be a second rate mystery writer who imagined himself to be one of the great ones. (Write about what you know, my editor keeps telling me.) He would travel around the world and get involved in all kinds of adventures. Sounds like *Murder, She Wrote,* doesn't it? However, this was before the TV series came out. So I gave my hero the fanciful literary name of Somerset Joyce and decided to spice things up a bit by writing so that the reader wouldn't know whether the action was really happening, or whether it was part of a book the hero was writing, or whether he was simply fantasizing like Walter Mitty. Here's the first chapter (don't panic because it's mercifully brief):

CHAPTER ONE

Somerset Joyce was eating breakfast on the terrace of the Oriental Hotel in Bangkok. He was furiously scribbling in his notebook a profile of the man at the next table. "From his olive complexion and his fat lips, I'd known that he was French before he started waving his hands. He was trying to impress the woman who had just joined him. She was slim and elegant. Her white cotton dress highlighted her golden suntan. She'd clearly been the center of intrigue in many a capital of the world. He was probably a wholesaler of guns to the rebels in Cambodia. Making millions, but putting his life on the line every day."

He had been writing profiles of people for years now. He had stored thousands of them on his computer in California and had cross-referenced them by nationality, personality, build, or the way they spoke. One day they would appear as a colorful character in one of his books. Whenever he saw an interesting person he fantasized about them and then created a profile. His writing so absorbed him that he didn't notice the tall slim woman in strapless sun dress until her long black hair started to tickle his neck and her hands were over his eyes.

"Guess who?" she whispered with a Mata Hari accent.

"Angela? Barbara? Connie? Debbie?" She punched him. "Oh, it's you Tracy! Surprise, surprise. It would have taken me all morning to get to the Ts."

She flopped down in the chair across from him, checked to be sure that the men on the terrace were all noticing her, and tossed her packages onto the spare chair. "G'Day, Sum. How's the scribbling?"

"Tracy, what I happen to be doing is creating a great work of literature. Do you have to describe it as scribbling?"

"You and your bloody fantasy world! You've had two cheap mystery novels published. The only reason they sold so well was because of the kinky sex. Why you needed to drag us halfway up the world to this dump of a city for 'atmosphere' is beyond me."

"Are you kidding? This place is a writer's paradise! There's three of us here on the terrace writing profiles of each other, right now. I'll probably show up in two other books as the incredible handsome and fearless CIA agent, who has only two objectives in life. To save the world for democracy and get laid by beautiful women. And not necessarily in that order."

"Dream on, sport. I suppose that all of these literary geniuses are being inspired by this glorious piece of bullshit?" She picked up a table card that listed the famous authors that had stayed at the Oriental, assigning a special dish to each of them. Somerset had read it earlier and had been pleased to see "Somerset Joyce Pâté de Foie Gras" listed as an appetizer under "Noel Coward Squid in Puff Pastry."

"They've all stayed here? Somerset Maugham, Noel Coward, James Michener, John Steinbeck. How come you're not on here, hotshot? And while I'm having a go at you, whatever happened to discretion? I stayed at the Hay Adams in Washington once, when they sacked a desk clerk for letting on to a reporter that a celebrity guest was staying at the hotel. And the poor sod had been working there for 18 years."

Somerset was still bristling about the "hotshot" comment. "Tracy, you're my literary assistant and researcher. I need you to be supportive. Not putting me down all the time. And please knock off the Aussie slang. It doesn't sound right in a classy place like this."

"Literary assistant, baloney. Researcher, bullshit. That's just a line that you spun Daddy so that he wouldn't set the dogs on you when I told him I was coming up here with you. You know how Australians feel about Yanks blowing up the world with nuclear bombs and screwing their women. The truth is, you only brought me up here for one thing, to get laid, something I happen to do for you exceptionally well, old sport. I still can't believe I bought that line about literary assistants having to sleep with the author, to develop the rapport that's needed. Anyway, as wide open as this town is, bringing a woman with you is like taking coals to Newcastle. . . ."

Much too mundane, thought Somerset, my editor will never let me get away with a phrase like that.

". . . is like taking sheep to an outback station . . ."

Not good, but I'll work on it.

". . . The doorman, a cheeky blighter who only seems to open doors as a sideline to his pimping business, let on that tonight was a special night on the Pat-Pong and that all the women were free. Buggers me how they can stay in business giving it away."

"He didn't mean that they were free, although they're never very expensive here. He meant that if I were to take you there tonight, they wouldn't charge for your drinks. Like happy hour in the States, before the women's libbers filed suit that it was discriminatory."

Tracy was laughing at the bellman walking onto the terrace from the restaurant. He was dressed in a bright red uniform with loads of gold braid and a pillbox hat. He carried an instrument that looked like a glockenspiel and was banging out tones with a small hammer. "Have you ever seen anything so bleeding ridiculous. Oh, Sum, you should put this in your book. Where on earth did they get the idea for this? From watching Fred Astaire movies?" The pager had a bulletin board on it, and he had assembled "Mr. Joyce" out of white letters. Somerset kicked Tracy, who was now biting her tongue to stop herself from laughing and turning bright red in the process, and beckoned him over.

"Oh, Somerset," she giggled, "are you still having yourself paged?"

The bellman handed him an envelope with his name on the front, and he turned it over before opening it and reading the message inside. The note seemed harmless enough, but it would change their lives for the next six months and would nearly get them both killed.

Okay, so it's not great writing, but considering the overall quality of writing in the genre I thought it had possibilities. Anyway I felt good enough about it to show what I'd written to a friend. He didn't like it. "A novel ought to have power, sex, and violence in it if you want it to sell," he told me.

I said, "Something along the lines of 'Come in,' said the captain, 'and take all your clothes off or I'll have you flogged'?"

"Well you don't have to put it all in the first sentence, but you know what I mean."

> *Why don't you write books that people can read?*
>
> NORA JOYCE TO HER HUSBAND JAMES JOYCE

Here's the point of what I'm saying: My friend had never had a word published in his life, much less a book, yet here I was letting him pass judgment on something he knew nothing about. In spite of that I never added another line to my novel. To whom should I have been talking? I should have been talking to someone who had already had a novel published. They probably wouldn't have liked it much either, but at least they could have given me some valuable suggestions. People who don't know how to do it themselves are ten times more likely to pour cold water on your ideas than someone who has some experience in the area you're quizzing them about.

> *A manuscript, like a cake, is never improved by opening the oven and showing it to somebody before it is done.*

So Power Performers have this firm rule in life: Whenever we have an objective—a mountain to climb or a sea to sail or a company to start—we never ask someone who hasn't already done it. We get an opinion only from those people who have already done what we plan to do. Seek out a Power Performer who has been successful in that area and see what he or she has to say—that person will probably tell you to go for it.

HOW THIS PRINCIPLE SAVED LIVES IN VIETNAM

There's a fascinating story about some troops in Vietnam during the war. Four soldiers were driving their jeep through a very narrow path in the jungle. Suddenly the jungle erupted with enemy fire. They braked the jeep to a halt and jumped quickly into the cover of the jungle, two on each side of the road. The jeep made a great target as it sat in the middle of the raised jungle trail, with its engine still running as the bullets came whistling in. The sergeant couldn't see his men, but could hear them, and he called out, "Men, as I see it, we have three chances to get out of this mess. The first thing is to run back onto the road, jump into the jeep, and drive straight on—but we'll be driving right into the enemy fire. Our second choice is to try escaping through the jungle, but we all know how dangerous that is, so I don't like our chances there either. The third thing we can do is jump back on the road, and each of us pick up a corner of the jeep, turn it around, jump in, and drive back to safety. That seems like the safest course, and I think it's our only chance."

The other three men agreed. "There's one thing, though," said the sergeant. "We must all believe we can turn that jeep around. If we get up on the road, and just one of us believes we can't lift it, all of us will die. So I want to make absolutely sure each of you believes we can do this."

He called out to his men, "Do you believe we can do it?"

"Yes, sir."

"Yes, sir, we can do it."

"Yes, sir, let's do it."

"Okay, men, one-two-three, back to the jeep!" They scrambled back to the jeep. They each picked up a corner of it and turned it around. Then they jumped back into the jeep and drove off at top speed, back to safety.

That's not the end of the story. When they got back to camp and told everyone what had happened to them, nobody believed them. Nobody could believe it was possible for four men to pick up a jeep. So the other soldiers started betting on it. Eventually there was $900 worth of bets that said those four men couldn't walk out to the parade ground and pick up that jeep again.

If you were in Vietnam, you know that $900 was a huge amount of money, so there was a tremendous amount of motivation. These men also knew that their reputations were on the line. They wanted to prove to their friends they hadn't been lying. So, while the motivation might not have been the life-or-death kind, as when they were under fire, there was still a great deal of pressure for them to do what they said they could do.

When they got out to the parade ground, however, they found they couldn't lift the jeep!

Why could they lift the jeep out in the jungle, but not in the middle of the parade ground? The difference was that on the parade ground there were dozens of men standing around telling them they couldn't do it, whereas out in the jungle there were only three other people, and they were all telling them they *could* do it.

WALK AWAY FROM PEOPLE WHO ARE DRAGGING YOU DOWN

The same applies to the accomplishment of any of your objectives. It's very difficult to accomplish anything when everyone is telling you, "It can't be done." If you want to make a change in your life you should make a conscious effort to ignore all those people who would love to drag you down to their level of nonaccomplishment.

You know people like that, don't you? They seem to spend most of their lives looking for something bad to talk about. If they can't wake up in the morning and hear some bad news on the radio or catch a disaster on television or read about it in the morning newspaper, they'll rush on down to work and find someone with whom to play, "Ain't it awful!" Who needs it? Power Performers learn to walk away from people who are trying to drag them down to their level. I'm as courteous as the next person, and I go out of my way to be polite, but when someone wants to poison my mind with their negativity, I've learned simply to turn around and walk away.

For example, when I'm speaking it's great to have people come up and chat with me during the breaks, but sometimes I'll see someone coming who's obvious bent on ruining my day. He or she wants to tell me about a typo in the seminar outline or complain about the people smoking in the hallway. With a little practice, you can spot these people at 100 yards. As Alice Roosevelt Longworth said, "They look like they were weaned on a pickle." Now I may have 500 people in the seminar, and 499 of them are having a great time. Is it fair to let this one person get to me and risk the chance of affecting my performance in the second half of the seminar? I'd rather turn my nonsense detector up to high, turn around. and walk away before he or she can get to me.

I love the story Earl Nightingale used to tell about being on a lecture tour in Australia. He recounts the story in the Nightingale-Conant audio-cassette program *The Compleat Speaker:*

> I accepted a request to appear on an interview television program several years ago in Sydney, Australia. It was an evening program and while I was greeted cordially in the studio by my young smiling host, it was not until the program was underway that I discovered my mistake in agreeing to appear. It was the kind of program on which the guest is put down while the smiling, sarcastic host is made to appear as a kind of District Attorney who proves that all his guests are, at heart, avaricious phonies. All replies to questions, however truthful, are met with a derisive, tongue-in-cheek response. I'm sure you've seen one or two. Fortunately, I detected my mistake almost immediately in the way my smiling host's attitude changed the moment we were on the air. Perhaps it was my own long experience in radio and television, but I immediately realized I was in for a difficult and demeaning half-hour. Luckily my host then asked me the question, "Well, Mr. Nightingale, you have such a hopeful, positive attitude toward life and the world, isn't there anything at all that you don't like?" To which I responded, "Oh, yes, there are some things. This program

is one, and you." Whereupon I smilingly removed my lapel mike and walked off the show. My open-mouthed host was left with twenty-five minutes of air time to fill as best he could. What was most interesting and surprising were the smiles and handshakes of the rest of the television people.

Isn't that a great story? Don't let other people drag you down to their level. Nobody has the right to destroy your positive attitude for his or her own petty gain. You have an obligation to walk away from these people.

DON'T LET ANYONE WHO HASN'T ALREADY DONE IT THEMSELVES TALK YOU OUT OF SOMETHING

So Power Performers make this a firm rule—don't let anyone who hasn't already done it him or herself talk you out of something. Remember this if you have a "once before I die" kind of ambition. Thinking of backpacking from Katmandu to Beijing? Anybody in the world is entitled to talk you into it, but the only person qualified to talk you out of it is the person who's actually been there and done it.

Thinking of quitting your job and moving to Connecticut to paint landscapes? The whole world is allowed to say, "Go ahead and do it." Only someone who has done it is qualified to tell you, "You have to be out of your mind."

> *Anybody in the world is entitled to talk you into reaching for your objectives. The only person qualified to talk you out of it is the person who's actually been there and done it.*

This is particularly so with someone like a bank loan officer. If you're going to listen to the advice of a bank loan officer sitting there in a polyester suit, K-Mart shoes, and white socks, you might as well go down to the post office and ask the clerk behind the counter for advice on your future.

Do you have a dream of starting your own company? Do you dream of being an inventor? Do you think you could make a good living as a consultant? Even if it's something more mundane like opening a car wash, don't let anyone who hasn't done it talk you out of it.

Incidentally, I know a man who made a fortune in the car-wash business, so don't laugh. When he divorced his first wife, she got a $19,000-a-month alimony settlement. She's hilarious when she sits in the bar of the country club and tells the story of the divorce case. The judge called her into chambers and said to her, "I can't believe you're asking for this much. I can't approve $19,000 a month—it's immoral!" She smiled sweetly and said, "Judge, why don't you keep on doing what you do best, and I'll just keep on doing what I do best."

Her ex-husband, on the other hand, has never looked back. He now owns a chain of car washes, and the alimony is a drop in the bucket. He loves it when a clerk in a department store asks him to apply for a credit card. When they get down to occupation he says, "I wash cars."

Discipline yourself to lock out negative thoughts and to turn your back on negative people. Instead, train yourself to really believe that something great will happen to you and you will change your life.

◆◆◆

The Sixth Secret of Power Performers is:

They don't let other people drag them down to their level.

◆◆◆

7

POWER PERFORMERS KNOW THAT FOR THINGS TO CHANGE, THEY HAVE TO CHANGE

Everyone thinks of changing the world, but no one thinks of changing himself.

— Leo Tolstoi

Things do not change, we do.

— Henry David Thoreau

Don't give me all that positive-thinking stuff. I've read all those books too, and it's not going to work.

— Roger Dawson

After I'd been in this country for about six years, a friend of mine visited me from England. He asked me, "Roger, how do you like America?"

I said, "Oh, it's fantastic. I just love it. The thing I love most is they don't have a class system here. In England, where you were born, your parents and the schools you attend, all limit the possibility of your becoming a Power Performer. In England, a

143

person could drag himself up from the ghetto and end up owning a nationwide chain of stores, but in the eyes of the aristocracy, he'd still be just a shopkeeper. And most of the so-called aristocracy have never done a productive thing in their lives."

As I explained to my friend, "My father drove a London taxicab for most of his life, so I'd probably never have gone very far in British society. In this country, however, it doesn't matter where you were born or what kind of school you attended. Here, successful people brag about their humble beginnings, or of lack of a formal education. The only thing that matters to Americans is what you're doing with your life right now—and where you're going. I love that about this country."

"Roger," he said, "you told me before you came here that the streets of America were paved with gold—the land of opportunity, you said. Do you still believe that?"

"Well, I have to tell you," I replied, "as much as I love it here, I'm having a tough time of it financially. I'm an operations manager in a department store, and I'm not even earning enough to support my wife and two young children.

"An embarrassing thing happened to me last week. We normally get paid on Fridays, but the computer broke down and they told us the checks wouldn't be ready until Monday. Head office told us they would make an advance to anyone who absolutely had to have the money, but not to ask for it unless we really needed it. To my shame, I had to get an advance. I couldn't believe it. After living for six years in the country with the greatest opportunity on earth, I had to get an advance on my salary to last from Friday until Monday.

"A couple of days later, a well-intentioned neighbor lady came by to drop off some used clothes for my children. I was so ashamed to think she thought I couldn't clothe my own children."

"What are you doing about it?" he asked me.

"I'm trying for a promotion at work," I answered. "I want to get promoted to merchandise manager at a larger store. However, I've been trying so hard for so long now, I'm beginning to wonder if that promotion will ever come."

"If I gave you a technique that would give you that promotion within 30 days, guaranteed, would you do it?"

"Of course I'd do it," I told him. "I'll try anything."

"Then do this: Write down in precise detail the promotion you want them to give you. Carry that piece of paper around with you in your pocket for 30 days and act as though it's impossible for you to fail." Do you know what my reaction was? "Aw, come on. Don't give me all that positive-thinking stuff. I've read all those books too, and it's not going to work."

He smiled. "Do you have a better idea?" Of course I didn't, so I tried it. I wrote down exactly the promotion I wanted. I carried that piece of paper around with me every day, acting as though I could not fail. Within 30 days, I got that promotion—exactly as I'd it written down. For years I was convinced my friend had lain on me some type of metaphysical magic. I couldn't believe it had really happened.

Many years later, I began to understand what had really taken place. Here's what really made it happen for me. When I prepared for work the day after I spoke to my friend, acting as though it were impossible to fail, I started thinking, "I'll bet a merchandise manager gets to work just a little earlier than I've been getting to work. He probably gets down there early, so he can get most of his paperwork out of the way, and then he spends the day out on the sales floor with the customers, getting a feel for buying trends." So I went to work just a little bit earlier and started spending more time on the sales floor.

"I'm sure that a merchandise manager dresses a little better than I've been dressing, and I'll bet he doesn't take half-hour coffee breaks twice a day. And I'm sure he doesn't sit in the lunchroom complaining about the way the company is being run." So I started dressing a little better, taking shorter coffee breaks, and being more grateful toward the company.

So what happened? The big difference was that I was beginning to change. At the end of 30 days, the people who were making the decisions must have said to each other, "We've seen a big change in Roger lately. Maybe he's finally ready for that promotion." In order for things to change in your life—you have to change.

Power Performers know that for things to change in their life, they have to change. They develop an attitude of positive expectancy, formulate objectives that will lead them to what they want in life, and then they intensify their belief that they will succeed.

◆◆◆

The Seventh Secret of Power Performers is:

They know that for things to change they have to change.

◆◆◆

POWER PERFORMERS KNOW HOW TO CREATE OPPORTUNITIES

A wise man will make more opportunities than he finds.

— *Francis Bacon*

The opportunity that God sends does not wake up someone who is asleep.

— *(Senegalese proverb)*

There is a tide in the affairs of men
Which, taken at the flood, leads on to fortune;
Omitted, all the voyage of their life
Is bound in shallows and in miseries.

— *William Shakespeare in* Julius Caesar

A hundred thousand miracles are happening every day, and those who say they don't agree, are those who neither hear nor see!

— *Oscar Hammerstein*

The opportunities are there all the time. It's our burning desire that enables us to see them.

— *Roger Dawson*

To everyone else Power Performers seem to have all the luck in the world. Opportunity always seems to knock on their door. While others grind it out, they seem to move effortlessly from one success to another. Is it possible that they can create their own opportunities?

A CHURCH FOR POSITIVE THINKERS

Let's see what members of the Church of Religious Science say about this. The church was inspired by the writings of Ernest Holmes, who was a student of the New Thought movement. New Thought goes back to the middle of the nineteenth Century, when Phineas P. Quimby of Portland, Maine, practiced healing with the power of the mind. One of the people he healed was Mrs. Mary Patterson, who later founded the Christian Science movement as Mary Baker Eddy. She stressed the spiritual side of New Thought. Another person that Quimby healed, clergyman W. F. Evans, went on to stress how mental power alone could heal. The interest in the possibilities of creative power through constructive thinking continued to grow, and believers started holding national conventions in 1894.

The possibilities fascinated Ernest Holmes and his brother Fenwicke so in 1915 they started to publish a magazine called *The Uplift,* which spread their belief that power of mind could heal and lead to fulfillment of life. In 1926 Ernest published a work that was to become a classic: *The Science of Mind.* The following year he established The Institute of Religious Science and Philosophy in Los Angeles so that his teachings would become widely available. Some of the graduates from this institute started churches based on his teachings, and in 1949 he reluctantly agreed to form the United Church of Religious Science.

Because it often confuses people, let me stress that apart from its common roots there is little connection between Religious Science and Christian Science. Religious Scientists are not Christians, since they believe that Jesus Christ was one of several religious leaders who was able to achieve oneness with universal intelligence. The other major difference is that Religious Scientists believe in doctors as a manifestation of universal intelligence. They believe that many illnesses are psychosomatic and can be cured by the mind, but unlike Christian Scientists, they don't hesitate to seek medical treatment if it would help.

Religious Scientists are metaphysicians who believe that each human mind is an expression of the Universal Mind (some call God) and that the universe is a material manifestation of Universal Mind. This is monistic thought—that we and nature are one with God. Since all humans are one with God, they are intrinsically good and what appears as evil to us is really just ignorance of the truth. So Religious Scientists are very open and trusting people. At one with the universe (Christians would say in a *state of grace*), they do not seek to succeed by taking away from anyone else. If you visit a Church of Religious Science the feeling of love among the congregation could overwhelm you. It's an awesome thing to be with a large group of people who feel themselves to be at one with you and the universe. They truly believe that your success and happiness is also their success and happiness. Whereas some religions invite their followers to pray to God to give them what they want, you won't get that feeling around Religious Scientists. They know that their mind, working with creative faith and knowing that it is one with infinite intelligence, can manifest anything it desires without depriving anyone else.

Of course you don't have to be a Religious Scientist to be a Power Performer, but Power Performers like the way Religious Scientists think.

If you were to ask me to tell you in three minutes or less what Religious Science is all about, I'd point out the following.

First, Religious Scientists have no argument with any other religion. They feel that any pathway that leads you to God is wonderful. So they embrace the philosophy of Buddha, Mohammed, or Confucius as readily as they do the philosophy of Jesus Christ. In their view these religious leaders are those few in history who have seen more clearly than any other human beings that God exists throughout the universe in every living thing and therefore also in us. Power Performers tend to embrace this type of liberal religious thinking. They find it hard to condemn the 460 million Hindus in the world to eternal hell or the 250 million Buddhists simply because these people haven't embraced Christianity. They're certainly not about to burn up much of their valuable internal energy by arguing with them, much less fighting a war over religious beliefs.

Furthermore, Religious Science is not in the purest sense just a religion. Founder Ernest Holmes described it as a blending of religion, philosophy, and science. As such, it has no dogma. They have cast nothing in stone. Since we're still uncovering scientific knowledge, it follows we can never say, "This is the truth and will always be the truth." A philosopher is literally a lover of knowledge and one who seeks it—the opposite position of the dogmatic believers in many other religions who regard any new information as being sent from the devil to pollute their minds. Power Performers also tend to have this type of open, inquiring mind.

The other important thing about Religious Scientists is that they believe thought can change the world and that collective thought is a potent force that can do incredible things. "You become what you think about," said Earl Nightingale. To which a Religious Scientist would respond, "Well, yes, of course that's true."

It's a very unusual church. The members believe thought controls the environment, so they have no membership drives and no one attempts to convert you to their beliefs. They certainly wouldn't criticize anyone else's religious beliefs. Should they wish to fill their church with members, they would only have to use collective thought (or prayer if you prefer) to do so.

They ask for contributions only when they pass the plate at services—and even then it's made clear all contributions are completely voluntary—so nobody asks you to tithe a part of your earnings. Members believe that, since their own thoughts can control events, it would be counter to their philosophy to push for contributions. Should they feel it necessary to increase their finances, they could do so by collectively making mental contact with Infinite Intelligence, the life force some call God, and it would satisfy their needs. Religious Scientists won't debate this with you: To try to change someone else's mind is counter to their beliefs. True Power Performers are also very comfortable with this kind of thinking.

Whether the Religious Scientists are right or wrong, the fact remains that those people who do believe their thoughts have an impact on the world around them are capable of accomplishing interesting things. A friend of mine uses this theory to find parking spaces. As he drives into a parking lot he concentrates on believing a space will appear close to his destination. Most people would feel justified in telling him he's crazy. "That may be so," he usually responds, "but I'm parked, and you're not."

HOW POWER PERFORMERS CREATE THEIR OWN GOOD FORTUNE

Is it possible that Power Performers appear lucky because in some mysterious way they can control their circumstances? It certainly appears that way, but perhaps there's a reason for it.

Let's examine whether we can control our world, and therefore our lives, or whether we must accept our world the way it is.

In the last 200 years, the human race has radically rethought its relationship with the planet on which it exists. Thirty years ago it took me four weeks on a ship to travel from Japan to California. This year it took me ten hours on a Boeing 747. Not long ago I stayed in a castle in Salzburg that was built in 1340. Meanwhile, in the New World restaurants in Beverly Hills and Newport Beach start bragging about how long they've been in business if they've survived their first year.

> *Is it possible that Power Performers appear lucky because in some mysterious way they can control their circumstances?*

Progress and change are relatively new concepts to us. Two hundred years ago people didn't think about change. The river would always be a river, and nobody would dam it to create a reservoir. The hill would always be a hill. Nobody was going to cut a slice of it away for a freeway or for a housing development. People periodically got sick and died. People always got old and died. There was nobody running around saying, "Hey, I don't think people have to die. Maybe we can change the way this thing is set up."

No wonder civilization developed the attitude that there were elements and forces outside the human race running things. Now, because technology is capable of influencing things so much in our lives, we're beginning to believe that there is very little in our universe that we can't change.

A MEETING OF WORLD-CLASS POSITIVE THINKERS

In Anchorage, Alaska, a few years ago, there was a meeting of world-class Power Performers—scientists from around the world, who met at the Global Infrastructure Projects Conference. The criterion for getting something onto the agenda was that the project be too big for any one single nation to tackle on its own, even the United States.

Wow! Can you believe that?

Among the topics scheduled for serious discussion was a dam across the Bering Strait linking Russia with the United States and providing an unlimited world source of hydroelectric power. Other projects would bring water from Canada to make the deserts of Mexico agricultural centers. Or develop a sea-level canal across Panama. Or make the Sahara desert bloom.

One of the most interesting projects they discussed was a road from the North Slope oil fields of Alaska, over the North Pole to the markets of Northern Europe and Russia. It turns out road building in the Arctic could not be simpler. You simply send through a convoy of vehicles that spray a fine mist of water over the intended roadway. Each film of water freezes solid and forms a roadbed as firm as asphalt. Several dozens of these films of ice, which become permanent almost instantly, form a road as reliable as any concrete freeway. The only difficulty is that the polar ice cap rotates clockwise several feet each year. The roadway wouldn't always be in the same place. "No problem," said Harold Heinze, the proponent of the plan. "The construction process is so inexpensive we can quickly develop another road. Eventually the ice cap would look like a wagon wheel, with the roads being the spokes of the wheel."

Sounds way out, doesn't it? The people who attend a conference such as that must be a bunch of kooks who get together to share their illusions of grandeur, right? Not exactly. Harold Heinze is the president of Arco of Alaska. The Panama Canal project was researched with a grant from the U.S. government, and Masaki Nakajima, who organized the conference, established and directs the research arm of the huge Mitsubishi corporation.

In a universe with so few absolutes, doesn't it make sense that we would have a great ability to influence our world? That we ought to be taking more control of our lives? If there's one common thread that has followed the path of progress of the human race for the last 200 years, it's that we're taking more and more control of our lives and our environment. Power Performers don't feel inclined to wait for this trend to develop any further. They know that they're in control of their lives now and eagerly seize the day.

WHY WE CREATE OUR OWN FATE

Let's play a game to illustrate that we control our lives and that fate does not. I want you to think back to the two most important things in your life so far. Perhaps one would be the person you wanted to marry. Another might be the job you wanted to get or the child you yearned to have. You choose. Let's not degrade the conversation by talking about material things. If you tell me that the thing you wanted most in your life was a 1974 Buick, you'll really disappoint me. However, do be specific. Don't say love or health, Okay? Think about it for a minute, write down the two key things in your life, and then continue with part two of the exercise.

The two most important things in my life:

1. _____

2. _____

The second question to answer is—did those two things come true for you? If you're like the thousands of people with whom I've done this exercise at my seminars, the answer is almost certainly "Yes!" Isn't that strange? Invariably the two things we wanted most in our lives we got. Perhaps all we need to do to get what we want is to want it intensely enough.

Now analyze the circumstances surrounding those dreams that came true for you.

How did those things come about?

1. _____

2. _____

Isn't it true that a weird set of circumstances brought you face to face with the love of your life or that great career opportunity or the chance to travel to an exciting destination?

That certainly was the case with me. When I was 20 I was selling appliances and televisions in Bognor Regis, a seaside resort in England. The owner of the store became interested in aggressive marketing techniques and sent Jack Harvey, the store manager, to the United States to study their merchandising methods. He spent two weeks in New York and Chicago analyzing why American retailing methods were the best in the world. He brought back so many exciting stories about the United States. He told me that living in the United States would be as different from living in Europe as the difference between Europe and the Orient. That certainly turned out to be true. I found myself developing a burning desire to travel and see the country that had excited him so much.

Then, it seemed like an impossible dream. I had never been out of England, a country that is so small that you can never be more than 50 miles from the sea. Neither had my parents, their parents, or their grandparents. One or two of my distant relatives had crossed the 26-mile-wide English Channel and visited some other European countries, but America? That seemed like a distant dream. Far too distant for anyone in our circle to contemplate.

A couple of weeks later, though, I received a postcard from Roger Kendall, who had become a friend when we both attended the London School of Photography. He was working on a passenger liner as a photographer, traveling between England and New York with occasional Caribbean cruises thrown in. The postcard he had sent me was from the Virgin Islands. Not only was this not costing him anything, he was getting paid for his work. For me, this was the golden opportunity for which I'd been looking: a chance to go to America and get paid for it. I wrote Roger to ask how I could get a job like his, and he wrote back to say that he didn't work directly for the cruise line but for Marine Photographic, a company that owned the photographic franchise on ships that traveled throughout the world. I called them for an interview and drove up to Colchester, which is about 50 miles northeast of London, to meet with the owner. He somewhat reluctantly offered me a two-week cruise job as a fourth photographer on a ship leaving at the end of the month. It would mean that I would have to quit my job as an appliance salesperson. That caused some mental agonizing about security versus adventure, but I decided to ignore my fears and take the job. Not wanting to appear that I wanted the job only to travel, I hadn't even asked where the ship was going. I called a travel agent who mistakenly informed me that it was going to the Canary Islands. After we sailed I found that we were going to Dubrovnik, in what was then communist Yugoslavia, stopping on the way at Messina, Sicily, and on the way back at Majorca and Gibraltar.

My next assignment was as first Photographer on board the S.S. *Orcades,* and this led to the voyages I mentioned earlier. What an adventure that was for a 20 year old! Ultimately this led to my moving to California in 1962.

Now doesn't that seem like an incredible coincidence? Within a few weeks of cultivating a desire to go to America, but with virtually no hope of being able to do so, an opportunity had presented itself where I could do the traveling I wanted—and get paid for it. Isn't that amazing?

I'm sure there have been times in your life also when coincidental things have happened that opened up new opportunities for you. Perhaps it was the way in which you first met the person you married or the way that big breakthrough in your career came about.

A friend of mine told me about moving to California and desperately looking for a job as a radio scriptwriter. When he was close to the end of his rope and willing to take any job to survive, his wife asked him if he'd looked in the help wanted ads in the paper. He said, "Do you realize how many scriptwriters there are in Hollywood looking for work? Of course they wouldn't advertise a job like that in the paper." However, he hunted through the classified ads and while there wasn't one for a radio scriptwriter, there was one for a retail writer. He had no idea what a retail writer was, but was curious enough to call about it. "Oh, that's a typo," they told him. "We're really looking for someone with radio writing experience." So he got the job. Isn't that a remarkable coincidence?

I'm sure you can think back to several such coincidences in your life. Why does this happen? And how? Do we really have the mental power to control our environment as Religious Scientists claim? Can we make things happen in our lives? Or could it be that those opportunities are there all the time, and we see them only when we have the burning desire to accomplish something. That only then do we reach out to grab them?

> *The opportunities are there all the time.*
> *It's our burning desire that enables us to see them.*

Let's say my friend had sent me that postcard from New York several months earlier, before Jack Harvey had stirred my imagination with visions of the New World. What kind of impact would it have had on me then? Probably not much. I would have thought it an interesting postcard and would quickly have forgotten it. I would have missed that opportunity. However, because I first had the burning desire to travel, when that postcard came it jumped out and presented itself to me as an incredible opportunity. I firmly believe you can do anything and go anywhere you want to in life—these opportunities are all around you—and that you simply need to activate them with burning desire. When someone has a negative attitude about his or her life and his or her future, it's as though the person has lowered a screen that hides those opportunities from view. While positive thinking may not always get you what you want, of one thing I'm absolutely sure: Negative thinking causes that screen to come crashing down. It works every time! You will never see opportunities through a screen of negativity.

It really is true: A hundred thousand miracles are happening every day, and those who say they don't agree are those who neither hear nor see.

MEETING THE FIRST BIG LOVE OF MY LIFE

Let me tell you of another personal example that seems to be right out of *The Twilight Zone*. It happened when I was the first photographer on board the S.S. *Orcades* and we were sailing between Hawaii and Japan. As first photographer I typically spent my time working with the first-class passengers, and the second photographer, Norman, handled the tourist class. The third photographer handled the darkroom. One night Norman asked me to help him work at a big ball they were having in tourist class, which was something I'd done many times before. On that night, however, for some reason I told the third photographer to get his tuxedo on and take the assignment. I would stay in the darkroom and process the film for him as they fed it back down to me during the evening. They took dozens of rolls of pictures that night and took turns to bring them down to me. I would unwrap the rolls of negatives in the dark and hang them in the huge processing tank. As soon as I had developed and dried the negatives I would start feeding them through the enlarger, which was suspended from the ceiling to counter the movement and vibration of the ship. Soon the huge developing tanks were swimming with hundreds of prints of the ball going on two decks above my head. Suddenly one of the prints almost jumped out of the developer at me. A strange feeling overwhelmed me and time seemed to stand still as I picked this print of a beautiful young lady out of the developer and stared at it.

When the others came back, I asked them, "Who is this girl; what do you know about her?"

They replied, "Are you kidding? Do you know how many people were there? We didn't even notice her when we took the picture."

That print has now hung on my wall for over 30 years. I had found Gudrun, the Icelandic girl who would become my first wife and the mother of my three children.

Many years later, on the other side of the world, I met the girl who had been Gudrun's roommate before she sailed on the trip. She said, "So you're the photographer she was destined to meet!" Then she went on to explain, "On the night before she sailed, we had a going-away party for her, and somebody brought a Ouija board. We asked the board if she would fall in love on the trip, and it said, "Yes." We asked if she would marry the man, and the board said, "Yes." Then we pushed our luck and asked the board who it would be, and the board spelled out P-H-O-T-O-G-R-A-P-H-E-R." Her story astounded and confused me, and does to this day, especially since Gudrun had never shared this story with me, although she confirmed it later. Perhaps it happened because, as Charles Perkhurst said, "The heart has eyes which the brain knows nothing of."

WHY DESIRE CREATES OPPORTUNITIES

While these things may be of intense interest to the scholar or philosopher, why they happen is of only passing interest to the Power Performer. The important thing to us is that they do happen. Desire, intensified by a specific written objective. apparently creates opportunities. Once you add the emotional belief that it will come true, it's like magic. It seems as though we could make any wish come true, if only we could wish hard enough.

Of course, wishing for a white Mercedes to appear in your driveway, fully paid for by some unknown benefactor, is metaphysical madness. Any Religious Scientist will explain to you that such a thing can't happen because this power works only when it is according to the laws of the universe—which in simple terms means when everyone concerned can be a winner. What if someone else were simultaneously wishing your Mercedes would appear in his or her driveway?

If, however, you had an objective in writing that within 90 days you'd get the opportunity to buy a Mercedes at far less than market price and with excellent terms, I believe it would happen, and the way it would happen would amaze you. A coworker might ask you to take over his payments, or a salesman might remember you from years ago and call you with a fantastic offer. You might pass a bulletin board in a supermarket and there, jumping out at you, would be a card with exactly what you're looking for on it. Does positive thinking make the card pin itself to the board? Of course not. The card was always there. Positive thinking draws you to see it.

A FASCINATING GAME THAT COULD CHANGE YOUR LIFE

Several years ago I was skiing in Aspen with Julia and Dwight, my two older children, and a group of friends. One evening we were sitting around the fire when we decided to play a mind game. It's a fascinating game and one I want to play with you now.

I want you to give this question serious thought, so the answer you give is the one you would give if you knew your wish would be granted.

Here's the question: "What would you do with the rest of your life if you had only 60 days to live, with no possibility of reprieve. Money is no object, you have unlimited funds at your disposal, and you don't have others who would benefit from your saving the money. Also your health is not a problem—you'll stay active and free of pain until the last moment. How would you spend those last 60 days of your life?"

Stop reading for a few minutes while you think this through and write in your answer below. Continue only when you've made up your mind.

What would you do if you had only 60 days to live?

_____

_____

If you're having trouble with this, you might find yourself stimulated by the last words of a few famous people:

Go away, I'm all right.— H. G.Wells

Get out of here and leave me alone. Last words are for fools who haven't said enough already.— Karl Marx

Either this wallpaper goes or I do.— Oscar Wilde, dying in a Paris hotel

I owe much, I have nothing, the rest I leave to the poor — Rabelais in his will.

I'll give everything I own for one more moment of time! — Queen Elizabeth I

Dying is easy. Comedy is difficult.— Edmund Gwenn

I have had just about all I can take of myself.— S. N. Behrman at 75

My work is done, why wait? — George Eastman suicide note

I don't feel good.— Luther Burbank

All right, then, I'll say it: Dante makes me sick.— Lope de Vega when told that he was dying

Don't let it end like this. Tell them I said something. — Pancho Villa

I've conducted this exercise many times at my Power Performance seminars, and the intriguing thing is that seldom does anyone wish for a material thing. The responses are fairly uniform. The most popular response is, "to travel." They'd take a cruise on the Queen Elizabeth, or go for the first time to the little village in Italy where their grandfather grew up, or they'd fly to Rio de Janeiro or Hong Kong. Travel seems to be the one big unfulfilled desire of the people with whom I've done this exercise.

The second most popular response is to spend time with their family. These responses are particularly touching because they come from the heart—you can tell there's not a trace of sacrifice, penance, or guilt-purging in these answers. Someone might respond, "I'd spend two of the weeks alone with my daughter. We haven't spent much time together since the divorce. There's so much I want to share with her. I'd tell her of the places I've been and the reasons for the things I've done. I'd tell her about the people I've met and teach her what a grand adventure life can be. Then I'd tell her how much I love her and how very much I'll miss her."

Another will say, "I'd just like to spend the time together alone with my husband (or wife). As I thought about this, I realized that for the last 25 years we've put our children ahead of our own relationship. I didn't understand that it had been so long until I stopped to figure it out. I wonder if we've really influenced the kids that much—they probably would have turned out about the same anyway. I think I'd like to rent a small house by a peaceful lake and just have us spend the time quietly together."

Nobody ever responds with, "I've been dreaming for the last 5 years of getting a bright red Ferrari—I'd get that sucker and drive across country and see how many women I could pick up." Nor does anyone ever say, "For the last 30 years I've been clawing my way up the corporate ladder at my company, dreaming of the day I'd be president. If I had unlimited funds, I'd buy the company and at least see it run right for two months." Nor do you hear, "I'd do what I've always wanted to do. I'd buy the biggest house in the best part of town. I'd give the owners an extra million dollars to move out within an hour leaving everything intact. Then we'd spend two months having party after party. Boy, would that make the people in town sit up and take notice!"

The interesting thing about this exercise is to compare what we would really like to be doing if we were to focus on the now, and where we're really devoting our life's energies. How much energy are we devoting to a career, for example, that isn't really that important to us, if push came to shove? How much energy and effort are we using to acquire that new car or new house, and it's not that meaningful to us? Most of us spend a disproportionate amount of our time trying to acquire material things. Yet when the chips are down and there's nobody to impress but ourselves, material things no longer seem important.

So now complete the second part of this exercise. If what you want do if you had only sixty days to live is the most important thing to you, why aren't you doing it now?

Why aren't you doing it?

_____

_____

The game is so interesting to play because it causes us to focus on the now, the present moment. Power Performers live their life in the now.

They never think, "Yes, it's true I hate my job, it's boring and the idiots with whom I have to work drive me up the wall, and it's all I can do to stop myself from throttling that imbecile supervisor of mine—but I have ten years to go to retirement—I can't quit now! If I can stick it out for ten more years, I'll have the cabin at the lake paid for and I'll sell our home that I never did like much anyway, but it's close to work, and buy a huge recreational vehicle with a motorcycle strapped to the back, and then I'll be happy!"

That may seem humorous to you, and sad at the same time, but unfortunately it's the way all too many people think. That if they can put up with now for just a bit longer, they'll store up enough happiness chips so that at some time in the future, they'll become happy—and stay that way!

Is it any wonder that we're achieving only 15 percent of our full potential when we're devoting so much of our energy to things that aren't important to us? Power Performers know when we devote our internal energies to the things that are really important to us, miracles can happen.

A CHILDHOOD FANTASY FULFILLED

Let me tell you about my response when we played the game sitting in front of the fireplace in Aspen. I told them, "If I had only 60 days to live, I'd get in a plane tomorrow and fly to New Delhi in

India, and from there east to Katmandu. Then I'd hire some Sherpas and have them take me up to the base camp of Mount Everest."

My friends said in astonishment, "You'd do what?" I could understand their surprise, but that had been my dream ever since I was 13 years old and saw a movie called *Conquest of Everest*. In 1953, on the eve of Queen Elizabeth's coronation, the news reached London that the John Hunt expedition had reached the summit of the world's highest mountain. It was a magnificent coronation present for the Queen because it was a British expedition that finally conquered Everest, and New Zealander Edmund Hillary was the first to the top.

A year later they released a movie of the triumph, and it was mandatory viewing for schoolchildren throughout the country. Our school class marched off, dressed in our uniforms of gray flannel shorts and blue blazers with matching beanie, to see the movie *Conquest of Everest*. Wow, did it capture my imagination! Now, 24 years later, whatever had enraptured me about the adventure had surfaced again.

The experience in Aspen was merely a harmless party game, but in the weeks that followed, I thought about it more and more. I had no aspiration to climb Mount Everest, which is more than 29,000 feet high, but an expedition to the 18,000-foot-high base camp, where the serious climbing starts, was practical. I'd read Sir John Hunt's account of the 1953 climb, and it inspired me so much that I made up my mind to do it one day.

About five months after that, another of those remarkable coincidences occurred. I was glancing through the Los Angeles *Times* one Sunday afternoon when a brief item in the travel section caught my eye. A woman in Los Angeles was organizing a trip to the base camp of Mount Everest.

Her name was Katherine Whitley, and I tracked her down to discuss it. Yes, she was planning on getting a group of friends together and traveling to Mount Everest in November of that year. It seemed a strange time of year to go, but she explained the snow in the Himalayas falls mainly in the monsoon months of July, August, and September. Although it'd be cold in November, she told me, the mountain trails would be free of snow.

Eventually a group of five of us agreed to the trip. We made the arrangements, and we all flew in different directions, finally to meet up in Katmandu, Nepal. From there we went by a small air-plane to Lukla, a grass airstrip at 9,200 feet built by Sir Edmund Hillary. During his climbing days in Nepal, he had fallen in love with the mountain Sherpas and had spent much of the rest of his life doing things to improve their way of life. Many of them suffered from a swelling of their thyroid glands that caused huge goiters on the front of their necks. An iodine deficiency in their diet caused the swelling, so they could cure themselves with simple iodine injections, but they'd never been taught this. To help ship in med-ical supplies, Hillary and a village of Sherpas had built by hand this tiny airstrip on the side of a mountain.

It was at Lukla airstrip that Sir Edmund once stood waiting for his wife and daughter to fly in from Katmandu to join him. He'd been in the mountains for many months and they were joining him from their home in New Zealand. As he waited, anxious moments turned to tormented hours. Finally the word came. The plane had crashed upon take-off from Katmandu, and both his wife and daughter were dead. Distraught beyond any meaning of the word, he spent many months alone in the mountains, a lonely her-mit, until he finally came to grips with the tragedy. A lesser man would have turned his back on this remote country that had caused him so much pain. However, he determined to make some-thing good of it, so he strengthened his resolve to spend the rest of his life helping the mountain Sherpas, who had become his closest friends.

At Lukla we met the Sherpas we'd hired and their yaks—the big, buffalo like animal that would carry our supplies. Then we headed out along the trail and our long trek to Mount Everest. We spent the nights at small Sherpa villages or in tents set up by our porters next to the roaring river.

At Namche Bazar, the small village where most of the Sherpa guides were born and raised, we spent a few days acclimatizing our-selves to the 11,300-foot elevation. The process of acclimatization is essential to avoid serious injury from the two most serious forms of altitude sickness, cerebral edema and pulmonary edema. The lack of air pressure and oxygen causes the red corpuscles in the blood-stream to deplete, and the body needs time to adjust. Above this altitude, we wouldn't advance more than 1,000 vertical feet a day.

Sherpa Tenzing Norgay was born near here in 1914, although as a boy he ran away to Darjeeling in India, which is the home of the Himalayan Club and the starting point of most expeditions. He became a legendary porter and took part in more Everest expeditions than any other climber. Eventually he became a sirdar, or organizer of porters, and it was in this capacity that John Hunt hired him for the Everest expedition. Because of health complications caused by an ill-fated Swiss expedition to Everest the previous year, Norgay didn't expect to go higher than the icefall. It was amazing that Hunt assigned him to the second summit team and a quirk of history that the first team failed and he and Edmund Hillary became world famous. After the climb he returned to Darjeeling and became director of the Mountaineering Institute there.

When our acclimatization process was complete, we climbed on—to one of the most remote and beautiful buildings in the world, Thyangboche Monastery. This is where many of the Buddhist monks claim to have seen the Yeti, or Abominable Snowman of the Himalayas. It's also the place where the John Hunt expedition of 1953 spent two weeks in preparation for the climb. I remembered it vividly from the movie I had seen as a boy in England, 24 years before. Here's how John Hunt described it in his book about the climb *The Conquest of Everest:*

> Thyangboche must be one of the most beautiful places in the world. The height is well over 12,000 feet. The monastery buildings stand upon a knoll at the end of a big spur, which is flung out across the direct axis of the Imja River. Surrounded by satellite dwellings, all quaintly constructed and oddly medieval in appearance, it provides a grandstand beyond comparison for the finest mountain scenery that I have ever seen, whether in the Himalaya or elsewhere.

From the monastery, it was one more week's trek before we reached the base camp at 18,000 feet and stood at the bottom of the awesome Khumbu Icefall. This massive coulior, filled with blocks of ice bigger than houses, had been the major nemesis of all expeditions to Everest. True, the Shipton expedition of 1951 and the Swiss expedition of 1952 had made it through, but they had been unable to move enough supplies through it to mount a successful summit attempt. Only John Hunt's organizational genius found a way to tame it.

This was an adventure I'd dreamed about for 24 years, and it all happened to me within nine months of my determination to do it. How unbelievable that I should have seen that particular notice in the Los Angeles *Times* so soon after developing a desire to go to Mount Everest. If you believe in metaphysics, then you'd say my mind created the opportunity. However, I believe that opportunities such as that are flashing past us constantly, and it's only when we're convinced they're there that we see them and reach for them. As Wayne Dyer says, "You'll see them when you believe them."

CREATING OPPORTUNITY IN HOLLYWOOD

Let me give you another example of how Power Performers "create" opportunities. Bill Wolf is a friend of mine, a writer for CBS news in Hollywood. He's always wanted to be a stand-up comedian, and he has a great sense of humor. He wrote a comedy routine and rehearsed it before some of his friends in the entertainment business. They told him the material was okay but his routine would never be a success because his jokes were too sophisticated and intellectual for the average comedy audience. This opinion enraged Bill so much he determined he'd give his routine to an "average comedy audience" at an important event within a short time.

One day as he drove to work he was listening to a radio talk show on the NBC affiliate station in Los Angeles. The station was having a contest for amateur comedians, and listeners could call in and do a few jokes over the air. They would give the winner the opportunity to do his entire routine in public. Now what was Bill's response? Did he think, "When I get to work I'll give them a call and find out what it's all about?" No! Bill's a Power Performer and loves life, and he's always waiting for exciting opportunities to appear.

He immediately swerved over to a gas station, ran to a pay phone, and called the radio station. He recorded a minute of his routine over the telephone and did so well he won the contest. That success led to another, and eventually he was able to present his material as the opening comedian for singer Kenny Rogers at the prestigious Playboy Club in Century City.

Did positive thinking cause that radio station to run the contest and cause Bill to tune into their station at exactly the right moment? Of course not. However, if Bill hadn't set his objectives so firmly in his mind and believed he would succeed, he probably wouldn't have paid much attention to the contest information on the radio that day. But his determination compelled him to "seize the day" and make the most of that opportunity.

For all practical purposes, you can create opportunities by determining in your own heart and mind that opportunities will appear. And they don't happen to just a few lucky people. You can create opportunities by setting objectives and working to achieve them by taking a positive attitude toward your life. Power Performers learn to be aware of all the opportunities that are constantly passing by, and they're able to reach out and grab those they find exciting.

Power Performers are no luckier than anyone else—they just appear to be!

◆◆◆

The Eighth Secret of Power Performers is:

They know how to create opportunities.

◆◆◆

In the next chapter I'll teach you how you can avoid having to spend the rest of your life working for money.

POWER PERFORMERS KNOW HOW TO MAKE MONEY WORK FOR THEM

He that is of the opinion money will do everything may well be suspected of doing everything for money.

— *Benjamin Franklin*

Money is like a sixth sense, and you can't make use of the other five without it.

— *W. Somerset Maugham*

My life is a bubble; but how much solid cash it costs
to keep that bubble floating!

— *Logan Pearsall Smith*

You must make money work for you, or spend the rest of your life working for money.

— *Roger Dawson*

Money is important. You need a great deal of it to create a pleasant environment in which to live, to buy a few fun toys, and to give you freedom to enjoy life. However, if you become obsessed by money and the things it will buy, you'll end up being miserable. A key part of Power Performance is putting money into perspective. That's what this chapter is about.

IT SHOULDN'T TAKE THE END OF THE WORLD TO LEARN THIS LESSON

One of my favorite books is *On the Beach,* written in 1957 by Nevil Shute, a British author who in the middle of his life moved to Australia. While there he wrote lovingly about the life and people of that continent. He wrote 25 books over a 30-year span but is best known for *A Town Like Alice* in which an Australian soldier caught up in World War II in Asia talks lovingly about his home town of Alice Springs, and *On The Beach.* I named my son Dwight after the lead character in the book, the American submarine commander, who was played in the movie by Gregory Peck. The character of this man, who logically knew that his wife and children in America were now dead but whose heart refused to accept it, appealed to me so much that I decided that if I ever had a son, I would name him Dwight. Coincidentally a quarter of a century later my son found himself dating a girl named Moira, who told him that her parents had named her after the Ava Gardner character in the movie.

On The Beach is set in Melbourne, Australia, at a time when nuclear war had killed everyone in the Northern Hemisphere and the people in that city were the last survivors on earth. Even they had only a few weeks left to live, because clouds of nuclear dust were blowing south with the trade winds, and all the people knew they were going to die. Since death from radiation would be painful, the government was issuing suicide pills to everyone. In later life Nevil Shute, who had an incredible love for people, became increasingly pessimistic and ultimately despairing about the future of the human race. He died in 1960 in Melbourne only three years after he wrote *On The Beach.* That year, 1960, was the year that Nikita Khrushchev, banged his shoe on the table at the United Nations and it seemed to many observers inevitable that nuclear war would break out one day between the Soviet Union and the United States. Shute was only 60 and, sadly he never knew that the nuclear holocaust would be averted. The world would back away from the brink of nuclear war, and Shute would never know how much he alerted us to the danger by writing *On The Beach* .

The characters in the book knew that they were going to die and this changed their perspective on the importance of money. Money had no value, because if you wanted something you just went down to the store and helped yourself; and because you didn't need money, for most people there was no point in going to work.

One of the most interesting characters in this story was the man driving the trolley car on Queen's Street in Melbourne. This man chose to spend the remaining days of his life driving his trolley car up and down Queen's Street, even though there were few passengers and he didn't need the money. This character really affected me as an illustration of a person so content with what he was doing that he'd rather do his work than anything else in the world. Wouldn't it be wonderful if everyone saw that much value in what he or she does?

YOUR WORK HAS TO MEAN MORE THAN MONEY

It's so sad that the vast majority of people—some say as many as 90 percent—hate their jobs. If they weren't getting paid, they'd quit on the spot. Can you believe that?

I saw a television program once about the shipyards in Northern England. There they lock the giant gates of the docks every day after the workers arrive, and they don't unlock them until the whistle blows that tells the workers to go home for the day. In the last few minutes of the day the workers press up to the gates, waiting for the whistle to tell them they may leave.

Why is it that so many people cling to jobs they don't enjoy?

Let's take someone who gets out of college at the age of 22 and chooses a career based only on how much it pays, not on how stimulating the work may be. He works for the same corporation until he retires at the age of 65. He may earn several million dollars during those 43 years. But at what expense?

He began his career full of excitement, imagination, and vigor, ready to take on the challenges of corporate life. But if he was working only for money, at 65 he will have lost his enthusiasm and probably his health and be left a faded shadow of the person who started out at 22. He's sold himself to the corporation just as surely as if he cut off a finger or a toe, and he sold it for a million dollars. What kind of life is that? Today's successful corporations know that you must offer employees far more than money. Today you not only have to be on the cutting edge of new ideas and technology, you must also be a leader in creating a rewarding work environment.

Just as the attitude of employers to their employees has changed, so has the relationship that employees feel they have with their employer. Today's astute employees know that the company does not give them a job. Instead they sell their skills to the company. The job doesn't pay them, their employer doesn't pay them—they develop salable skills that they take into the marketplace. Power Performers understand this and are constantly working to improve their skills. When you have marketable skills, you need not cling to a job you no longer enjoy.

It always amazes me that employees expect their company to train them in skills, such as selling, negotiating, writing letters, or dealing with difficult customers, or any one of a dozen different other skills it takes to be successful in today's business world. Some employees even expect their company to motivate them—can you believe that?

In my mind, a company should be responsible for giving knowledge to the employees, such as product features and policies and procedures of the company. However, the company isn't responsible for teaching skills. Skills are something the employee should bring to the job and should refine at his or her own expense by listening to tapes, reading books, or attending seminars.

Power Performers understand this. Because they're constantly working to improve their skills, rather than looking to the employer to do this for them, they never become dependent on the company. They know they can break free at any time and market those skills somewhere else.

BREAKING FREE OF THE CORPORATE MOLD

Let me tell you the story of how I broke free of the corporation. I'd worked for this large department store chain for 13 years, had fulfilled every assignment, and had faithfully transferred whenever they told me to. I had a perfect track record. Whenever the regional office called me and said, "Roger, we'd like you to be at the other end of the state a week from Monday," I did exactly what they asked me. However, after 13 years I still wasn't earning enough to support my wife and three children adequately.

At that point I became interested in real estate. I'd accumulated a few rental houses because as I transferred from city to city I'd rented out my homes instead of selling them. By the time they transferred me to Los Angeles in 1974 I owned rental houses elsewhere in California, in Napa, Auburn, and Bakersfield. Every year the houses would go up in value, the mortgages would go down, and I wasn't having to pay any income tax because of the tax shelter they provided me. So on the one hand I was working like the devil to earn a paycheck. On the other I was depositing a few rent checks each month and getting rich. It suddenly occurred to me that I was making more money from these accidental real estate investments than from my corporate position. So I made up my mind to quit my job and go full time into real estate investing.

> *How little you know about the age you live in if*
> *you think that honey is sweeter than cash in hand.*
>
> OVID, WHO DIED IN A.D. 18.

> *There is nothing so absurd but some philosopher*
> *has said it.*
>
> CICERO, WHO DIED IN A.D. 43.

At the last minute, however, I got cold feet. I started thinking, "The job doesn't pay much, but at least I have security. I have health insurance, a profit-sharing plan, and a retirement program.

I decided to give the corporation one last chance. If they'd promote me, I'd stay. If they wouldn't, I'd be history. I set up a meeting with the regional personnel director in charge of the seven western states, Dave Cooke, and said to him, "Dave, you know that I've been a good corporate soldier for the last 13 years. I have a good record, and I think it's time you promoted me to store manager."

The story he gave me is one I'm sure most people who work for large corporations hear all the time. It goes something like this: "Roger, we think an awful lot of you at this company, and you'll be a store manager one day, but not just yet. You're going to have to be a little more patient." A little more patient—after 13 years.

Trying not let him see how upset I was, I politely said, "Dave, I want you to know I'll probably be reevaluating whether I want to spend the rest of my life with this company."

What he did astounded me. He leaned back with a look of complete astonishment on his face. Then he said, "But, Roger, where would you go? What would you do?"

He insulted me so much that I quit the next day and left within two weeks to pursue my real estate investment program. I quickly found that I could make in a month what it took me a year to do in retail management. (I found out later that Dave also quit the company a few months later, so when he asked me where I would go, he may just have been looking for leads.)

Often I wonder, though, what would have happened if Dave had handled the interview a little better? What if he hadn't insulted me so deeply? Would I still be working for that company? Still not making enough to support my family? The sad thing is that there's a good chance I'd still be there today, trapped in a job I didn't like and still not earning enough on which to live.

Power Performers will tell you there was such a day in their life too—a split-second moment of decision when they determined never again to be dependent on other people or on a company. Even if they made a decision to stay with the company they would work to develop enough marketable skills so that they wouldn't be dependent on the company.

It's the moment that changes your life.

For some people that moment happens very late in life, for example, Harlan Sanders, who founded the Kentucky Fried Chicken empire. He'd accomplished very little in his life and seemed destined to spend the rest of it in poverty. The day that turned his life around was the day he walked out to the mailbox and found his first social security check. He looked at that check, turning it around in his hands, and finally said in an explosion of rage, "I'm not going to do it! I'm not going to spend the rest of my life dependent on the federal government." Of course, you know the rest of the story. He took his recipe for fried chicken around the city, from restaurant to restaurant, cooking samples in the trunk of his car, and eventually had success greater than his wildest dreams.

MAKING MONEY WORK FOR YOU

What else can we do to ensure that we're never dependent upon other people for the money we need?

Here's a lesson too few people ever learn. Simply put, it's the attitude that you must make money work for you, or you'll spend the rest of your life working for money. It's really sad that our educational institutions spend so much time teaching our children how to *earn* money, but almost no time teaching how to *make* money.

> *You must make money work for you, or spend the rest of your life working for money.*

When my children were young, I decided I'd teach them this lesson myself. By the time she was 15 my daughter, Julia, understood the principle of working for money. I never gave my children an allowance without their having to do something in return for it, so she was accustomed to earning money. Now I wanted to teach her to make money.

I had an old Plymouth automobile that ran well but looked terrible. I offered to sell her the car so she could fix it up and resell it for a profit. We negotiated the price very professionally. I think I offered her the car for $500, she offered me $100, and we finally settled on $200.

She didn't have $200 to buy the car from me, so I proposed to loan her the money at an interest rate of 10 percent. Then I showed her how to set up a profit-and-loss statement. At that point she had assets of $200: the automobile. She also had liabilities of $200: her debt to me. That left her with a net worth of zero.

ASSETS	LIABILITIES	INCOME	NET WORTH
$200	$200	0	0

She and a friend took the car down to the car wash and steam cleaned the engine. She polished the car and fixed it up a little. Then she ran an ad in the paper—again borrowing the money from me because she had none—and eventually sold the car for $400.

At this point she paid me the money she owed me and then adjusted her profit-and-loss statement. After paying off her debt to me, she had assets that totaled $170, and no liabilities; so she had a net worth of $170. At 15 she now understood how to make money, rather than just earn it.

ASSETS	LIABILITIES	INCOME	EXPENSES	NET WORTH
$200	$200	0	0	0
$170	0	$400	$230	$170

Then I asked her what she wanted to do with the money. Did she want to buy clothes with it, or did she want to invest it in something else? Maybe I phrased the question in a little different way, because she said that since she wanted to continue living in our house she wanted to invest the money again! I helped her acquire a piece of real estate. Using some creative financing, I was able to buy a $39,000 house for her with no money down. So Julia found herself with assets of $39,000 (the house), and liabilities of $39,000—leaving her an unchanged net worth of $170.

ASSETS	LIABILITIES	INCOME	EXPENSES	NET WORTH
$200	$200	0	0	0
$170	0	$400	$230	$170
$39,000	$39,000	0	0	$170

Julia worked to fix the house up, advertise it, and rent it out. A year later we were able to sell the house for $59,000. By then Julia had assets of $20,000, which was the profit on the house, no liabilities, and so a net worth of $20,170. Not too bad for a 16 year old.

ASSETS	LIABILITIES	INCOME	EXPENSES	NET WORTH
$200	$200	0	0	0
$170	0	$400	$230	$170
$39,000	$39,000	0	0	$170
$20,000	0	$59,000	$39,000	$20,170

From there, she reinvested the money and bought a half-interest in four rental houses. Julia had learned a lesson too few people ever learn: how to make money rather than just earn it. Who knows what influences children to develop into what they become? I think it's more than a coincidence she went on to get a degree in business finance from University of Southern California, and become a Beverly Hills stockbroker.

Not many people realize that if you start out with only $1 of working capital, you'd have to double that investment dollar only 20 times to become a millionaire. If you don't believe me, then stop a minute and figure it out:

Imagine a dollar and start doubling it:

$1

Step 1. × 2 = $2
Step 2. × 2 = $4
Step 3. × 2 = $8
Step 4. × 2 = $16
Step 5. × 2 = $32
Step 6. × 2 = $64
Step 7. × 2 = $128
Step 8. × 2 = $256
Step 9. × 2 = $512

The tenth time you double it you will have $1,024.

Step 11. × 2 = $2048
Step 12. × 2 = $4096
Step 13. × 2 = $8192
Step 14. × 2 = $16,384

Step 15. × 2 = $32,768
Step 16. × 2 = $65,536
Step 17. × 2 = $131,072
Step 18. × 2 = $262,144
Step 19. × 2 = $524,288

By the twentieth time you double it, you will have $1,048,576.

As you can see, it is true—you have to double a dollar only 20 times to become a millionaire. However, there's the problem—very few people know how to double that first dollar.

In my Power Performance seminars, I challenge the people in the audience to take a dollar and double it within the next 24 hours without working for the money. In all the years I've been proposing this experiment, I've heard of only one person who was able to do it. He took the dollar to a local drugstore where they'd been selling collector's postage stamps. There was an assortment of loose stamps left in the bottom of the bin, and he asked the manager if he would take $1 for all of them. The manager agreed, and my student returned to the office where he worked and found someone who would buy the stamps from him for $2. It seems so simple, doesn't it? However, hardly anybody has the experience of buying something and reselling it at a profit.

So I want to challenge you—sometime within the next 48 hours—to take just $1 of working capital and figure out a way to double it, without working for it.

Remember that the more capital you have, the easier it is to begin on any investment program. So if you can double $1, you'll be able to double $2, and $4, and $8, right up to a million. Don't skip any steps in between. It's a temptation to say, "I'll jump start this program by starting with $1,000 of capital." It's harder to make a million dollars when you start with $1,000 because you haven't had the experience of doubling your money the ten times that it would have taken you to get that far.

The day that you make the transition from thinking that the only way you can get money is to work for it to realizing that you can make money work for you will be a magical day for you. You don't have to quit your job. Just realize that you're not dependent on your job.

The big challenge for you is to become a real entrepreneur—that is, someone who loves to prove that his particular talents and abilities are marketable—to make that transition from working for other people to working for yourself in a company that you started. It's not for everyone, but if it is for you I promise you that once you've done it you will never look back.

THE THREE STAGES TO BECOMING AN ENTREPRENEUR

Here are the three stages to becoming an entrepreneur:

STAGE ONE: CATALOG YOUR TALENTS

Take a day when you can be completely alone, get away from everyone else, and make a list. Don't think of what you are, such as beautiful, handsome, wealthy, educated, or athletic. Think of what you can do. If a friend were describing you to a stranger, what would he or she say you can do? If it still stumps you, get in your car and drive by your house, answering the question: "What kind of a person lives in that house? What can he or she do better than other people?"

- ◆ Can you persuade other people?
- ◆ Are you good at foreign languages?
- ◆ Can you bake cakes or tell jokes?
- ◆ Can you sing or paint?
- ◆ Can you keep cool under pressure?
- ◆ Can you read fast, sail a boat, or ride a wave on a surfboard?
- ◆ Can you explain complicated things in a simple way?

All of these things are talents that you can market. Think back to when you were nine years old. What did you have a natural talent for when you were that age? If I went back to your classmates and asked them what you were good at, what would they say? So many people have natural talents that were obvious at that age, but they got caught up in the herd mentality and drifted off into another career for which they were totally unsuited. When I look back to when I was nine I can tell you without a trace of hesitation what I was good at. I know what my classmates would tell you. I was the best in class at writing. It was always my essay that the teacher would read to the class. If I'd have known how important it was to pursue one's natural talents, I would have focused my education on that, gotten a job writing for a local newspaper, and started writing books in my spare time, instead of getting sidetracked into half a dozen other careers that ill suited me. I probably would have had my first book published when I was 25 instead of waiting until I was 45. I could have done a great deal of writing with those extra 20 years.

To get you thinking about your natural abilities consider how you feel about yourself in the following areas. Rate yourself on a scale of 1 (low) to 10 (high).

Physical

Strength. I am stronger than most people in my age group. If necessary I can do manual labor for hours at a time. In fact, I kind of like it.

| 1 | 2 | 3 | 4 | 5 | 6 | 7 | 8 | 9 | 10 |

Energy. I always seem to have a high energy level and can stay active even when others are drooping.

| 1 | 2 | 3 | 4 | 5 | 6 | 7 | 8 | 9 | 10 |

Coordination. I have always been good at sports that require coordination. I can connect easily with a baseball, and the first time I played golf (or baseball) it seemed like such a simple game.

| 1 | 2 | 3 | 4 | 5 | 6 | 7 | 8 | 9 | 10 |

Manual dexterity. I enjoy working with small models, I'm good at dealing cards, and think I'd probably make a good magician. (Terrific talents for a surgeon.)

| 1 | 2 | 3 | 4 | 5 | 6 | 7 | 8 | 9 | 10 |

Endurance. I enjoy activities that take a long time. I can hike up in the mountains for 12 hours a day. I could play 36 holes of golf effortlessly. I never crash.

1   2   3   4   5   6   7   8   9   10

Mental

Concentration. I've never had a problem with this. If I lose myself in a good book or if I'm working to solve a difficult problem, hours can pass and I won't know it.

1   2   3   4   5   6   7   8   9   10

Imagination. My mind races with wild ideas. At school I was always getting into trouble for daydreaming.

1   2   3   4   5   6   7   8   9   10

Endurance. You won't find me quitting a project because it tires me mentally. If I have to I can stay up most of the night studying or cramming for a test.

1   2   3   4   5   6   7   8   9   10

Emotional

Staying calm. Nothing seems to rattle me. In an emergency you can count on me to stay cool and do the right thing.

1   2   3   4   5   6   7   8   9   10

Feeling and expressing passion. I love life. I love people. My heart is bursting with all the great things I want to share with other people.

1   2   3   4   5   6   7   8   9   10

Feeling and expressing warmth. I'm never happier than when I'm close with someone I care about. I make friends easily and enjoy being with them and helping them if they need me.

1   2   3   4   5   6   7   8   9   10

Ignoring people's feelings in order to get the job done. I'm a friendly person but if you need someone to bang a few heads together to get the job done, you can count on me. I don't think it's mean. Some people need shaking up for their own good.

1   2   3   4   5   6   7   8   9   10

Artistic

Writing. If I have to communicate something to a friend or business acquaintance I'd much rather sit down and write a five page letter than I would pick up the phone and call the person.

1   2   3   4   5   6   7   8   9   10

Oral skills. If I have something to communicate to a friend or business acquaintance I'd much rather call the person than to take the time to write it all down. That takes me forever.

1   2   3   4   5   6   7   8   9   10

Painting. I enjoyed painting or drawing in school and did better at it than most of the other students.

1   2   3   4   5   6   7   8   9   10

Music. I have a good sense of rhythm and seemed to have a talent for playing an instrument in school. (There's more to this than rhythm, of course. You need good pitch and timbre discrimination, and good tonal memory.)

1   2   3   4   5   6   7   8   9   10

Self-expression. I don't have a problem communicating with other people. Most of my friends and coworkers will tell you that they know exactly where I stand. I'm a good supervisor and enjoy teaching skills to the employees.

1	2	3	4	5	6	7	8	9	10

Intellectual

Mathematical. I'm a natural with numbers. When the other kinds were struggling with algebra and trigonometry I could breeze through the course and not understand why they were having trouble.

1	2	3	4	5	6	7	8	9	10

Abstract concepts. I enjoy brain teasers and working through problems that require me to juggle complex thoughts in my mind.

1	2	3	4	5	6	7	8	9	10

Language. English language came naturally to me at school and I've enjoyed learning foreign languages. My friends would agree that I use a broad vocabulary when I'm speaking.

1	2	3	4	5	6	7	8	9	10

Interpersonal Skills

Gregariousness. I love being around people and people love being around me. In school I had more friends than anybody.

1	2	3	4	5	6	7	8	9	10

Persuasiveness. I can usually get my way with people so I don't get uptight if things don't appear to be just the way I want them. I'll be able to talk somebody into doing it for me.

1	2	3	4	5	6	7	8	9	10

Self-confidence. Nothing bothers me about dealing with people. I'd be the last person you'd describe as shy. In school I didn't have any problem knocking on doors for fund drives or standing on the street corner and waving people into our car washes.

1   2   3   4   5   6   7   8   9   10

What you've just completed isn't a scientific analysis, and there are no right or wrong answers. However, there's a good chance that you ran across a talent that you forgot you had and you're wondering why you're not in a line of work where you could take advantage of it.

STAGE TWO: INSPIRE YOURSELF

Read about and surround yourself with successful entrepreneurs. For reading, I'd suggest:

Grinding It Out, by Ray Kroc. Berkley Medallion Books 1977. Ray Kroc sold paper cups for 17 years until an opportunity to make money, not just earn it, came up. He quit his secure job to buy the rights to distribute Multimixers, a machine used by restaurants and snack bars to make milk shakes.

In 1954 he became curious about a hamburger stand in San Bernardino, California, that used eight mixers at a time. Since each mixer had six spindles, that meant they could make 48 milk shakes at once. Kroc flew out to what was then a sleepy desert town, to see what was going on. The name of that fast-food place was McDonald's, and the crush of people trying to buy their 15-cent hamburgers overwhelmed him. The customers ranged from laborers on their lunch break to a beautiful, fashionably dressed blonde in a convertible. "It was not her sex appeal that made my heart pound with excitement," he was fond of saying. "It was the obvious relish with which she devoured the hamburger."

Ray Kroc bought the right to use the McDonald's name and their assembly-line preparation methods, and he made over $500 million. The first line in his autobiography stresses the cornerstone of Power Performance: "I have always believed that each man makes his own happiness and is responsible for his own problems . . . it works as well for me now that I am a multimillionaire as it did for me when I was selling paper cups for $35 a week and playing piano part time to support my wife and daughter."

Be My Guest, by Conrad Hilton. Prentice Hall 1987 (free in most Hilton hotel rooms). Unlike Ray Kroc, who discovered how to make money late in life, Conrad Hilton was an entrepreneur almost from the start. Raised in the desert just south of Albuquerque, he owned his own produce business as a youngster. "I hoed the corn, watered the vegetables, and then toured the town selling my harvest from door to door. I got 10 cents for 12 ears of corn and thought I was doing very well." When he was 20 his parents were facing bankruptcy, and he used his entrepreneurial talents to help them turn the family home into a hotel.

By the time he was 25 he'd raised capital and started his own bank. Then one of those strange things happened that we talked about in the last chapter. He went to Cisco, Texas, to invest in another bank but ended up instead buying the hotel in which he stayed. From that chance happening grew the Hilton Hotels empire. His advice: "Find your own particular talent; think big, be honest, and assume your full share of responsibility for the world in which you live."

Marriott, by Robert O'Brien. Deseret Book Company 1977 (free in most Marriott hotel rooms). The book describes how J. Willard Marriott built his empire. (The first nine chapters cover his youth as a member of the Mormon Church. If you're interested just in the business part of it, you can start at Chapter 10.) In 1928 he and a friend put together $6,000 and started an A&W Root Beer Stand on 14th Street in Washington. They did well during the hot summer, but faced failure as they went into the winter because their A&W franchise did not permit them to sell food. However, Bill Marriott was a Power Performer, and understood that within every problem is the seed of success. He went to the franchiser and received permission to be the only outlet in the country authorized to sell food.

They decided to specialize in hot Mexican food and called it the Hot Shoppe. They had problems in the early days, and his partner was happy when Bill bought him out for $5,000. The first Hot Shoppe turned into a small chain, and Marriott opened his eighth restaurant near the old Hoover Airport. Then one of those strange coincidences happened. Bill was visiting the restaurant one day when an Eastern Air Transport employee came in and asked for a quart of coffee to go. Bill asked him, "Driving to New York?"

"No, flying to Atlanta," he replied. "We'll drink this on the way."

The restaurant manager told Bill that more and more people were buying coffee and sandwiches to take with them on flights because the airlines didn't offer anything. Bill immediately picked up on this and went to see the people at Eastern. This was the start of one of Marriott's most successful divisions, Host Foods, which is now a major caterer of food to airlines, hospitals, and colleges. If you have a drink or a sandwich at an airport, chances are you're buying it from Host. Bill Marriott also stressed what I believe is a key point for Power Performance: "Keep your sense of humor. Make the business fun for you and others."

To find out about key groups of entrepreneurs with whom you can meet, try calling your local Chamber of Commerce, which keeps a list of all the clubs in the area. See if you can find organizations such as The Winner's Circle, which meets in Costa Mesa, California. Call local churches to see if they have classes for entrepreneurs. The University of Southern California has a separate division of its business school specializing in the subject.

STAGE THREE: GET STARTED!

Once you've done that, you're halfway there. You don't have to quit your job or sell your home just yet. Do something small. Write the first page of that novel you've been planning for years. See if you can't sell that oil painting you did years ago by putting it on consignment at a local store. Call up someone who is doing well in a field that interests you and see if you can buy the person lunch. Set an objective to make $10 during the next 30 days by performing some activity outside your present occupation. Ten dollars may seem like a drop in a bucket, but it's a start. That drop may well turn into a trickle, the trickle will turn into a stream, and, just maybe, that stream will turn into a torrent.

> *The Three Stages of Entrepreneurship.*
>
> *1. Catalog your talents.*
>
> *2. Inspire yourself.*
>
> *3. Get started!*

I made my first $10 as an entrepreneur when I gave a talk at a real estate convention I was attending in Atlanta. I was recording my talk so that I could critique myself afterward. When I finished talking, a member of the audience approached me and said, "I saw that you were recording your talk. Could I buy a copy of the tape?" I had no idea what to charge him, so I suggested $10. I duplicated the tape on the machine at the office and sent it to him. I called my real estate investment company Plaza Properties, so I asked him to make the check out to Plaza Productions. When the check came, I opened up a bank account under that name and deposited the check. That's a key rule for entrepreneurs: don't commingle your funds. Each business should have its own accounting system and its own bank account, right from the first dollar you take in.

The next time a local real estate board asked me to give a speech, I took a few copies with me and sold over $200 worth. Apparently I'd stumbled upon a talent I didn't know I had. Soon afterward I decided to become a full-time speaker, and in the first full year of my new career I sold over $500,000 worth of my cassette tapes.

I'd discovered a key to Power Performance: If you want to make a dramatic change in your income, you have make a dramatic change in what you're doing. There's an expression in real estate that says, "Changing use changes value," Which means that if you own a house and you can get the zoning on it changed from residential to commercial, and you turn the house into an office or store, the property changes value. Instead of getting a steady increase in value from appreciation, you instantly get a big jump in value. If you own an apartment building and convert it to condominiums—changing use changes value. If you own farmland and can get it zoned commercial for a shopping center—changing use, changes value.

> *To make a dramatic change in your income*
> *remember the real estate adage:*
>
> *"Changing use changes value."*

People are like that too. Our value increases steadily over the years because we get better at what we do and because of inflation. However, if we want to make a dramatic increase in our income, we must change what we're doing. Lee Iacocca understood this when he switched from engineering to marketing at Ford Motors. Ray Kroc understood it when he switched from selling Multimixers to developing a restaurant franchise. When I left retailing to go into real estate, I found I could make in a month what it took me a year to make before. When I went from real estate to speaking, I found I could make in a day what it took me a month to make in real estate and a year to make in retailing. Changing use changes value. Often we've trapped ourselves in a situation from which we see no way to escape. We need to learn how to break free of the self imposed restrictions stopping us from becoming Power Performers.

Let me tell you a story to illustrate this point of breaking free from self imposed restrictions.

Many years ago some friends and I spent a week in Rome. It was my first trip there. We stayed at one of the finest hotels in the world, the Excelsior on the romantic Via Veneto, where they filmed *La Dolce Vita* (The Good Life). We were the guests of a couple who'd just sold their company for $13 million, and they were celebrating in grand style. For a week we indulged ourselves with all the finest things the city had to offer.

You can argue that Paris has more atmosphere and Salzburg has more charm, but Rome! Rome is the most fascinating city in Europe because of its grand history and its great works of art and culture.

The city exists on three levels: the ancient Rome of the Caesars and the early Saints; the Renaissance Rome that produced the great works of art filling every park, museum, and church; and the bustling metropolis of the modern city.

It's an intriguing city at every level. The Catacombs reverberate with the strong voices of the early Christians, fighting bravely to maintain their faith amid horrible persecution; the imposing force of the Coliseum rules the city with the power of emperors dead for a millennium; the works of Michelangelo and Leonardo da Vinci still vibrate with their strokes of genius.

There are simpler things too. The unmatchable pleasure of an extended lunch at the sidewalk cafés in the Piazza Navona, or spending an afternoon sitting on the French Steps as people from all over the world pass by.

One of the greatest experiences I had in Italy was discovering the works of the great sculptor Michelangelo Buonarroti. The largest church in the world, St. Peter's Cathedral, is in Rome. Michelangelo designed it in the early sixteeth century. Walking into the cathedral, through the large front doors, I was drawn to the right where, set aside in an alcove, sits one of the world's most priceless treasures: Michelangelo's Pieta. This indescribable sculpture depicts the dead body of Christ lying in his mother's arms, as Mary looks with sorrow and serenity into the face of her son. It has an unbelievable emotional appeal. I don't believe I ever really understood the love a mother can have for a child until I saw that statue. The work is perfect—every square inch is faultlessly beautiful.

In Southern California, the people at Forest Lawn cemetery in Burbank have re-created the "Pieta" with incredible care. Craftsmen went to the same Italian quarries near Peitrasanta, where Michelangelo quarried Carrera marble for the "Pieta," and found marble identical to that which he used centuries before. Then they electronically reproduced the sculpture with a new process, forming an exact replica of the "Pieta." There's not one single centimeter's difference between the two, but there's no comparison between them. The original simply glows with the work of the master, and regardless of how many duplicates they make, the original Pieta remains unique.

We human beings are also unique. Each of us glows with the work of the Master, with unique talents and abilities. Our worth as a human being comes from what we do, not who we are. Each one of us is a unique creation of the Master, whom nobody should compare to any other. Who we are is sublime.

Michelangelo's "Pieta" impressed me so much that I decided to search out more of his sculptures—the tombs of the Dukes in the New Sacristy of San Lorenzo; the magnificent Pope Julius II's mausoleum in the Church of St. Peter in Vincoli, which features the incredible statue of Moses. The marble statue appears to be so full of life that Michelangelo stood before it and cried out, "Why don't you speak?"

A few days later I drove up through the beautiful green hills north of Rome to the city of Florence, to see the world famous statue of David. It stands in a museum called the Academy, built in 1873 just to feature this Michelangelo masterpiece. (For the previous 369 years the statue had stood in the square in front of the Palace.) The Academy has a long entry way lined on both sides with magnificent works of art. At the end of the hall is a glass-roofed rotunda, in the center of which stands "David," sling in hand as he stands prepared to attack the giant Goliath. I stood before it, overwhelmed by its magnificence. Michelangelo had taken a block of marble that other sculptors had discarded because a large piece was missing from the mid-section of the column. Where others saw scrap, however, Michelangelo saw beauty, and he planned the curve of David's stance as he stood facing Goliath to perfectly complement the missing piece. In a lyrical moment I wondered if a master such as Michelangelo could look at me and see past my imperfections to find something of greatness within.

Look past your imperfections to see the greatness within.

A tourist was gauche enough to ask a guide if David's right hand was too large and out of proportion to the rest of the body. This visibly pained the guide, who said softly, "Please, sir, you are in the presence of one of the finest works of art the world has ever known. How can you desecrate such beauty with an observation such as that?"

As magnificent as the statue of David is, there are two other pieces in the Academy that made an even greater impression on me. They were also by Michelangelo, and he called them both "The Prisoner." The sculptures are two of four pieces he did with the same theme. A third is in the Louvre in Paris, and it would be several years before I would see it; nobody has located the fourth. Michelangelo took four solid blocks of marble, and from each he carved the figure of a slave emerging from the confines of the stone. From the bases of the uncarved blocks these slaves thrust themselves upward, as if struggling to free themselves of the chains of their enslavement.

Michelangelo was depicting the drama of the soul imprisoned in the body. However, it symbolized to me how we must throw off the confines of our own self-imposed restrictions if we are to become Power Performers. Have the courage to examine your life and see if changing your use—what you're doing now—wouldn't dramatically change your value and therefore your income.

Power Performers understand that, although we should never work only for money, we do need a great deal of it to finance this adventure called life. There are many ways to get money, and straight salary is absolutely the worst. Straight salary is addictive. If you can't be an entrepreneur, work on commission. If you can't work on commission, in some way get a piece of the action, so that your Power Performance gives you the financial rewards you deserve. Having a great deal of money isn't everything—but it sure helps!

> *There are many ways to finance the adventure of life.*
>
> *Straight salary is the worst.*

Here are the six rules about money that Power Performers always follow:

1. Money begins to flow to us when we find something we love to do so much we'd do it even if we weren't getting paid.

2. We earn money because we have developed marketable skills, not because we have a job.

3. The company for which we work is responsible for giving us information. We are responsible for developing skills.

4. We must learn to make money work for us, or we'll spend the rest of our lives working for money.

5. Whether we work for a corporation or for ourselves, we need to develop an entrepreneurial spirit. That means analyzing our talents, motivating ourselves, and above all getting started.

6. Changing use changes value. Moving to a different division in your company or in some way branching out in a new direction can make a dramatic increase in your income.

◆◆◆

The Ninth Secret of Power Performers is:

They know how to make money work for them.

◆◆◆

In the next chapter, I'll tell you how to survive a mid-life crisis.

10

POWER PERFORMERS HAVE LEARNED HOW TO DEFINE THEIR FUTURE

The secret to success is constancy to purpose.

— *Benjamin Disraeli*

Many persons have a wrong idea of what constitutes true happiness. It is not attained through self-gratification but through fidelity to a worthy purpose.

— *Helen Keller*

The great and glorious masterpiece of man is to know how to live to purpose.

— *Montaigne*

Success is making a fortune doing something you'd choose to do even if you weren't getting paid for it.

— *Roger Dawson*

If you haven't done so already, one day you'll go through a mid-life crisis. If you've been through it already, you know exactly what I'm talking about. If you haven't been through it, nothing I can say will prepare you for its devastating impact.

It usually happens to men in their early forties and to women in their late thirties. Your mid-life crisis is the day when you wake up and suddenly understand, with a flash of savage insight, that you're going to die someday.

It usually hits women in their late thirties because that's when their children start to drift off to college or get married or in some other way become independent of the family nest. Then women suddenly lose the identity of being a "mother," a role with which they've lived for so long.

> *My parents have been visiting me for a few days. I just dropped them off at the airport. They leave tomorrow.*
>
> MARGARET SMITH

Men get hit a little later in life, in the early to mid forties. A thirtieth birthday will give them a little jolt, when they suddenly realize with astonishment that they're about half-way through their life. Until then, they've been thinking like a teenager, that their life is just getting started and there's all the time in the world to accomplish the things they want to do. Then 40 hits and it's becoming abundantly clear they're not going to accomplish all the material objectives they've set for themselves. Any time now, they're a prime candidate for a mid-life crisis—the day when they suddenly realize life doesn't last forever.

As I finished speaking to a group in Seattle, a woman came up to me and said, "Can you tell me what the problem might be between my husband and me? We've been married for 24 years, and I didn't think anyone in the world had a better marriage. However, suddenly it all changed. Now he's moody and wants to be by himself a lot. It's not just that he wants to be away from me. He's quit golfing with his friends and has even dropped out of his weekly poker game."

I could see that the possibility that he had a girlfriend tucked away somewhere concerned her, but it embarrassed her too much for her even to broach the subject. She was a fine looking lady who really seemed to "have her act together," as we say in California, however, so I took a wild guess in another direction. I asked her, "Has he been to any funerals lately?"

> *They say such nice things about people at their funerals that it makes me sad to realize that I'm going to miss mine by just a few days.*
>
> GARRISON KEILLOR

"Why, yes," she said thoughtfully. "A friend of his from the Lions Club died, and he was one of the pall bearers. His friend was only 42, and seemed to be in perfect health. He went out jogging one morning and died of a heart attack. That was about a month ago. I bet that's what's bothering him!" I could sense a wave of relief sweep over her.

"It's not grief over the loss of a friend," I explained to her. "Nothing triggers a mid-life crisis in a man more than the unexpected death of a friend who's about the same age. He's brooding because he realizes he isn't going to live forever, either. Give him your love, and patience and understanding and he'll get over it—in another 10 or 15 years!"

> *Your mid-life crisis starts the day you suddenly realize that you're going to die someday.*

It's like the guy who goes to the doctor, and says, "Give it to me straight, Doc."

"Okay I will," says the doctor, "the way you're living your life, you're not going to last until morning."

The guy rushes home and tells his wife the bad news. "At least we'll make our last night together memorable," he tells her. "Let's go to the best restaurant in town. We'll have the greatest meal we've ever had, we'll dance until midnight, and then we'll come back and make love all night long."

"That's easy for you to say," she says. "You don't have to get up in the morning!"

WHAT IS TRULY IMPORTANT IS THE EXPERIENCE OF LIFE ITSELF

People do unusual things as the result of a mid-life crisis. Suddenly the material objectives they've set for themselves seem unimportant. This can come as a crushing blow to someone who's spent the last 20 years climbing the corporate ladder. The dream this person has held for so long of becoming the president of his or her company or of heading up a corporate division has become so much a part of him or her that distinguishing between accomplishing the objective and having feelings of self-worth is impossible. A mid-life crisis suddenly makes the person reshape his or her values. The person ends up sailing a boat across the Pacific or climbing to 20,000 feet in the Andes or starting a vineyard in the Napa Valley.

People often become Power Performers when they go through a mid-life crisis. That's when they suddenly realize that life starts one day and ends one day. Then, for the first time, they realize that the experience of life itself, the appreciation they gain from the unique experience of living it, is what's truly important.

Power Performers know that life is not about making money or the, "He Who Dies with the Most Toys—Wins," philosophy. Power Performance is about doing the most we can with the short time God gives us here on earth.

Ask people who work with the terminally ill and they'll tell you that whenever their patients' illnesses force them to confront their own mortality they realize that it's not the number of years they live that's important—it's the quality of life that counts.

THE DIFFERENCE BETWEEN INTELLECTUAL BELIEF AND EMOTIONAL BELIEF

It's an unchangeable law of nature that all living things have a life span—eventually they die. The life span of living things varies tremendously, from one day for the mayfly to 4,900 years for the bristle-cone pine. Among mammals, human beings have the longest life span, which is 115 years. It has always been 115 years, and as far as anyone knows, it will always be 115 years.

"Wait a minute, Roger," I hear you saying. "That's not true. Human beings are living far longer now than they used to."

Yes, that's true. *Life expectancy* has increased dramatically. At the time of Christ, it may have been only 25 years. As recently as the start of the twentieth century, life expectancy in this country was only 47 years. Today it's over 75 years. It's true that improvements in hygiene, nutrition, and the prevention and cure of disease have extended life expectancy. However, life span has always remained the same—you're born, and if nothing goes wrong, you'll die 115 years later.

So why on earth should this sudden realization that we'll die someday come as such a shock? The answer lies in the difference between intellectual belief and emotional belief.

Since we were young and we first heard about someone dying, we've understood intellectually that we will die someday. On the day of our mid-life crisis, we understand it emotionally for the first time.

To illustrate the difference between intellectual belief and emotional belief, let me tell you a story. A few years ago I went white-water rafting on the Snake River in Wyoming. It was such an exciting introduction to the sport that in subsequent years I found myself rafting in the Andes, Taiwan, and New Zealand.

We had a local guide, Matt, to guide us through the rapids. Experts grade rapids on a difficulty scale of one to six. Six is unnavigable, down to one, which is a calm flow. We would be going through class-five rapids. Matt told me the flow that day was as fast as any he'd ever seen in the 11 years he'd been working on the river.

"How many times have you flipped the raft in those 11 years?" I asked him.

"Only once," he said. "I'll tell you about it later."

As we went through the rapids on the toughest part of the river, I couldn't believe that the boat stayed afloat. I have a video tape of the run, and it astounds people who watch it that we came through without sinking. Churning white water surrounded us, and the boat completely submerged before we came roaring out of the ravine. After we came out of the thunder of the chute, into the more peaceful waters downstream, Matt told me, "Now I'll tell you about the only time I've ever flipped a raft in 11 years. It was this morning!"

"Matthew!" I teased him. "If I'd have known you were having a bad day, however, then I never would have come!"

I didn't really realize how dangerous the waters were that day, until I heard that he'd taken another boat through later in the day and had flipped it also.

In town that evening I ran into Michael, who had been in the raft that flipped. To my surprise, he was furious with Matt. Hours later he was still shaking with the kind of rage you'll only see with people who've been scared to death and need to release the tension by taking it out on someone.

At first his anger puzzled me because I know that white-water rafting can be a dangerous sport. You understand the risks involved, or you don't do it. There's a good chance you'll get dumped into the water, and anytime that happens there's a danger that you'll drown. The difference between Michael and me was not that I'm more courageous or even that I think more logically. The big difference was that Michael understood drowning emotionally, and I understood it only intellectually. We both knew intellectually that if we're trapped under water too long, we'll die. However, he had experienced the fear of being hurled into the tumultuous water, of coming to the surface with his lungs bursting and fighting for air, only to find himself trapped under the raft. He was the one who'd faced the shock of realizing that it was finally happening to him, that he was going to die. My belief in drowning was at a superficial level, while his belief had ripped into him and become a permanent part of his consciousness.

A mid-life crisis affects us in the same way. When we go through it we replace the intellectual belief that we'll die someday with the emotional belief that it really is going to happen. Life takes us to the edge of a cliff, dangles us by the ankles and says, "This is what's going to happen to you one day."

WHO DO YOU THINK IS THE WORLD'S MOST POWERFUL PERFORMER?

Let me share with you my reaction to my mid-life crisis. I was forty-two when I suddenly became obsessed with the realization that I was going to die someday. For over a year I found it difficult to think of anything else.

I spent my days wondering about the quality of my life and reevaluating my definition of success. One day I asked myself, "Who do you think is the most powerful performer in the entire world?" The person I chose will surprise you. In my opinion, it's movie director Stephen Spielberg, the man who made *Jaws, Raiders of the Lost Ark, E.T., Jurassic Park,* and *Schindler's List.* Why do I think he's so successful? Because he's doing something with his life that he loves to do so much he'd do it even if he weren't getting paid—and yet he's able to make a fortune doing it. That, to me, is the ultimate success—to make a fortune doing something that you'd choose to do, even if you weren't getting paid for it. Ronald Reagan brought that aura to the presidency. Never once did we doubt that he was loving every minute of it.

> *Success is making a fortune doing something you'd choose to do even if you weren't getting paid for it.*

Power Performance isn't just money and toys. It's achieving stratospheric success and loving every minute of what you're doing.

WHAT DO YOU ENJOY DOING MORE THAT ANYTHING ELSE IN THE WORLD?

So as I went through my own mid-life crisis, I asked myself, "What do you enjoy doing more than anything else in the entire world?" The answer was that I enjoy speaking in front of groups. There's a stimulation to public speaking to which I'm apparently addicted. I'm never happier than when entertaining and sharing important ideas with a responsive audience. The next question I asked myself was, "Can you make a lot of money doing that?" I decided that with a bit of luck, I could. That's when I made the decision to become a full-time professional speaker. I quit a high paying job as president of a large real estate corporation and cast my fate to the wind to see if I could make it as a speaker. It was scary at first, but within weeks I knew that I'd made the right choice, and I have never for a moment regretted the move.

I was finally doing something with my life simply because I loved to do it; rather than doing something for the promise of future rewards. I didn't fully understand the reason, but from then on success was easy for me. What I had unknowingly done was to align my talents with my desires. When you do that, everything drops into place for you.

What is it you enjoy doing more than anything else in the world? Could you make a lot of money doing it?

To help you explore your response, let me ask you three questions:

1. *What were you good at when you were nine years old?* Remember what I told you in the previous chapter? Let's suppose I tracked down your fourth-grade teacher and all of your classmates. Then when I asked them what they remembered you for, what would they tell me? Was it the drawings you did? Was it your leadership skills? Your athletic prowess? Often our natural talents are apparent when we're that young, but we forget them in our rush to conform with our peer group. For example, when I was nine it was the essays I wrote that made me stand out in my class. It was always my stories that the teacher would read in class. As I told you, I made the mistake of shelving this talent for more than thirty years, finally rediscovering it during my mid-life crisis.

Enter your response here. When I was nine years old I was one of the best in my class at: _____

_____

2. *What is not work to you?* What are you willing to put a lot of effort into that you don't consider work? When I tell people that climbing Mount Kilimanjaro in Africa took me four long days, they say, "That sounds like a lot of work!" That may be so, but it wasn't work to me. When I tell people that it takes me nine months of 18-hour days to write a book, they say, "That sounds like a lot of work!" Yes, but it wasn't work to me!

When I want to retreat from the pressures of my business life, I rent the Villa Michelle in Puerto Vallarta, Mexico. It's a beautiful three story villa built onto a hillside overlooking Mismaloya Bay where John Huston filmed *The Night of the Iguana*. Every room has a balcony with fabulous views up and down the Mexican Riviera. Early each morning I get up while the servants are still cleaning the house, pour myself a cup of coffee, and write out on the patio deck, with my portable computer balanced on my knees. Once Gerardo, the houseman, watched me for a while and then said, "Mr. Roger, could I ask you what you do?"

"I write books and give seminars all over the United States. Why do you ask?"

"Because you are different than the other guests who come here. They all come to have a good time. You work every morning."

"Gerardo, it looks to you as if I'm working, but I'm not. I'm having fun. Work is only work if you don't want to do it."

When Francis Chichester became the first person to sail across the Atlantic alone, he worked 18 hour days, seven days a week, for 40 days straight. Hard work? It wasn't work for him.

So look for something that isn't work to you.

Enter your response here. What activity can you lose yourself in so much that even though it takes effort, it doesn't seem like work? _____

_____

3. *What would you do with your life if you were assured of success?* If you knew that no matter what direction you took with your life you'd be successful, what would you do with the rest of your time on earth?

Enter your response here. If I knew it was impossible to fail, I would:_____

_____

TURNING DREAMS INTO REALITY

Let's say you're currently teaching school in San Diego, but when you think back to fourth grade you recall that it was your photographs that people would remember. Your parents had given you a small camera and for some reason you had a natural talent for taking pictures. You were always taking your latest efforts to your teacher and hearing her rave over them.

When you think about what you don't consider work, you think of how much fun it is to stay up all night processing pictures in your darkroom. As for what you would do if you knew you couldn't fail, you decide that you'd move to Jackson Hole, Wyoming, and open up a photographic gallery. You'd have a little shop in the town square where you'd market your work. Although you'd be willing to work hard, you'd never be afraid to hang up the closed sign if the fishing was good up the valley or the aspen trees were in full glow and aching to be photographed against the background of the snowcapped Grand Teton.

In the winter you might take a long lunch hour and ski at Snow King, or take a couple of weeks off to go elk hunting. You'd shop around for a few acres out on the butte overlooking the river and then build a beautiful rustic cabin on the land. For you it's the perfect vision, an absolutely ideal way to spend the rest of your life. Many people have dreams like that, don't they?

Power Performers know how to turn those dreams into reality.

> *I used to work at the International House of Pancakes. It was a dream and I made it happen.*
>
> PAULA POUNDSTONE

So if your dream is a photographic gallery in Jackson Hole, how do you go about turning that dream into a reality?

The first thing you should do is write it down on a piece of paper and start carrying it around with you. Oh, oh! How many times have you heard that? That you should write down your objectives and carry them with you all the time? So why don't you quit giving it lip service and start doing it? Your subconscious mind is so much more aware of objectives when you have them written down.

One evening when my son Dwight was a teenager, I took him out to dinner and we talked about the future. Sometimes parents have to play little games to catch the attention of teenagers, because the youngsters' minds are full of other things. I said, "Dwight, I'm going to do something for you only 3 percent of the people in this world can do." With that I pulled my list of objectives out of my pocket and showed them to him. Study after study has shown only 3 percent of people carry their objectives with them, despite having been told to do so, time after time after time.

Only 10 percent of the people in this country can even tell you what they'd like to be doing five years from now.

Isn't it amazing that you could walk up to 100 people on any city street and say something such as, "Pardon me, but here we are, travelers together on Planet Earth spinning through the heavens; would you mind telling me exactly what you're doing here?"

Ninety percent of them—if they didn't have you hauled away—would have to answer, "Well, I don't know. I haven't really given it that much thought." Ninety percent of the people in the world have no more direction in their life than that.

HOW TO PLAN YOUR OBJECTIVES

So we know your objective is the photographic gallery in Wyoming, or whatever else might be your vision of a perfect future. So we know you should have this as a written objective, but how do you go about writing it down? There's quite an art to writing objectives. An objective doesn't need to be all-encompassing or profound, but it does need to have a precise format. First it must include an action verb: this is any verb; with a "to" in front of it—to do, to have, to become, to attain. A well-written objective also needs a time-frame. "To have established a photographic gallery in Jackson Hole, Wyoming by January 1, three years from now." That's a well-written objective because it has a verb and a time frame. Remember that without a time frame it's not an objective, it's just a daydream.

For a business objective, you must also include the phrase, "at a cost of . . . ," because in business you can accomplish almost any objective if you lavish enough money on it, but you'll probably go broke trying to do it. So "to have established a photographic gallery in Jackson Hole, Wyoming, by January 1, three years from now; at a cost not to exceed $50,000, which will show a net return after my salary of $10,000 a year" is a good business objective. Anyone can do anything if his or her pockets are deep enough, but in business you must always consider the cost.

Write down your objective here:

My objective is to:

I will accomplish this by:

(If business) *The cost will not exceed:*

Having learned how to format your objective, I now want you to create a form on which you'll write your objectives, so you can carry them with you always. It should look like this:

OBJECT PLANNER

My one-year objective is:

My five-year objective is:

Skills and qualifications I'll need:

What I'm willing to give up:

What I'll do this month:

It's an excellent format for the sheet of objectives you'll carry around with you in your pocket. As you can see, it includes a one-year objective as a part of a much longer-range five-year objective, detailed information to help you accomplish your objective, and an immediate activity objective.

Take the time to photocopy it and make 21 copies. My purpose is to get you in the habit of looking at your objectives every day. If I can get you to do it for 21 consecutive days, it'll become a lifetime habit.

Pavlov, the man who could make a dog salivate just by ringing a dinner bell, told us it takes 21 days for anyone to develop a new habit. You'll notice that if you move the wastepaper basket to the other side of your desk you'll throw paper on the floor for about 21 days until you break your old habit and start a new one. If you move to a new home, it takes about twenty-one days before it starts feeling like home. If you start a new job, it takes about 21 days for it to switch from feeling as if it's a new job, to feeling as if it's what you do for a living. Amputees know that it takes about 21 days for their mind to realize that the limb is missing—until then they continue to get feelings in the phantom limb.

In California we decided that motorists must wear seat belts, and so I found myself faced with this new law starting on the first of the month and having to break a lifelong bad habit. Here's how I went about it: I promised myself that I would always buckle up, even if I didn't realize I hadn't put it on until I was pulling into my own garage. Once or twice I switched the engine off and went to get out of the car before I realized that I had not buckled up. So I would force myself to sit back in the car, buckle up, and then remove the seat belt. In behavioral psychology terms I was removing the benefit from not buckling up. Failing to put on my seat belt was not going to save me any time or make things more convenient because before I could get out of the car I would have to put it on anyway. Then one day I was driving off down the street from my office, and suddenly I remembered to buckle up. I reached down to find out I already had the seat belt on. I'd put it on instinctively, without realizing it. Guess what the date was? The twenty-first of the month. Pavlov was right—it does take 21 days to start a new habit.

So if you get into the habit of looking at your objectives every day for the next twenty-one days, you will have created a new habit, and what a difference it will make in your life!

HOW TO COMPLETE THE OBJECTIVE PLANNER

So on the first of the 21 days, use one of the sheets to write out your objectives. Here are some things to consider as you fill it in.

Your one year objective. It may be that your objective will take five years for you to accomplish; however, you need guideposts along the way. You need some intermediate stops on which you can set your sights and pause to revel in your accomplishment. Be sure that your one year objective is consistent with your five-year objective. Don't give yourself an objective to own that Cadillac Seville in one year and an objective of having $100,000 cash in the bank in five years. Unless in some way you must have the Cadillac to earn the $100,000, the two objectives are conflicting. Better to set an objective of having $10,000, $15,000, or $20,000 in the bank within the year.

Your five-year objective. Of course this would be an extension of your one-year objective. Be sure that you've read this entire chapter, including the reasons why we don't make our objectives, before you firm it up. Stretch yourself, but make the objective believable. If you don't believe that you can achieve it now, while it excites you and while your right-brain creative mind is in control, you'll never be able to maintain a positive attitude when your left brain starts to present all the obstacles to you.

Skills and qualifications I'll need. Skills you'll need may include:

◆ Public speaking skills
◆ Writing skills
◆ Persuasion skills
◆ Selling skills
◆ Computer skills

Qualifications you'll need may include:

◆ College courses
◆ Professional designations
◆ State licenses
◆ Published articles or books
◆ Citizenship
◆ Residency in a city or state

What I'm willing to give up. The measure of your desire is what you're willing to give up to accomplish your objective. (As a metaphysician, I don't really believe in this. I believe in the law of unlimited abundance—that you can have anything without having to give anything up. However, I don't want to complicate this too much, so let's just go with the generally accepted view that to get something, you have to give something up.) This section may include:

- ◆ Expensive vacations
- ◆ My bowling league so that I can attend class
- ◆ Buying a new car this year
- ◆ Buying lunch instead of packing a lunch
- ◆ The trip to visit friends that we'd planned

What I'll do this month. Getting started is half the battle. Haven't you found that to be true? Perhaps you've dreaded the thought of doing your income tax return and have been putting it off for weeks. However, once you start, you realize that it's not half as much work as you expected.

Writing a book like this takes a tremendous amount of time. Writing on a computer, rather than on a typewriter or in longhand, saves a tremendous amount of time, but even so there may be 600,000 keystrokes in this book before I get it finished. It will take me at least nine months of constant effort to get it done (I don't call it work, remember, because it's so aligned with my natural talents that I find it fun to do). It's a daunting challenge. How do I do it? I get started. I promise myself that at 7:00 A.M. the next day I will be sitting in front of my computer with a hot cup of coffee. I will call up a new page on my word-processing program and set the margins and the type style. Then I will do a title page, "The 13 Secrets of Power Performers by Roger Dawson." Then I'll set a page break and list "Other books by Roger Dawson." Then I'll switch to an outlining program and start dropping in all my thoughts on the topic, and then I'll start to rearrange them into a coherent outline. Soon it will be evening and I'll have a fairly good idea of the direction in which I want to go and a bare bones outline of what I'll cover. That first day is so valuable. It may produce the equivalent of a month's work later on, as I pore over the rewrites. Once you commit to getting started, you're halfway there.

So this section on your objective pad may include:

◆ Sign up for a college course.
◆ Get a part-time job to gain experience.
◆ Buy and read three books on the topic.
◆ Make contact with three people who could give me guidance.

On the second day take out a new piece of paper—throw away the old piece of paper—and rewrite your objectives. It will take you only a few seconds, and the results are amazing.

You'll find that during the first week you will reformulate your objectives. Things that may have seemed important to you on the first day may not seem important any more, because your subconscious mind has been playing with these ideas. Now you're beginning to formulate a plan that you're really enthusiastic about, and you're getting excited. By the middle of the second week you'll probably find yourself doing something unconsciously that's a step toward your objective. You may find yourself reading a college catalog, for instance, and as you glance at the courses you realize these are some of the skills you'll need to be successful in your new venture. You didn't consciously pick it up for that reason, but your subconscious mind is pushing you in the right direction. As you near the end of the three-week period, you'll find you've made substantial progress toward making your objectives happen.

DON'T SET OBJECTIVES FOR MORE THAN FIVE YEARS

Notice I didn't give you a place to write anything longer than a five-year objective. There's no space for lifetime objectives, and with good reason. Power Performers know that you can accomplish anything you want in five years. If you make longer-term objectives, you may limit yourself instead of enhancing your progress. For example, you take a new position with a company and after studying the way things work there, you decide that your objective will be to become vice-president in charge of operations for the corporation. After asking some more questions, you learn it generally takes about 15 years for someone to become a vice-president, so you set yourself a 15-year objective. You'll probably accomplish your objective within that time, but the question is: If you'd made it a five-year objective—could you have made it much sooner? Sure you could. If you set an objective for longer than five years, you'll limit your accomplishment to a slower time schedule than you need. Give yourself the credit you deserve, and set your objectives for a shorter time—no more than five years.

> *You can change the world in 15 years.*
>
> *You can certainly change your life in 5 years.*
>
> *Don't set objectives for longer than that.*

It's sad to meet people whose main objective in life is to prepare themselves for retirement. Harry might work for the county, and in 15 years he'll retire. By retirement, his objective is to have a little cabin up in the mountains with a boat and a recreational vehicle. That's Harry's objective for the next 15 years. Fifteen years! A person could change the whole world in 15 years! Don't set objectives for more than five years.

What if you decided that, rather than lose tenure as a teacher in San Diego, you would set your dream of moving to Wyoming back to your retirement years. You rationalize you can take and sell pictures just as well at 65 as you can at 55. Then you finally make the move, and you don't like it! You move up there at the end of the school year, and the place is swarming with tourists. It's not the peaceful rustic experience you expected. A bad winter starts right after the tourists leave. It's fun at first, with snow on the ground and everything looking so beautiful. You never saw snow in San Diego. However, when the snow is still on the ground in May, you're longing for the other kind of flakes, the ones in California. You've had an acute case of cabin fever most of the winter and get the distinct impression the locals are laughing at you behind your back. Now what are you going to do? My advice is to throw out those lifetime objectives and go ahead and get it done in no more than five years.

Richard Bach, who wrote *Jonathan Livingston Seagull,* had a romantic notion that an author couldn't be successful in the first ten years of writing. He felt he'd have to pay his dues to the industry for ten years before he could be successful. Before Bach was finally able to find a publisher for Jonathan Livingston Seagull, he had to take the manuscript to 27 publishing houses—the first 26 of which turned him down. The book became an overwhelming best seller, and Bach found himself reexamining his career. He realized his success had taken him ten years and one month. He announced publicly, "If there is a next life, when I come back I'll never do that again. I'll never limit myself so much that I say, 'It's going to take ten years,' when I could have done it much quicker."

Incidentally Richard Bach tells one of the greatest stories in the annals of publishing. He finally succeeded in getting *Jonathan Livingston Seagull* published, but it wasn't a good seller, because the publisher was trying to promote it as a children's book. Connie Clausen, a friend of mine who is one of the best book agents in the industry, saw its potential as an adult fable and started to talk it up in the industry. "Kahlil Gabran with feathers," she called it. It started to sell, unknown to Bach, who was barnstorming old airplanes in Iowa. Almost by chance he called into his publisher. They yelled at him, "Where have you been! Your book is selling like crazy. We've been depositing royalty checks to your account, but we haven't been able to find you. We need you for television talk shows."

As he hung up, he started to fantasize about the amount of money in his account. Ten thousand, twenty, maybe even fifty thousand? He called the bank in New York to find out. When they told him he couldn't believe it. His publisher has deposited almost $1.4 million into his account! Now do you still want to put off the book you've been meaning to write all these years?

WHY WE DON'T ACCOMPLISH OUR OBJECTIVES

Now let's come back down to earth and examine the four reasons we don't accomplish our objectives. They are:

1. They're unrealistic.
2. They're false objectives.
3. They're too vague.
4. We lack the motivation.

Let's take a close look at each one of these:

1. *They're unrealistic.* The first reason is: they're unrealistic. Many people go through life setting unrealistic objectives and never accomplishing any of them. It's an interesting phenomenon: People who set unrealistic objectives often have negative self-images. Their subconscious minds think of themselves as losers. However, they like to go through the motions of setting objectives, so when they fail they can say to themselves, "Poor me, I'm such a failure, I keep trying but I never seem to make it." In this way, they feed their self-image as a loser. When someone visits a weight-loss doctor and says, "I want to lose fifty pounds," the doctor usually tells him or her: "Let's set an objective of ten pounds first and see how it goes." A good doctor pushes the patient back to reality because he or she realizes it's essential that objectives are realistic.

2. *Our objectives are false.* Be sure that you set objectives only for those things you really want. Power Performers set objectives that are important to them and don't care what the rest of the world thinks. My son would give his right arm for a Porsche, and yet, having been through the foreign sports car phase myself, I have no interest in impressing others in that way anymore. My daughter once let the engine overheat on my 12-cylinder Jaguar XJS and had it towed to a repair shop. They called me to let me know they had it and what it would cost to fix it—$11,000.

I must have given it the longest pause before I finally said, "Did you realize you just said $11,000, when you must have meant $1,100?"

"No," they said. "You heard right. $11,000. These aluminum engines freeze up real easy." Maybe that's when I decided I didn't need any more fancy imported sports cars.

Unfortunately we live in a world where advertising messages constantly bombard us telling us what we should want out of life. Too often they overwhelm us and we never stop to determine what it is we really want. You wouldn't let someone else sit down and write out your objectives for you, would you? Then why should you let yourself be controlled by subliminal advertising messages?

3. *They're too vague.* The third reason we fail to accomplish our objectives is that they're too vague. Be specific. For example, if one

of your objectives is to acquire a luxury car, don't word it vaguely. Even to say you want a Cadillac Seville is too vague. Feed your sub-conscious all the details; you should be able to feel the objective in all its reality: "I want a navy-blue Cadillac Seville with a white stripe and tan leather interior, white lambswool carpeting, and a wormwood dashboard and a compact disc player." See the objective clearly and you'll be that much closer to accomplishing it.

For example, don't set an objective just to "open a dress store." State specifically: "I'll start a chain of clothing stores within the next two years, with capitalization of $500,000. The first branch will be in the Century City Plaza. We will appeal directly to the upscale woman executive with lines suitable for business wear, with separate boutiques for business cocktail dresses and convention sportswear." Start now to think of a name and to design your logo and business stationery. Put together some sample ads. None of these will be good enough to use, but you're beginning to build a visual image in your mind. Start finding out about the manufacturers who might have the appropriate lines. Start talking to them and to the shopping-center management. Don't worry about people stealing your ideas, because people who have the courage, drive, and initiative to steal your idea and make it work are already too busy implementing the ideas with which they're in love. Don't let worries about financing stop you. When you have a powerful idea, offers of capital venture money will find you. Perhaps one of the manufacturers will finance you, or the shopping mall will know someone who has capital available. When you can really feel and see the store and the clothes in your mind it will be that much easier to reach.

> *Don't worry about people stealing your ideas. If they're capable of making it work they're already in love with what they're doing.*

4. *We lack the motivation.* Lack of motivation is the fourth reason so many objectives fall by the wayside. Motivation always follows desire, doesn't it? Do you have enough desire? Do you have enough reasons to pursue your objective? There's a story about Socrates that tells of a young man who approached him and asked, "How do I become as wise as you? How can I get the knowledge?"

Socrates walked with the young man to the beach, and when they reached the ocean Socrates pushed him under the water and held him there with his hand. The young man pulled himself out of the water, gurgling for breath, and Socrates pushed him under again. Again the young man surfaced, and Socrates pushed him under a third time. Finally, when the young man's lungs were nearly bursting and he was on the verge of passing out, Socrates freed him and the man lay there, gulping for air. Socrates stood over him and said, "Young man, when you want knowledge as much as you just wanted air, you'll get it."

There's an old proverb that says when a student is ready, a teacher will appear. Power Performers understand that when the desire to fulfill a mental picture is strong enough, the opportunity will appear. Be sure your objectives excite you so much that they give you a driving desire to accomplish. When you've trained yourself to review your objectives daily and you've started to build a mental picture in such detail and with such clarity that it demands to become real, you'll be already on the road to Power Performance.

Setting realistic, specific, and motivating objectives is the only way any of us can begin to define the direction of our lives. Power Performers believe this with every fiber of their being, and they apply it on a daily basis throughout their lives. They know that only with sharply defined, imaginative, and stimulating objectives will they be able to achieve their dreams.

Before you go on to the next chapter, define and write down your five-year and one-year objectives. Commit to thinking about them for a few minutes every day for the next 21 days. Then start to act as though it's impossible to fail.

◆◆◆

The Tenth Secret of Power Performers is:
They have learned how to define their future.

◆◆◆

Next I'll teach you how to take control of your life by taking control of your time.

11

POWER PERFORMERS KNOW HOW TO ENHANCE THEIR TIME

Dost thou love life? Then do not squander time, for that is the stuff life is made of.

— *Benjamin Franklin*

Time is at once the most valuable and the most perishable of all our possessions.

— *John Randolph*

I'll give everything I own for one more moment of time!

— *Queen Elizabeth I*
(on her deathbed)

Time is the one and only nonnegotiable thing in our lives! You can never buy it or sell it, and other people can't give it to you! You can only organize time better!

— *Roger Dawson*

To Power Performers, nothing is more valuable than time. Their high energy level gives them a strong desire to see everything, to do everything. Financial success gives them all the material things they need, but there's always a burning desire to have more time to enjoy the good things of life. John Denver had to post a sign outside his Starwood in Aspen home that said bluntly, "You're not welcome here." He didn't like to do it, but he had so many people who felt they had the right to take up his time. "Even very successful people, who ought to know how valuable time is," he'd say. So let's not talk about managing time—I'm always uncomfortable with the term *time management* because it sounds like people frantically trying to cram in as much as they can. All successful people know how to manage time. Power Performers need to learn how to enhance time, to smoothly concentrate their actions on what's most important to them, so that they never feel pressured from having too much to do. Getting out from under the pressure of a rigid time-management system releases the internal energy needed for Power Performance.

Power Performers believe time enhancement is one thing that's essential to their ability to enjoy life. It's critical for five important reasons:

1. Time enhancement enables you to get more done in less time, which frees up your time for creative thinking and strategic planning. People who don't understand how to enhance their time will approach a loaded desk first thing in the morning with a sense of dread. They finally plow into the mess and may well spend the entire day thinking they have been busy, when in truth they haven't done anything of importance. Power Performers can take no more than an hour and swiftly get everything of importance handled.

The willingness to work long hours may be noble, but it is foolish. Your ability to do good work goes down dramatically after eight hours on the job. Also when you know you'll be working late that night you tend to be less efficient during the day because you know you'll be able to get the work done after hours.

2. Time enhancement takes the pressure and stress out of working, making it more fun. Whenever I have met people in a work environment who seems tense and frustrated, it soon becomes apparent that they are lousy time managers. They feel a constant pressure from the fear of not getting to something they

need to get done. Since they spend their day handling emergency situations that arose because they didn't take care of the situation when they should have, they are constantly moving from one crisis to another, never feeling that they are making any real progress.

3. Time enhancement enables you to plan time for recreation and family life, to enrich your experience of life.

Dietrich Bonhoeffer was a Protestant minister in Germany who led the opposition to the Nazi movement. In 1939 he took refuge in New York City but after only two weeks chose to return to Germany to continue the fight. He was the leader in the plot to assassinate Hitler, for which the Nazis imprisoned and subsequently executed him (I assume from this that Hitler took the assassination plot personally). While he was in prison Bonhoeffer wrote many letters and papers that were published posthumously in 1951. In one he gave an interested perspective on time, from the point of view of a prisoner forced to waste it. He said, "Time lost is time when we have not lived a full human life, time unenriched by experience, creative endeavor, enjoyment and suffering."

Your perspective of people who manage time well may be that they are capable of taking on monumental amounts of work but can still get everything done. However, my perspective of someone who manages time well conjures up a vision of a father whitewater rafting with his children on a Saturday morning. It also conjures up a picture of a mother who has all the time in the world to spend with her young children despite being a successful business person and a great housekeeper.

4. In your business life a good program of time enhancement makes you more promotable. There's an old myth that employers promote the person who works long and hard hours. The truth is that people who work 12-hour days are subliminally communicating that they're having a tough time handling the work load they already have. Why should their boss entrust them with even more responsibility?

5. Good time enhancement gives you an incredible reputation for reliability. If you say you'll call someone on Thursday afternoon, then the person can count on it. If you say you'll mail someone information, then the person can expect it. If you tell someone you'll take care of it, then the person doesn't have to

waste time following up on you to see if you remembered to do it. People with whom you do business will admire you so much for this that you will draw them to you. Employees will soon learn that if they committed to complete a project for you they should do it on time or you will be right behind them, following up.

Ten Rules for Good Time Enhancement

Rule One:
Concentrate on One Thing at a Time

First, Power Performers know the key element of getting control of their life is to constantly be breaking projects down into pieces small enough so that they can concentrate on "one thing at a time."

Once I went on a ten-day speaking tour that would take me from my home in La Habra Heights, California, to speaking engagements in Orlando, San Antonio, back to Orlando, on to Huntsville and New York, and then finally to Atlanta, before returning to California.

On that trip I gave six talks to five different industries, all of which I had to learn about, so that I could customize the talk to their particular needs. The talks ranged in length from a 30-minute keynote to an all-day seminar. My office had shipped home-study courses to each location to sell at the event, and I had to coordinate handouts and workbooks. Here's the point: If I had left on this trip and worried about all the things that had to fall into place for the trip to go well, it would have blown my mind. Instead of being the adventure it was, it would have been one big frustrating hassle.

> *I have a new philosophy. I'm only going to dread one day at a time.*
>
> Charlie Brown in *Peanuts*

I've learned to handle schedules such as this by concentrating on one day at a time. I make a plan for the entire trip and double-check it before I leave. Once I leave, however, I worry about only one day at a time. Today I worry only about getting from San Antonio to Orlando, and giving the best talk I've ever given. Tomorrow I'll worry about getting from Orlando to Huntsville, and doing the best job there. By taking each day as a separate unit, you can handle the most incredibly complicated schedules.

Let me pose this question to you: If, when you were born, someone had magically appeared in front of you and told you all the things you'd have to face throughout life—all the problems, the trials, the tribulations that a lifetime would bring you, you'd prob-ably have crawled back into the womb, wouldn't you? You would have looked up at the doctor that was hanging you by your ankles, and said, "Get me out of here!" However, taking one day at a time you can handle just about anything.

Learning how to concentrate on one thing at a time may take a great deal of personal discipline. So try to objectively observe how you do things in your personal life. Do you get easily side-tracked? Perhaps you go outside to get the morning newspaper from the driveway and see some trash that needs picking up so you end up doing that "as long as you're there." You take the trash into the garage and notice some tools that you didn't put back in their place, so you take a few minutes to do that. You notice that the windshield on your car is dirty so you go into the house to get some glass cleaner from the laundry room. There you notice that clothes are still in the dryer so you get them out before they wrin-kle. All this may well use up half an hour and you still don't have the newspaper. If you have gotten into bad habits like this, you need to force yourself to do one thing at a time. Notice the trash in the driveway but force yourself to say, "I'm here to pick up the newspaper, and I'm going to finish this task. I'll make a mental note to come back out later and pick up the trash." Obviously this is going to have the short term disadvantage of taking longer, but you'll be building the ability to concentrate on one thing at a time, and that will pay off for you in the future.

You may even be a person who has a hard time doing only one thing at a time. Perhaps you feel that you're productive only if you're attempting to do two or more things at once. How many of the following habits apply to you?

- ◆ I don't like to eat alone unless I'm reading too.
- ◆ If I'm watching television I like to being doing something else too.
- ◆ As I'm putting on my shoes, I reach for my belt and put it on at the same time.
- ◆ I have a television in my bathroom or a magazine rack next to the toilet.
- ◆ I can shave (or put on makeup) while I'm driving to work if I'm running late.
- ◆ When I'm cleaning house I have the television on or play motivational tapes.
- ◆ I can squeeze in a telephone call while I'm fixing breakfast.
- ◆ I listen to the radio or tapes while I'm exercising. (Okay, so maybe that's smart, but once in a park in Hawaii I saw a couple jogging who were both wearing Walkmans®. That's obsessive!)

If many of these habits apply to you, you may have a hardcore problem. Practice doing only one thing at a time for a while. It'll pay off for you because you'll be increasing your power of concentration.

A good time-enhancement system encourages you to concentrate on each task separately. It breaks down all of your responsibilities into pint-size pieces, so you can concentrate on "one thing at a time." You trust your system to bring the right thing to your attention at the right time.

If it weren't for the last minute, nothing would get done.

RULE NUMBER TWO: USE A DAILY PLANNING SYSTEM THAT YOU CUSTOMIZE TO COMPLEMENT THE WAY YOU WORK

Don't attempt to change the way you work to fit a prepackaged time-management system. I'm quite sure that you've had the experience of getting so frustrated by being disorganized that you went out and bought an expensive time management system. You probably spent hours learning how to use it and days setting it up. Then you found that it was more trouble than it was worth. It simply didn't complement the way you work or the type of work you do. The time-enhancement system that I'm going to teach you is very flexible. Start by using the forms that are in this book, but after you have used them for a month or so, I encourage you to go to your computer and adapt these forms to your own needs.

RULE NUMBER THREE: PRIORITIZE YOUR WORK

Before you do anything it is essential that you prioritize your tasks. It's the only way that you'll force yourself to do the most important things first. If you don't prioritize your duties, you'll find yourself looking down your list and gravitating to one of two categories:

1. The most enjoyable things. "I have to call Mike and set a golf date. That sounds best to start with," you might think, because you enjoy talking to Mike. It's not a threatening situation to you. So you follow that phone call up with another call to a friend, and after that you might write some letters. Probably you'll never get to the more important things.

2. Those things that take the least time. You say, "It'll only take me a minute to open these letters, so I'll do that first." Then you'll spend the first hour of your day opening mail addressed to occupant, which is probably the least important thing you need to do—with the possible exception of your sitting there

not being able to decide whether to open occupant mail or not.

You've probably heard the story of Ivy Lee and Bethlehem Steel, but it bears repeating. Charles Schwab was the president of the company and a real Power Performer—he was the first man ever to earn a salary of more than $1 million a year, and that was back in the 1930s when a million dollars was a great deal of money (Incidentally he died penniless, after spending the last few years of his life on borrowed money. He never learned the lessons we talked about in Chapter 9.) Ivy Lee was a management consultant who wanted a contract with the company. Schwab rebuffed him, saying that they already knew more about producing and selling steel than Lee would ever know. Then he gave Lee a challenge that would go down in business folklore. Schwab told Lee that the only thing he himself lacked was the time to implement all the ideas he had and that if Lee would show him a way to get more things done with his time, he would pay him any fee within reason. According to management expert Donald Schoeller, Lee replied, "Write down the most important tasks you have to do tomorrow and number them in order of importance. When you arrive in the morning, begin at once on Number 1 and stay on it till it's completed. Recheck your priorities; then begin with Number 2. If any task takes all day, never mind. Stick with it as long as it's the most important one. If you don't finish them all, you probably couldn't do so with any other method, and without some system you'd probably not even decide which one was most important. Make this a habit every working day. When it works for you, give it to your men. Try it as long as you like. Then send me your check for what you think it's worth."

What he was saying is so unbelievably simple that you may find it hard to grasp its importance. Charles Schwab loved it. He sent Ivy Lee a check for $25,000, calling the advice the most profitable lesson he'd every learned. He credited this system with turning Bethlehem Steel around and making it, in its day, the biggest independent steel producer in the world. Business experts later chided Schwab for his extravagance in sending Lee so much more than he expected, but Schwab insisted that it was the best investment he'd made all year, saying that it was only once he'd adopted this system that he found all of his people doing the most important things first.

RULE NUMBER FOUR: GIVE YOURSELF DEADLINES BY SCHEDULING BLOCKS OF TIME

If you're up against a deadline, you can get an incredible amount of work done. Haven't you noticed that? If you have to leave for the airport in an hour and won't be back for a week, you can skim through a large pile of work that might take you all day if *you had all day.* C. Northcote Parkinson's Law says, "Work expands so as to fill the amount of time available for its completion." So a key to getting more done is to force yourself to work against a deadline. If you have a stack of mail to answer, allocate an hour to it and when the hour is over set it aside for another day. Don't let meetings be open-ended. Tell everyone when you start that the meeting will last until a set hour and that they'll have to work hard and stay on track to get everything done in that time.

I disagree with Ivy Lee that you should stick with one task all day if you have to. If you take that approach you find other issues piling up so much that it may take you several days to climb out of the hole you've dug for yourself. Better to say, "I'm going to take the hour after lunch to get caught up on my other work, but at exactly 2:00 P.M. I'm going to return to this task."

Forcing yourself to work against deadlines like this dramatically increases your effectiveness.

If once a man indulges himself in murder, very soon he comes to think of robbing; and from robbing he next comes to drinking, and from that . . . to procrastination.

THOMAS DE QUINCY

RULE NUMBER FIVE:
CONTROL INTERRUPTIONS

Without doubt this is the number-one frustration of people trying to get organized. Everybody who has been to one of my time-enhancement seminars has said to me in one way or another, "If I could control the interruptions, I wouldn't have a problem managing my time." Managers have the biggest problem with this because they naturally want to be accessible to their people. They secretly want their people to bring their problems to them rather than solving them on their own because this elevates their feeling of self-worth. Let's take a look at some common interruptions and see what we can do about them.

◆ *Stop people from dropping into your office.* Try to position your office so that fellow workers can't see you from the hallway. An open door policy is fine, but permit people to get carried away with it and it will destroy your efficiency. In a couple of offices I've had the door to the hallway taken out and the wall sealed up and have then routed the traffic to my office through anterooms. If you can't do that, have a screen built or put in a wall of plants. If you don't do these things anybody who wanders by with time on his or her hands will be able to see that you don't have anybody with you and will feel free to drop by for a visit. At the very least turn your desk so that your back is to the hallway.

◆ *Permit yourself an occasional closed-door policy.* See if there's a block of time in your organization that seems to be a "let's wander around and see what's going on" hour. Very often it's first thing in the morning when people are getting coffee and haven't really gotten into their work yet, or it might be the last hour of the day when people have tidied up their desks but it's not time to leave. If you find that there's one hour of the day when people are more likely to drop in, make it your closed door hour. Certainly if you've come in early to get caught up, you're not obliged to let anybody know you're there. Hole up, hide out, and don't feel guilty about it.

◆ *Signal your secretary when you don't want any interruptions.* I don't have these problems now that I'm a writer, but when I ran the real estate corporation my secretary knew that if I closed my door, she was to hold all calls and visitors. Other than that she could put calls through. I realize that this is controversial, but I would take calls even if someone were in my office because I found that I could dispense with most calls in 30 seconds or less. An office manager or department head would call me and I would say, "Joe, I have someone with me right now. Is it a quickie or should I call you back?" Nine times out of ten Joe would say, "I just need an okay to . . . ," and I could take care of the call with a quick response. Joe appreciates my accessibility and doesn't feel that I don't have the time for him. You have to point out that you have someone with you and offer to call them back if they'd prefer. If you don't tell them they think you have all the time in the world and that 30-second phone call could turn into a 5-minute rambling conversation. Consider the alternative. If I had a policy of holding my calls any time I was with someone, I would finish a half-hour meeting with the person only to have my secretary hand me three or four telephone slips where I'd have to return their calls. This can be very time consuming, as you know, because when you return the call the other person may not be there and the whole cycle starts again.

I know what you're thinking. You're thinking: Isn't it rude to take calls when you have someone in your office to see you? Certainly if it's a sensitive conversation, or an important caller, I would close my door—the signal to hold my calls. After the third brief interruption, or if I saw that my taking calls was irritating my visitor, I would get up and close my door. However, I seldom had a problem with handling calls like that, and it made me accessible without tying up a great deal of my time.

♦ *Discourage people from responding to your queries by coming to see you.* Why have someone come to your office with a reply when a short note from them would give you the information you need. Here's the system that Bruce Mulhearn, the owner of the real estate company I ran, taught me, and it worked beautifully. Every executive at the company (we had 28 offices, 540 sales associates, 50 support people, and 5 subsidiary companies) had a different-colored note pad with his or her name on it. If I had a question for a vice-president or a department head I would scribble a quick note on buff-colored paper and put it in my out basket. If I expected a reply I would write ANS. (for answer) and circle it under my name. Because of the color paper others would immediately spot a note from the president. They would scribble a reply on their colored note pad, staple it to the front, and return it to me. I would quickly spot the reply coming back because of the color of the paper. Sometimes I had a further question, and I would scribble another note, staple it on top of the other two, and send it back. If any of these notes were confidential, we would simply fold up the bottom of the note to obscure everything except the name of the person to whom it was going and staple it shut. Note that there are no copies for follow-up and everything stays together until it gets resolved so that each side can review everything that's gone on before. If it concerned me that others might not respond to my note, I would make a brief notation in my daily planner to remind me that I was expecting a response (more about that later).

Naturally there would be times when the matter was important or complicated and I wanted the other person to come and see me. Then instead of ANS. under my name, I would put SEE ME (or CALL ME) and circle it.

I found that I could resolve 95 percent of everyday issues in this very time-efficient way. Looking back, we had created a type of electronic-mail system, long before the first personal computer. If you have an electronic-mail system, you're comfortable passing messages back and forth like that. You're using the same system without the paper.

• *Get comfortable with voice mail.* Remember when answering machines first became popular in the early 1980s? We would curse the machines that caused us to pay for the call even though we couldn't reach the person we wanted. Now we have become so comfortable with them that we curse if they don't have a machine on which we can leave a message.

We need to make the same transformation with voice mail. Instead of cursing that you can't reach the person, start valuing a system that allows you to make a detailed presentation to almost any executive in the country. That's the biggest complaint I get from salespeople these days. They tell me that it's almost impossible to make contact with a prospect these days because they're hiding behind their voice mail. I say that's great! Learn to take advantage of this incredible system that enables you to make a sales presentation to almost all the buyers in the country. In the old days you couldn't get past their secretaries. This is much better. True, they could fast forward through your call or erase your message with a punch of a button, but that's your challenge—to make your presentation so intriguing that they'll want to listen to it all.

I have half a dozen people with whom I deal that I know I'll never be able to reach in person, but I can still get the information I need, or I can get my point across to them. The voice-mail neophyte calls and says, "Joe this is Harry Smith. Please call me at 555-1234" (often rattling off the number so fast that Joe has to back space a couple of times to get it)." The voice-mail pro calls and says, "Joe, this is Harry Smith. I'm the production coordinator at James Tools, and we buy moldings from you. I have three things I'd like an answer on. They are:" (Harry goes on to leave a detailed message and slowly spells out his telephone number and repeats it.)" In this way Joe can research the information that's needed and call Harry back with a concise message. If he gets Harry's voice mail it's not a problem because he can leave a brief message that gives Harry all he needs to know.

RULE NUMBER SIX: READ PAPER ONCE

Break the habit of reading a sheet of paper more than once. Here's what typically happens: Your secretary brings you a stack of the morning's mail. It includes a letter from a corporation with which you do business, and they're asking you for some action. You say, "Okay, I'll need to take care of that later on today," and you put it into your pending basket. Then later in the day, you'll go through your pending basket and see the letter again and say, "Oh, how urgent was that?" So you read the letter again, and then, maybe then, you'll schedule it for some positive action. However, very often you'll find yourself reading the same letter three or four times.

Here's a system to break that bad habit. Every time you read a piece of paper, tear off a corner. It will amaze you how often you'll tear off all four corners before you get around to taking action on that particular item.

Instead of wasting time by rereading letters like that, get into the habit of quickly reviewing what you need to do and making a decision about when and how you're going to do it. Then put it behind the appropriate 1–31 divider, and cross-reference it to your Daily Plan sheet; or put it into your "P" file. Then move on, so you don't read the paper a second time. You'll free up a tremendous amount of time

RULE NUMBER SEVEN:
GO TO LUNCH AT AN ODD HOUR

Get into the habit of going to lunch from 1:00 to 2:00, rather than from noon to 1:00, or go from 11:00 to 12:00. You'll not only get faster service, you'll find the hour when everyone else is out to lunch and you're at your desk working will become the most productive time of your day.

RULE NUMBER EIGHT:
CALL, DON'T GO

If you have a problem with which someone else in the building can help, use the telephone—don't go! Going is a waste of time. Chances are you'll find yourself standing at the person's desk when his or her phone rings. The phone call's going to get priority, isn't it? So you'll get caught spending your time waiting for the person to finish the phone call. Why don't you be the one on the telephone? Use the telephone to call the person. You get priority that way. Also you won't get stopped by people as you walk to their office. How many times have you left your desk for a five-minute errand that turns into an hour's detour? Furthermore you won't return to a stack of telephone calls that you must then return.

RULE NUMBER NINE:
DON'T ASK FOR TIME TO THINK THINGS OVER

You either have enough information to make a decision, or you don't. I cover this in much more detail in my book *The Confident Decision Maker* (William Morrow, 1992), but it's a fundamental of good decision making that you first determine if you have enough information to make a decision. If you don't have enough information, don't ask for more time—ask for more facts. If you do have enough information, go ahead and make the decision.

RULE NUMBER TEN: DEVELOP A DAILY PLANNING SYSTEM THAT WORKS FOR YOU

Then you should believe in the system, trust the system, and always use the system. Over the last 15 years, I've developed a system that's simple, yet incredibly effective. Looking back I don't know how I was able to survive before I had it, when I was still frantically scrambling to put out fires. We have reproduced all the forms that you'll need in this section of the book, and you're welcome to reproduce them for your own use (you'll want to use a photocopier that enlarges, so that your forms come out full size). After you have used them for a month I suggest that you use your computer to create forms that you have customized to the way you work. These are the forms you'll find:

- ◆ *Daily Plan.* This is the sheet on which you'll list the things you have to do, and the phone calls you have to make. At the bottom there's a special section for follow-up with people with whom you have frequent dealings.
- ◆ *Appointments.* This sheet will face your Daily Plan in your planner, and on it you will schedule your appointments and any other activity that you have committed to do at a particular time of day. This is also the sheet on which you'll block out periods of time for specific activities.
- ◆ *Follow-Up Sheet.* On this sheet you'll keep a capsule look at each of your ongoing activities and move it through your planner.

SETTING UP YOUR DAILY PLANNER

Now let's get to work and I'll show you how to set it up. You don't need much, only a three-ring binder. I use an expensive leather one that a friend gave me, but a basic binder costs only a few dollars at the stationery store. While you're there get a set of 1–31 dividers, the kind with tabs on the edges numbered for each day in the month.

Place the dividers into the binder, with a Daily Plan sheet on the right-hand side behind each of the dividers (so you should three-hole punch them on the left side of the sheet). You'll see a Daily Plan sheet illustrated on the following page.

Note that the page includes three sections:

1. A Things to Do section labeled "Project"
2. A Phone Calls to Make section labeled "Telephone Calls"
3. Reminder Columns at the bottom for follow-ups.

Note that I have divided the follow-up section at the bottom of the Daily Plan into vertical columns. I call these the Reminder Columns. There is one for each of the people with whom you frequently communicate and one that says, "Home." Personalize those columns by writing in the names of people with whom you frequently deal.

Facing the Daily Plan sheet, you insert an Appointments sheet. You'll find one on the following the Daily Plan sheet.

Remember that to have the Appointment sheet face the Daily Plan sheet, you will 3-hole punch it on the right-hand side of the page, not the left. On this sheet you'll list the appointments that you make and plan your day by blocking off periods of time for activities such as golfing or exercising at the gym or taking your son to his Little League game.

I based my system on the principle that the simpler it is, the more likely you are to use it. The more complicated it is, the less likely you are to use it. Unlike other more complicated systems, you don't need any special pages other than these two and the Follow-Up Record that I'll show you later.

The key to a good time enhancement system is that it's tailored to your individual needs. That's why you may have invested a great deal of money in an expensive time-management system in the past and then become frustrated trying to make it work for you. It's because it wasn't tailored to your needs.

Once you've set up the binder, you'll have a 1–31 divider and a Daily Plan sheet for each day of the coming month. Facing each

DAILY PLAN

A	B	C	DISP	PROJECT

_____	_____	_____	HOME	TELEPHONE CALLS

© Roger Dawson

APPOINTMENTS

7	00			2	00	
	15				15	
	30				30	
	45				45	
8	00			3	00	
	15				15	
	30				30	
	45				45	
9	00			4	00	
	15				15	
	30				30	
	45				45	
10	00			5	00	
	15				15	
	30				30	
	45				45	
11	00			6	00	
	15				15	
	30				30	
	45				45	
12	00			7	00	
	15				15	
	30				30	
	45				45	
1	00			8	00	
	15				15	
	30				30	
	45				45	

EXPENSE	AMOUNT	EXPENSE	AMOUNT

© Roger Dawson

Daily Plan will be an Appointments sheet. At the top of each sheet of paper, write the day of the week and the date, for example: Tuesday, August 12. These pages will correspond to the days of the coming month for the next 31 days, so if you start on August 12 you will set it up through September 11.

When you've done all this your planner is ready to go, so turn to the next day's Daily Plan and write down everything you'll need to do, in the Things To Do section.

Phone calls you need to make get listed at the bottom right. Try to empty your mind, your purse, your pockets, and your in-basket of all the things you need to do and write them all on this one Daily Plan Sheet.

From now on anything that you need to do you will list on your Daily Plan. No more little notes tucked away in pockets. No more writing down phone messages on odd scraps of paper. You must *believe in the system, trust the system, and always use the system.* We had a real estate agent in one of our offices who was so paranoid that she would overlook something that she would staple notes around the shoulder strap of her purse. We could tell how much pressure she was under as she came across the parking lot just by the number of notes stapled to her shoulder strap. Once I showed her how to set up a daily planner and use it exclusively, half of the stress went out of her life.

If you come into the office and your secretary hands you a dozen little telephone slips to tell you that people called and you have to return the calls, immediately transfer them to your Daily Plan. Usually you can transfer the name and number and throw the slip away, but if there is a detailed message that you don't want to transcribe, stapled it to a piece of paper that has been three-hole punched and file it behind your Daily Plan. Don't forget to cross reference it to your Daily Plan by writing down "Call Fred. AT." AT means that there's a page attached that gives you more information.

Don't list more than you think you can reasonably get done in one day. If you find yourself looking at the list and groaning at the thought of all the work you have to do, you're attempting too much for that day. So list some of the things on one of the future days' Daily Plan sheets. Don't overload yourself. It's essential that you feel comfortable that you can get everything done, because during the day other things will come up and you need to have enough cushion in your plan to be able to take care of them.

Never put off until tomorrow what you can do the day after tomorrow.

MARK TWAIN

Some of the things you've been planning may not be for tomorrow, even if you would have time to do them then. They are things that it's better for you to take care of at a future date, for example, a reminder to follow up on something on which you're working or to call someone when he or she returns from vacation. In that case, simply turn to the appropriate daily divider and list it on the Daily Plan sheet behind it, to be done on that particular day.

From now on take notes only on a full-sized pad of paper that has been three-hole punched. (You can buy them at the store that way.) When you answer the phone or make an outgoing phone call, have it handy. Make notes as you listen. Jot down the person's name, his or her number, and anything else the person might tell you. When you meet with someone have a pad with you and make notes from the first thing he or she tells you. If the telephone call or personal conversation turns into something that needs further action, you're ready to insert it into your daily planner and start moving it through the system. If it doesn't require further action throw the paper away. Yes, you'll be wasting some paper but you'll be making a lumberjack happy and you'll be saving time. I'll bet you that there have been hundreds of times when you have started a conversation with someone only to realize after a minute or two that this requires some action. Then you have to go back over the conversation, ask the person his or her name again, the name of his or her company, and all the other pertinent facts. Write it down first and throw it away if you don't need it. Paper is cheap compared to your time.

SETTING UP THE APPOINTMENTS PAGES

Now go through your annual calendar and write down on the Appointments sheet all your appointments for the next month, as well as any other promises you have made. Any time you make a commitment to do something at a particular hour, it's an appointment, not a Thing to Do. For example, if I tell you, "I'll call you on Thursday," I list it on Thursday's sheet as a Thing to Do. However, if I tell you, "I'll call you on Thursday at 3:00 P.M.," I treat it just as seriously as if I'd agreed to meet you then. I list it on the Appointment sheet at the appropriate time.

Soon you'll have all of your commitments in one place, organized by the day on which you should take care of them.

At the bottom of the Appointments page there is a place for you to write down your expenses for the day. Just using this will repay you for any expense that you incur in setting up your time-enhancement system. We all tend to overlook many little expenses and never get reimbursed by our company or submit it as a deduction to the IRS. The $2 you spend for coffee with a potential client, the 50-cent bridge toll on the way to an appointment, or the dollar you tipped the parking attendant, are all too easily overlooked. Since this section is next to the appointments that you'll be referring to throughout the day, you'll remember to jot them down. Recap them onto your expense statement at the end of the week.

Also on your Appointments sheet you will block out the periods of time that I talked about in rule number four. Set aside an hour to prepare for that big meeting, or 30 minutes to organize your desk. Set aside time for exercise and time to be with your family. I also suggest that you write in the television programs you want to watch. Highlight the guide to TV programs each week and put them onto your Appointments page. Nothing is a bigger time waster than aimlessly turning on the television to "see what's on." Better yet, program them into your VCR and watch them when you can fast-forward through the commercials. It will amaze you to find out how short your favorite program is without the commercial breaks.

PRIORITIZING YOUR COMMITMENTS

The next thing to do with your Daily Planner is to turn to tomorrow's page and begin prioritizing the commitments you have. Do this in the columns just to the left of your list. See the four vertical columns on the left-hand side? Leave the fourth column blank for now. First give the items an "A," "B," or "C," priority by writing one of those letters in the appropriate column.

- ◆ "A" projects are those that you must accomplish that day, although they may not all be the most important commitments. For example, making a deposit to your checking account may be an "A," while calling a real estate agent in Pittsburgh about the new location of your plant may be a "B," simply because you must make the deposit today. The call could wait until tomorrow.
- ◆ "B's" are those projects you'd like to get done that day.
- ◆ "C's" are those projects it would be good to get done, but they aren't essential.

Be sparing with your "A's." Fifteen "A" priorities is probably the maximum load you can carry, and I hope you'll have far fewer. Only the truly critical things get an "A." You must do them or else. These are the projects that if you don't have them done by 5 P.M., you'll have to call home and tell the family that you'll be working late to get them completed.

When you're prioritizing, don't give something a high priority just because it has been sitting on your desk for ages. Always prioritize with these two things in mind:

1. How much closer it will bring you to your long-term objectives.
2. What is the consequence of its not getting done today.

Having prioritized "A," "B," and "C," now go back and number them for importance. "A–1," for example, would be the most important thing to do that day. "A–2" is the second most important and so on. Again, think strictly about moving yourself closer to your objective, instead of how many people are bugging you to get it done.

- ◆ Prioritize the "B's" only when you've completed all the "A's."
- ◆ Prioritize the "C's" only when you've completed all the "A's" and the "B's."

At this point you may be thinking, "I'm much too busy to go through that prioritizing process. It would take me at least 15 minutes a day." Perhaps it will, but remember that if you work an eight-hour day, you have to become only 5 percent more effective in your use of time to make the 15 minutes you spend prioritizing a good investment.

Once you've prioritized your list, begin with "A-1." Don't begin your day by rereading the list. You've already done that. Just begin your day with the most important task and work on it until it's completed. When you've done that, automatically, without reading the list, move on to task "A-2." From there, move to "A-3" and so on. That's another point on which I disagree with management consultant Ivy Lee. Remember that he told Charles Schwab at Bethlehem Steel to: "Begin at once on No. 1 and stay on it till it's completed. Recheck your priorities; then begin with No. 2." I find that rechecking your priorities really slows you down because it distracts you. Certainly reorder your priorities if you need to, because your system must be flexible and you shouldn't become a slave to it. However, I think you'll get much more done if you move right on to the next task without rechecking your priorities.

There may be a project that you're not able to complete. Perhaps you have to set it aside for a while and get more information. In that case you should renumber it or reassign it to another day for completion. Don't jump around on your list. Consider and deal with each item in order. Don't worry if you have 15 "A's" on your list and you get only five of them accomplished that day. At least you'll have done the five most important things on your schedule.

Be careful, as you prioritize, that you don't assign tasks a low priority just because they're things you'd rather not do. If you have an unpleasant job to do, such as calling a client to tell him that his project fell through or that you've been unable to perform the way he wanted, then get that job off your desk the first thing in the morning.

This means giving the worst jobs the highest priority. This will release you from dreading them all day long. As my friend Danny Cox says, "If you have a lot of frogs to eat, you should start eating them first thing, and begin with the biggest frog!"

FILING ADDITIONAL INFORMATION BEHIND THE DAILY PLAN SHEETS

The beauty of the 1–31 system is you'll be able to file things behind your Daily Plan sheets. That's what's missing from most commercially prepared time-management programs. Here's why it's so valuable: Suppose an acquaintance has invited you to a meeting, a party, or a luncheon and has mailed you a flyer. You simply three-hole punch it and turn to the day of the event and file it there, making a notation on your Appointment sheet that it's attached. You do this by writing (AT) next to the notation of the appointment. So any time you file a separate piece of paper like this, indicate that there's some additional material by putting (AT) for "attached," after its corresponding entry on the daily list or if it's an appointment, on the Appointments sheet.

How many times have you walked out the door to some function, only to realize you can't remember where it's being held? So you hunt through your desk or briefcase but you can't find the invitation. Then you have to search through your address book and call the host and ask for directions. Or how many times have you been heading for the theater and can't find the tickets? You know you've put them somewhere, but where? With this system you file everything behind the appropriate day's page so that it's always with you and it's easy to find.

MOVING PROJECTS THROUGH YOUR DAILY PLANNER

Let's say you've received a letter from someone asking you to call on the fifteenth of the month when she gets back from a business trip. She wants to talk to you about the project on Main Street. You'd have listed that task on your Daily Plan sheet for the fifteenth and filed the letter behind it for reference. When you come down to the task on your list, which says, "Call Stacey Jones— Main Street project—AT," you find the telephone number on the attached letter and call her. However, her secretary tells you that Ms. Jones has extended her business trip and she won't be back until Monday. You simply remove the letter from its place in the file, move it to behind Monday's page, and write it down to do that day. Don't reprioritize it now. Remember it'll be reprioritized with your other commitments on Monday.

What happens if someone says, "Call me on the fifteenth of next month after our committee meeting"? You've set up for only 30 days ahead of time, so you won't have a page for that. What you need is a little holding area at the back of your three-ring binder where you hold things for the following month. Indicate at the top right hand of the page the days on which you must handle them, so that when you set up next month's binder, you won't have trouble putting them in order.

You might want to schedule the telephone call first for the thirteenth of the month, so that you call and remind the person that he should recommend the project in question to the committee when they meet. Then you move the reminder back to the fifteenth of the month, so that you call him after the meeting to hear their decision.

USING FLOW CHARTS WITH YOUR DAILY PLANNER

This system works beautifully with flow charts. If you have a background in engineering, you know all about flow charts. For example, at Boeing or McDonnell-Douglas Aircraft Company, they don't take the project to the workers; the workers go to the project.

When a worker starts work on a project, it's very important to know what other workers have already done to it so that, for example, the new worker doesn't install the electrical system or the instrumentation before other workers have completed the preliminary steps. So at each project there'll be a flow chart, and as each new specialist approaches, that person can see where the project stands on the flow chart and what other people have done so far. When the specialist has completed his or her work, he or she also marks down the work done, so that those who follow him or her are aware of what has been done.

This flow-chart system is wonderful for any ongoing project you may have. Take a look at the Follow-Up Record that I use—you'll find it on page 239.

Any time you start a contact, reach for one of these forms and start to fill it in as you talk. The first line, "Source," means how you made contact with this person, so you might indicate:

- ◆ Cold calling
- ◆ Incoming call
- ◆ Referral from John Doe
- ◆ Walk in
- ◆ Newspaper ad

If you mailed the person some information, show the date. The rest of the top section is self-explanatory.

Take a look at the bottom section, where there is a slim vertical column running down the left hand side. On the first line and in the left-hand column write the date of the first action. For example:

> 8/11. Called Mr. Smith. He told me to call him back on the 15th of the month. He was leaving to watch his son play Little League.

Then take the flow chart and file it behind the fifteenth of the month, ready to remind you to call Mr. Smith on that day. Then if you call him and he asks you to mail him a prospectus, you jot down on the flow chart:

> 8/15. Mailed prospectus. Follow up on the 25th.

Then you move it behind the twenty-fifth divider and list it for action on the sheet for that day.

This sheet will become an outline of your business dealings on this project. As you move it through your binder from day to day, you'll always have a complete and current record of the project. If you must reassign a project to another day, be sure to move any "attached" sheets as well.

On this one sheet you'll have all of your contacts with this person. Whenever you call the person you'll be able to quickly review the form and be able to make it sound as if that person is the most important person with whom you deal. You'll sound so efficient and professional when you call and say, "Bob, when we spoke on the tenth you asked me to call you back today. By the way, did your son win his Little League game?"

Eventually you may have several sheets attached to the Follow-up Form and it will be time to create a file on this person. When you do, staple or tape this Follow-up Form to the inside of the folder and create a second Follow-up Form to move through your Daily Planner.

FOLLOW UP RECORD

SOURCE:

DATE: / / .   COMPANY or ORGANIZATION:

CONTACT PERSON: PHONE (   )

ADDRESS:

CITY: STATE: ZIP: MAILED INFO:

TOPIC:

YOUR PROJECTS FILE

If you have some extra material that's too bulky to fit into this filing system, for example, a manila folder that can't be three-hole punched, write "P" by the task on your list. The abbreviation "P" stands for "Projects." Somewhere in your work area you should find a place to keep all of these "P's"—a file drawer or a specific basket, or anything handy. I use a Pendaflex hanging folder. When you work your way down to this project, you'll see the "P" and know exactly where to find the extra information. (Once a week go through your projects file to be sure that nothing is in there that isn't on your Daily Plan.)

INDICATING THE STATUS OF A TASK

Take a look at the Daily Plan form on page 229 and I'll teach you how to indicate the status of each task as your day progresses.

Completed tasks. Once you've completed each item on your day's list so that it no longer requires any kind of follow-up, draw a diagonal line through the priority letter and number (you'll find it in a column headed "A," "B," or "C"). This instantly signifies to you that you've completed the task.

Carrying forward tasks. If for some reason you need to continue a task to another day, say for follow-up or for confirmation, draw a horizontal line through the priority number and letter. As you review the sheet, you'll be able to see that you worked on that project but you needed to move it forward to another day.

With this system you can glance down the list to see which of the commitments you've dealt with and which still require some attention.

INDICATING THE STATUS OF TELEPHONE CALLS

There's a different code for indicating the status of telephone calls.

Left message. If one of your tasks is a phone call and you leave a message for someone to call you back, make a check mark (✓) by the priority. Do this in the other column, the one we haven't talked about yet, the fourth one on the left-hand side of the sheet that's headed up DISP for Disposition. There is also a narrow column for this purpose in the Telephone Calls section. Then when the phone rings and a voice says, "Hello, Roy Jones here, returning your call," you'll know immediately why he's calling, because you can glance at your list, looking for the check marks that tell you you've left a message for someone to call you back. Even on a busy day you won't have more than three or four of these check marks. So it doesn't take you very long to identify Roy Jones and figure out why you were calling him.

Otherwise you'll find yourself going through an embarrassing process of responding to his, "Hi, Roy Jones returning your call," with, "Ah, well, Mr. Jones, I'm not sure why I was calling you. Which company are you with? Why do you think I might have called you?" Now, doesn't that make you sound like an idiot? You wouldn't want to do business with someone who does that. However, the check mark on the side is an excellent way to identify anybody for whom you've left a message. When the person calls you back you'll immediately know why you called him or her.

If I have to leave a message on a machine or voice mail, asking for a return call, I put an "m" for machine by the check mark.

No answer. If you make a call and there's no answer, draw a circle meaning you'll have to try later.

USING THE REMINDER COLUMNS

Remember the vertical columns at the bottom of the page? There's one column for each of the people with whom you regularly deal, plus one column headed "Home."

Columns for people with whom you regularly deal. When you need to talk to one of these people about something, instead of immediately picking up the phone and calling him or her, just make a little notation in that vertical column. The column is narrow but it's still wide enough for you to make a notation that reminds you what you wanted to talk about. Then the next time the person calls you, you can say, "Oh, by the way, Joan, there are a couple of things I need to talk to you about," and you go through them.

It's great for follow-up too. If Joan says, "Okay I'll research that and get back to you on Monday," then you'd turn to Monday and make a notation to be sure Joan does get back to you. Once people realize that you have an efficient follow-up system, they learn quickly to keep their commitments to you. This simple system saves a great deal of time that you'd otherwise spend checking on them.

The home column. I have labeled the one of the columns at the bottom "Home." Sometimes, something will come up that you need to do at home—maybe to pull a book out of your personal library or to get something out of a file that may be at home. So in this column you list anything you may need to do there. Get in the habit of checking your "Home" file every morning before you leave for work and pulling the things out that need to be done there. That way, if somebody says to you, "Do you happen to have a copy of this week's *Time* magazine? Could I borrow it?" you know you'll be bringing it with you the next morning.

REVIEWING THE THINGS TO DO LIST AT THE END OF THE DAY

At the end of your work day, you should review the entire list of Things to Do and move ahead those tasks that you didn't complete during the day. You might want to move all of those tasks to the next day, or portion them out over the next week. The important thing is that once you've written each task onto its appropriate Daily Plan, you'll have a complete list of everything you need to do, all in one place.

If you have many things to carry forward it may tempt you to tear out today's Daily Plan sheet and attach it to the back of tomorrow's. There are two reasons why you should avoid that temptation:

1. Rewriting the item every day stops you from accumulating old items. Having to write it every day reminds you of it, and it eventually becomes a nuisance to the point where you'll either do it or decide that you don't need to do it. However,

there's almost no chance that it's going to get lost in the system.

2. You shouldn't throw away your Daily Plan sheets or move them out of sequence. Keep the last three months on file. Eventually you'll be frantically hunting for the name or telephone number of a person you need to contact and the only place it may be is on your completed Daily Plan sheets.

At first glance this system may seem complicated. However, making good time enhancement a habit is a real key to Power Performance. Nothing is more important than how you use your time, because however rich you become you'll never be able to buy any more of it. Queen Elizabeth I said on her deathbed, "I'll give everything I own for one more moment of time!" At some time or another, that thought will occur to each of us. Power Performer Vince Lombardi used to say he could win every game if only the clock never ran out. Power Performers know they could accomplish anything in life if they had an endless supply of time.

Time is the one and only nonnegotiable thing in our lives. You can never buy it or sell it, and other people can't give it to you. You can only organize time better.

Learn to organize your time better. Learn the art of getting the most out of every minute of every day. Remember, if you can take control of your time, you can take control of your life and channel your internal energy into Power Performance.

◆◆◆

The Eleventh Secret of Power Performers is:

They know how to enhance their time.

◆◆◆

Next we'll talk about a major problem every Power Performer needs to confront and overcome.

12

POWER PERFORMERS HAVE LEARNED TO TURN THEIR FEAR INTO FORTUNE

It is not death or pain that is to be dreaded, but the fear of pain or death.

— *Epictetus*

Talent is nothing. What really counts is courage. Do you have the courage to use the talent with which you were born?

— *Woody Allen*

God is good, there is no devil but fear.

— *Elbert Hubbard*

Fear has the largest eyes of all.

— *Boris Pasternak*

Neither a man nor a crowd nor a nation can be trusted to act humanely or to think sanely under the influence of a great fear.

— *Bertrand Russell*

Fear immobilizes and inaction compounds problems. It is action that solves problems.

— *Roger Dawson*

Let's talk about fear—the fear that stops you from acting when you should, the fear that paralyzes you, the fear that tears at your insides, the fear that keeps you from achieving your full potential as a Power Performer.

Fear immobilizes, and it's the greatest barrier you must face and overcome to release the energy that's within you and make your life a success.

Do this exercise with me. Imagine you're standing in the open doorway of a plane at about 4,000 feet. You're about to do your first ever parachute jump. You put your hands against the ice-cold steel of the doorway and look down. The wind is tearing at your head. The noise of the wind and the roar of the engines is deafening. Way below you, you can pick out buildings and roads. You spot the tiny circle that is your jump target. The jump master has his hand on your shoulder and is yelling, "Jump! Jump!" Feel the shakiness in your legs, the tightness in your stomach. Your mouth is dry and you're having trouble forcing air into your lungs. What you're feeling now is fear, fear telling you, "Don't jump!" More than that, fear is telling you, "Don't do anything! Freeze!"

Fear stands between us and all we could become.

In 1958 Woody Allen was a very successful comedy writer making $1,700 a week writing for television. The thing he feared most was appearing in front of an audience, but he pushed himself to do it, even though it meant working for only $75 a week. Before every performance he would be physically sick and often had to be pushed onto the stage by the stage manager. Although some of the audiences savaged him, everyone who knew comedy declared him to be the most talented comic of his time. "Talent is nothing," he would respond. "You're born with talent in the same way that basketball players are born tall. What really counts is courage. Do you have the courage to use the talent with which you were born?"

Of course, you don't have to stand in the open doorway of a plane at 4,000 feet or become a stand-up comedian to experience fear. Perhaps just thinking of giving a talk at your annual sales meeting will do it or making a tough sales call or quitting your job and starting the new business about which you've been dreaming.

Since fear stands between us and all we can become, let's examine fear. Let's take a look at what it is, and what it can do to us.

THE FIVE STAGES OF FEAR

Psychologists tell us that there are five stages of fear, and each one induces a different mental state.

Without fear:	Self-actualizing
Stage four fear:	Coping
Stage three fear:	Striving
Stage two fear:	Inertia
Stage one fear:	Panic

To be completely without fear is to self-actualize. To be totally controlled by fear is to panic. Let's take a look at those two and the three stages of fear that exist between them.

WITHOUT FEAR

Without fear we live in a state that Abraham Maslow called self-actualization. In this state we're happy, cheerful, confident, and feel that we're doing the things we want to with our lives. We can confidently move through life with the wonderful feeling that we are fulfilling ourselves, that we are being all that we can be.

STAGE-FOUR FEAR ALERTS

When trouble strikes, however, we move into a stage-four fear alert, which is coping, getting by. Here we know there are troubles, we know there are problems affecting our life. However, we feel that we can handle them, even though we're not as happy as when in the self-actualizing stage.

STAGE-THREE FEAR ALERTS

When we feel fear taking an even greater hold on us, then we're having a stage-three fear attack. This means striving. Here we must struggle to make an effort to cope, and often we're not very successful because we feel ourselves dragged down constantly by the fear and the stress of what's going on around us. Our bodies deplete their supply of vitamin B, we're a bundle of nerves, and our energy level drops way down. Everything is an effort for us.

STAGE-TWO FEAR ALERTS

The next level down, a stage-two fear alert, is inertia. We feel this on those mornings when we wake up and the pressure is so great that all we want to do is pull the sheet back over our heads, stay in bed for the rest of the day, and turn the world off. This is what we feel on those days at work when the problems begin to overwhelm us and we invent a sudden illness rather than stay to deal with the problems.

I'm not denying the existence of real disease and real viruses, but more and more researchers are finding that minor illness is really just a symptom of stage-two fear alerts.

I remember that when I had a "real job"—when I worked on salary—I was always getting sick. Three or four times a year I'd have to take a day off to recover from the sniffles or aches and pains. All of that ended when I became a professional speaker and I found out meeting planners don't pay you unless you actually give the talk. Can you believe people can be that heartless? They not only don't pay you, they expect you to refund the deposit they've given you. Furthermore, if you've already traveled to the meeting location, they don't even expect to reimburse you for your expenses. Can you believe that?

So when you wake up in a hotel on the other side of the country and you have a speech to give but feel awful, you lie there thinking to yourself, Do I want to stay in bed, in which case I'll lose the $5,000 speaking fee, and have to pay the $1,000 it took to fly here, or do I want to take some vitamins, pretend they're doing me some good, and go give the talk? Believe me, that kind of thinking snaps you right out of it. Suddenly, you feel great!

Inertia is the biggest problem that most of us face with fear—we have a tendency to do nothing when the pressure is high. It's a huge error in human thinking that when our problems desperately require action, when we need to be working hardest for a solution, we tend to do exactly the reverse and retreat from our problems instead. We tend to drop into inertia and do nothing.

If you've learned to snow ski, you know the feeling you get when you begin to lose your balance on a slope. You feel yourself start to fall, you feel catastrophe coming, and your immediate reaction is to try to stop yourself—to come to a standstill. Your ski instructor has to pound the opposite lesson into your head: "That's the worst thing you can do. That's when all the legs get broken. Safety lies down the hill, safety lies in speed and motion. You have to get yourself moving again, build up your momentum. That's what will save you." It's doing something that will be the answer to your problem.

If you've learned to fly a plane, you've learned about stalling. When my instructor told me we were going to practice stalls, I thought that he meant we were going to go up and switch the engine off. It's not that at all. A plane needs enough thrust or power to sustain its climbing angle. If it doesn't have enough thrust, it aerodynamically won't fly. It simply flutters and falls to the ground like a duck that has taken a full load of buckshot. That's what happened to a Galaxy airliner flying out of Reno a few years ago. One of the engines lost power, reducing the thrust during takeoff. By the time the pilot figured out what the problem was, it was too late to reduce the angle of climb to compensate for the lowered power and the plane went down.

Because you need maximum power for take off, there's a real danger a stall could happen at low altitude and be fatal. So your instructor must drill you on what to do should you experience a stall. He took me up and forced me to pull the nose sharply up and cut back the power. After a while, the stall alarm went off—a terrifying screech that warns you a stall is imminent. However, he made me keep the nose up until the plane simply couldn't fly anymore. It began to shake and flutter and then started to fall like a rock.

It was horrifying. I did what every person does in a panic situation, I fell into inertia as a response to fear: I froze up and did nothing. Soon we were falling in a terrifying spin. My instructor took over and got the plane back under control. However, he'd taught me a lesson I would never forget. When you're in difficulty, you must override your natural tendency to do nothing and force yourself into action. On every subsequent practice stall I didn't need any prompting to move quickly to get the nose down and the power up.

So a second-stage fear alert is inertia, the slide into inactivity that always compounds the problem.

STAGE-ONE FEAR ALERTS

A stage-one fear alert is panic. We reach this stage when something so frightening or so traumatic occurs that it causes us to lose control of our minds and body. Since fear is a very primitive emotion and panic is the worst form of fear, it gives us a good insight into the way we react to fear. Fear creates extensive bodily changes and causes us either to withdraw or to escape. We either take flight without any control of our actions or we withdraw and become frozen with panic. Most of us experience absolute terror only in our nightmares. What is interesting is that the same two responses are instinctive to a lesser degree with all the stages of fear: We either flee from the fear or it immobilizes us as we withdraw into inertia.

Power Performers know that fear is a problem because it immobilizes us. Even in small degrees, fear keeps us from doing the things we could be doing with our lives. Fear attacks stand between us and our being the Power Performers we're capable of becoming.

FEAR CAN BE USEFUL

Of course, fear can be useful. Fear is what tells us to leave a building that's on fire. Fear tells us to avoid dark alleys. Fear tells us not to make unfriendly gestures at a Hell's Angel. Fear becomes a problem, though, when it tells us not to do anything at all.

I learned about fear at a very early age. I was born in 1940 in a city ten miles to the south of London called Croydon. Apart from two evacuations, I spent the first years of my life enduring some of the worst bombing any city would undergo during World War II. They called it the Blitz, the Great Battle of Britain, the fight for survival. Every night hordes of Luftwaffe planes would fly over and drop their bombs on the city. The army put many of the perimeter antiaircraft guns in Croydon, and the German planes would frequently drop their bombs short of their main targets in London, turning around when they met the first heavy resistance. For this reason Croydon was the worst hit of all the cities surrounding the capital. When the raids started each night, my mother would scoop me out of my crib and hold me in her arms until it was over. I can still remember her shaking with fear.

> *Fear can be useful.*
>
> *Fear is what tells us to leave a building that's on fire.*
>
> *Fear becomes a problem when it tells us not to do anything at all.*

I can remember vividly walking through the city with my mother when I was about three years old and seeing a small German fighter plane came roaring down the street, only 50 or 60 feet above the ground, spraying machine-gun fire ahead of it. We raced for cover and dove under a bush. There was no military reason for strafing civilians in that way. It was simply a German fear tactic to "encourage" Britain to surrender.

> *The object of war is not to die for your country but to make the other bastard die for his.*
>
> GENERAL GEORGE PATTON

People who haven't personally experienced war tend to have a cavalier attitude about it. To them it's something that happens somewhere else, not here. Soldiers go away to fight the war, and the ones who come back are heroes. Let me tell you what war really is. Londoners lived through it for six years. War is husbands coming home from a day's work and wives coming home from the factory, knowing that they might turn the corner to find out that the bombing had killed their entire family. Sometimes it wasn't just a family, or their home, but an entire street that the bombing had demolished—it had transformed their neighborhood instantly into a pile of rubble. War is not knowing for a single night in six long years if you'd even wake up the next morning.

It's natural to fear when you're living through something like that. Fear that a bomb will hit your house, killing your entire family. Fear that your entire world will be turned upside down in a few seconds of unpredictable hell. Fear is when anxiety stretches your nerves to the breaking point. I'm not suggesting that you become so impervious to danger and anxiety that you no longer feel fear. You don't need to become fearless, but you must develop immunity to apprehension that immobilizes you.

DON'T LET APPREHENSION IMMOBILIZE YOU

Doesn't this happen frequently to you? Your boss calls you and says, "I want you in my office at one o'clock this afternoon!" Don't you usually worry that you're in some kind of trouble? It's quite natural to think you might get fired or that they might demote you, but the real loss is the morning that gets destroyed as you worry about all the possibilities.

It makes no sense to allow anxiety to overcome you to the point that "what-ifs," incapacitate you. What if your boss were leaving on a vacation and as she walked out the office door, she said to you, "When I get back in two weeks, I want to see you in my office at nine o'clock in the morning." Would you spend the next two weeks worrying? Would you let one statement destroy two weeks of your life? What if she said she was leaving for a year and wanted to see you when she returned? Would that ruin a whole year for you?

Don't let fear control your life.

IS YOUR FEAR BASED ON PERSONAL EXPERIENCE?

Most fears are imagined—totally and completely imagined. During the Vietnam War era, the Pentagon sponsored a study of LSD (lysergic acid diethylamide), the very potent synthetic hallucinogenic drug derived from lysergic acid. LSD has some limited use in the study and treatment of psychiatric disorders, but it is dangerous. Beside producing hallucinations and bizarre behavior, it can cause psychosis and chromosomal damage. Because scientists suspected that with LSD they could transform soldiers into aggressive fighting machines, the army performed experiments on volunteer soldiers. The results of the study proved to be just the opposite of what they expected, however. The drug LSD seemed to have the property of making fears real only when the subject had personally experienced those fears. When they placed soldiers under the influence of LSD and ordered them to hate Communists, for example, the soldiers gave no response at all—because they'd never experienced any harm from Communists. They feared only those things that they'd personally encountered.

Ninety-nine percent of our fears concern things that we've never personally experienced. I've religiously locked my car whenever I parked it for the last 30 years, and yet I've never had my car stolen—I have no actual experience of the event that's controlling my actions. My fear has come entirely from rumors I've heard or from stories in the newspapers or on television. How many of your fears do you base on actual experience? How many of them can you really justify? How many times have others implanted their fears into your mind, for you to adopt as your own?

> *Ninety-nine percent of our fears concern things that we've never personally experienced.*

A friend of mine, a very fine lady who lives in a lovely home in an area with very little crime, nevertheless refuses to walk anywhere without her large German shepherd dog. The animal goes with her everywhere. If she goes on vacation, the dog goes with her so she can feel safe walking on the beach. I asked her, "Why on earth do you feel that way? Has anyone ever attacked you?"

"Oh, no," she said. "I've never been attacked."

"Well, has anyone you know ever been attacked?"

"No, I don't think so."

Then why does she have this fear? Undoubtedly she's heard of terrible things happening to elderly women who live alone.

Many of our fears, while unfounded, are still reasonable—as long as we don't let them control us.

Isn't it strange that fears placed in our subconscious when we were very young can dominate us? Unless we're careful we pass them from one generation to another. I've always worked to avoid passing on my fears to my children with the result that they all appear to be totally fearless. I've never seen them hesitate at the top of a steep ski slope or fear to walk in a particular area of town. All of them have skydived, both my sons have bungee jumped, and John ran with the bulls in Pamplona when we attended the Festival of San Fermin.

FACING YOUR GREATEST FEAR

My most overwhelming fear had always been the thought of skydiving. I found it impossible to hold in my mind the idea of me standing in the doorway of an airplane and then jumping out into free space. It brought back memories of all my childhood nightmares when I was falling, falling, falling, and then woke up just as I was about to hit the ground.

My fears finally came to a climax when I was the president of a large real estate company in California. We showed a movie at our Saturday-morning sales rally entitled *Pack Your Own Chute* by psychologist Eden Ryle. It's an excellent film about a key principle of Power Performance: that each person should take complete responsibility for his or her own life. In the film, Eden Ryle— a woman in her mid-forties or so—performs her first parachute jump, especially remarkable because she doesn't know how to swim and parachute jumps into the ocean. However, she does it because she's determined to overcome her fears.

After the film I got carried away with all this and did a rash thing. I grabbed the microphone and said, "I challenge all of you to go on a first parachute jump with me. Who wants to go?" About 25 hands immediately shot up. So we arranged to go out to Perris Airport near Riverside, California, where they charged about $100 for a morning's training and an afternoon parachute jump.

Boy, did we get a lot of drop-outs from the original twenty-five! Everybody seemed to have more important things to do, or they were expecting mysterious visitors from out of town. Only eight people showed for the challenge and that included my two older children—Julia, who was 17 at the time, and Dwight, who was 16. Eleven-year-old John wanted to go too, but they said he was too young.

Part of the challenge with the salespeople was if I chickened out at the last minute and didn't make the jump, then I'd have to pay for everyone else's jump. That would cost me an extra $500. On the other hand, if anyone else chickened out and I didn't, then they'd have to pay for my day's training. Beside the financial incentives, I was feeling a great deal of peer pressure. As the leader of the group, it simply wouldn't do for me to weasel out of the challenge. Let me tell you, without those incentives I never would have made it.

We went through a whole morning of training, which included simulating the jump from a fake airplane door on the ground and learning how open the reserve chute if the main chute didn't open and so on. By the end of the day we knew exactly how to handle any emergency.

One of the most important lessons I learned at skydiving school was that knowledge conquers fear. Once I had some training in the thing that scared me most—even before I actually did it—I was much less afraid than I had been. That's a valuable lesson we can apply to business training. We can teach people knowledge by having them read a book or watch a movie. However, to learn skills, people have to get involved with role-plays and workshop sessions. This is what gets them over their fear of performing the task.

Parachute jumping brings out the worst kind of sadistic humor in people. Our instructor, who was 5' 8", claimed he was 6' 6" when he got into the sport! I nervously asked him, "If both chutes fail, how long will it take me to hit the ground?"

He answered with a big grin, "The rest of your life!"

He told us if both chutes did fail, we were to put our hands behind our heads and keep our elbows extended. He made us all stand up and demonstrate the position and then said, "Great! That makes it so much easier for us to unscrew you out of the ground!"

No amount of training could have prepared us for the sensation of the actual jump. It still absolutely terrified me. As we took off, I was in the back praying that the plane would crash before we had to jump, so that I could die honorably, without the imprint of the jump instructor's foot between my shoulder blades.

When you watch people skydiving you always see them hanging from the chute. Up there, it's different. All you can feel is the weight of the two parachutes. The only sensation you get is the feeling of jumping with nothing to hold you up. Finally, however, with peer pressure still holding me firmly in its grasp, I stood there in the doorway, closed my eyes, and jumped.

Then the wheels came off. Somewhere along the way I'd forgotten that I'd be stepping out into an 80-mile-an-hour wind that would spin me like a top. Everything seemed to go haywire as this hurricane battered me. Suddenly there was a tug at my shoulders and the chute billowed out above me, opened by the static line. It convinced me that in spite of all the training we'd received that day, if our chutes hadn't opened automatically all we beginners would simply have fallen straight to the ground and been flattened like pancakes. Not one of us would have had the common sense or clear thinking needed to do any of the things we'd spent the entire morning learning to do.

Our instructor had given us extensive training and detailed instructions on how to guide our chutes into the landing area, but we all landed together about a mile from the target, and the air field had to send a pickup truck out after us. Obviously, none of us had been able to affect our downward drift at all because we all landed where the plane had dumped us. But no matter how poorly we had performed, we'd done it.

For years afterward my youngest son, John, said to me, "Dad, that looked like fun. Will you take me when I'm old enough?"

"Let's talk about it when the time comes, son," I'd say, hoping he'd forget. I thought he'd forgotten, until he called me years later from the San Francisco Bay Area, where he was attending Menlo College.

"Dad," he said, "wish me luck. I've just completed training for my first parachute jump, and I'll be going up in about half an hour."

Let me tell you, I was much more nervous that afternoon than he could possibly have been. However, I knew what a valuable experience it would be for him. Children are born with only two fears, the fear of falling and the fear of loud noises. All other fears, we've taught them. Now here he was, learning to overcome one of these inborn fears. When he called me later to tell me that he'd had a great first jump, I was overwhelmed with pride and relief.

He had a bad experience with his third jump, getting into a strong gust of wind and being dragged across the ground by his chute. However, he got going again and ended up organizing a sky-diving club at his college.

WHY SHOULD WE TEACH OUR CHILDREN TO FEAR?

Now you may say this is irresponsible, that we should raise our children with fears of the bogie man and should train them that every stranger is a threat. However, I disagree. I've traveled all over the world, well off the beaten path, and sometimes in volatile situations, such as the time in Lima, Peru, when I was standing by the National Palace when the Maoists attacked it with rocket launchers. However, the worst thing that's ever really happened to me is to have a pickpocket lift my wallet in Mexico City and to go through an attempted mugging in Istanbul, which I thwarted. That's what I'd prefer to communicate to my children.

Once I spent the evening down at my office, getting caught up before leaving on a speaking trip. When I returned home John, who was 16, said, "Dad, you won't believe what happened to me while you were gone. I heard these footsteps pounding up the road outside and this man ran up our driveway and started pounding on the door. I opened it, and he was yelling, 'Somebody is trying to kill me, they're right behind me, and they'll kill you too.' He had blood all over him, and rope burns on his neck, as though someone had tried to strangle him."

By now I was sure John was pulling my leg. "What did you do?" I asked, trying to keep a straight face.

"Well, I let him in and started to call the paramedics. Then he collapsed while I was on the phone. There was blood all over the place." By this time I was looking over his shoulder into the hallway. There was no sign of any blood. "Oh, the paramedics cleaned it all up," he explained. "I'll prove it to you. After the paramedics and the police got here I switched on the video camera and filmed it all." Sure enough he had. The interesting thing was that my office was only ten minutes away and he could have called me, but he saw no reason to do that. It never occurred to this 16 year old to fear the man at the door; and I know adults who wouldn't have opened the door without a loaded gun in their hands.

It turned out the victim had met some people in a bar who had promised to sell him a great car at a bargain price. He agreed to meet them in a remote area not far from our home with $2,000 cash. They evidently planned to kill him and steal the money. The story was headline news in our local newspaper the next day under the banner headline, LA HABRA HEIGHTS USED AS A DUMPING GROUND BY CRIMINALS? No wonder the population is paranoid when the press exaggerates like that.

> *The best thing we can do to overcome our fears is*
> *to go out and face them head on.*

FACING YOUR FEARS HEAD ON

The question is: What can we do to stop even the most reasonable fears from overwhelming us and directing our lives? The best thing we can do to overcome our fears is to go out and face them head on.

I tackled my fear of the dark by camping in the wilderness. After living in the midst of civilization my whole life, it was a strange feeling to watch the sun go down and realize there would be no electricity, no light, no television, nothing to break up the darkness. What do you do when you usually go to bed at 10 or 11 o'clock at night and it becomes dark at 7 or 8? For me, it was a real learning experience. Now, having faced that fear, it's gone.

Another great fear of mine was the fear of being alone. You may never have thought much about it, but there probably haven't been many times in your life when you've been completely alone for long. I know I hadn't, and the thought scared me. So I took a trip to my favorite spot in the California Sierras, Mineral King. Remember I told you about it in the preface? I spent a total of 48 hours there, completely alone. Forty-eight hours without seeing another human being, even in the far distance. Forty-eight hours without newspapers, radio, telephones, or communication of any kind. This experience gave me a different perspective on life. It definitely gave me a different outlook on my own being, and it would be a good experience for you too. Experience being alone in the wilderness for a while, and you'll find out a great deal about yourself and your relationship to the world in which you live.

In later years, forcing myself to overcome my fears has led me to buying an around-the-world air ticket and taking off for a month, without any plans or hotel reservations. It's found me sitting in the jungles of Zaire in central Africa in front of a 500-pound mountain gorilla and learning not to flinch when it made a mock charge at me. It's taken me bungee jumping and walking over burning coals.

HOW OVERCOMING YOUR GREATEST FEAR TRANSFORMS YOU

What do you fear the most? Whatever it is, go out and do it. Overcoming what you fear the most will help you through the challenges that lie in your future. That's why the parachute jump was such a valuable experience for me. Ever since I made it, I haven't been afraid of anything. Every time I feel anxiety approaching, I just compare it to that moment standing in the doorway of the plane with the wind rushing by and me looking straight down to the ground 4,000 feet below; no other fear can compare. Nothing else can stack up. I think, "Gee, if I could jump out of a plane, I can do this." So you see, once you do the thing that scares you the most, you'll be able to overcome all the other fears in your life as well, and you'll have taken a major step toward becoming a Power Performer.

What is it you fear most? Many people fear public speaking. I know when I present my seminars and speak in front of hundreds and sometime thousands of people, afterward people often approach me and say, "How can you do that? How can you speak like that without being scared to death? Whenever I have to speak to my Rotary Club, I'm terrified!"

Well, I used to feel that way, too, but I learned to overcome it. I joined a local Toastmaster's Club, and I attended their meetings for 15 years. I learned to stand up in front of groups of 10, 12, or 15 people, and gradually erased my fear of public speaking.

Dale Carnegie found confronting this particular fear to be a magical thing. He developed the Dale Carnegie Course, which helps a person build up his or her self-confidence through public speaking. Carnegie's theory was if someone could make a fool of himself or herself in front of a group, then he or she wouldn't feel anxious in normal, one-on-one situations. So if public speaking is your fear, deal with it—you'll be much more self-confident in all areas of your life if you do.

Are you afraid of rejection? It wouldn't surprise me because that's a very common fear. I think that fear affects the direction of our lives. We never ask out the person we really want to date because we're afraid of rejection. There are many things we could have but never get because we don't ask for them. We're afraid of being rejected.

If this fear worries you, there's a very simple way to face it. Pick up the phone. Call six random numbers out of the telephone book and say, "Hi, I'm calling from the Universal Encyclopedia. Do you have a few minutes to talk with me?" Then let all six hang up on you. Don't call more than six people because when you get around to the seventh or eighth call, someone will answer, "Sure, why don't you tell me about it? How much does it cost?" You might find yourself having to hang up on him.

I suggested this exercise on my Nightingale-Conant cassette program, *Secrets of Power Performance,* and got a great letter from a young man in Xenia, Ohio. He said, "I tried that six-phone-call encyclopedia exercise today, and it was a blast. It really was fun. People actually believed I was a salesman and they would politely say no thank you. That was neat."

Then he went on to say, "One of my biggest fears is asking girls out on a date. But I'm getting better at it. I can now ask one a week, and I've done it for the last three weeks."

There's another reason that you must learn to face your fears and overcome them. William Glasser, the father of Reality Therapy, says the fear of something is just as damaging as the actual thing. You would be much better to face your fear once and get past it than to avoid it and suffer the bad effect on your nervous system every time you think of it. Your aim should be not to eliminate all fear from your life, but to free yourself from the debilitating effects of your fears. Learn to face your fears and overcome them.

Once you've stared at your fears straight on you can start to enjoy all the excitement life holds for you. As a Power Performer, an achievement-filled future is out there waiting for you. All you need is the courage to accept it.

◆◆◆

The Twelfth Secret of Power Performers is:

They know how to turn their fear into fortune.

◆◆◆

In the next chapter, we'll talk about love and how to find it.

13

POWER PERFORMERS HAVE LEARNED TO PUT LOVE IN THEIR LIFE

A coward is incapable of exhibiting love; it is the prerogative of the brave.

— *Mahatma Gandhi*

I never knew how to worship until I knew how to love.

— *Henry Ward Beecher*

Try to reason about love and you will lose your reason.

— *French proverb*

Immature love says: "I love you because I need you."
Mature love says: "I need you because I love you."

— *Erich Fromm*

If you would be loved, be worthy of love.

— *Ovid. A.D. 8*

Could it be that love and God is what we are? That we are love and we are God?

— *Roger Dawson*

Where does the Power Performer find that incredible love of life that sets him or her apart? From love, that amazing force in our lives, which no one has ever been able to define but which is so powerful that it can dominate our existence. A Power Performer is someone who loves life itself with all the passion and the intensity of an Antony with a Cleopatra, or a King Edward with a Wallis Simpson.

It's interesting that we're unable to define love and can approximate what it is only by describing the effect it has on people. My dictionary lists eight different definitions of the word, seven if we exclude the tennis score, and still doesn't come close to saying what it is, only what it does.

THE THREE THINGS THAT HUMAN BEINGS HAVE TROUBLE DEFINING

There are two other things we also have trouble defining. One is God. We can tell exactly the effects of the presence of God in our lives, but we have trouble expressing exactly who He is. The other thing we have a problem with is expressing exactly what we are. We know what we can do and the effect that we can have on our environment, but we're unable to say exactly what we are.

Three indefinable things in our universe—love, God and us. Isn't that an interesting combination? Could it be that we are all the same thing? That we are love, and we are God.

However, I didn't bring you this far to take you on a metaphysical mystery tour. I brought you here to give you some specifics on how to make your life more fun and more exciting so that you release the energy needed for Power Perforance. So back to our theme, that a Power Performer is in love with the very act of being alive.

"Okay I have it," you say. "A Power Performer is someone who has a deep love for life. Therefore if I want to be a Power Performer I need to find love and get me some. Where should I look?" There's a big problem with that line of thinking. Love is an elusive, shy creature. You can't go find it. You have to lie low and pretend you're not looking for it. Then it will come and find you.

So you say, "I didn't know that! What about all those singles bars down at the beach. I heard you can find love down there. Shouldn't I at least go and take a look?" Go ahead if you want, perhaps you'll enjoy the search, but you won't find love there.

> *The most romantic thing a girl ever said to me in bed was, "Are you sure you're not a cop?"*
>
> LARRY BROWN

If you don't believe me, think of the couple you feel are most in love with each other and go ask them. That for me would be Dottie and Henry Hoche. They are longtime friends of mine who have a beautiful home in the hills of North Carolina, that they've just turned into one of the finest bed and breakfasts in the country. It's called The Innisfree in Glenville, North Carolina. They're one of only a few couples I've ever met whose love for each other simply glows, like a warm fire on a chilly evening. It's a sheer delight just to be with them. Dottie had married twice before, and Henry once. Both spent years in a search for the perfect love. They are sophisticated, intelligent people who had experience in relationships and the way of the world. They knew what would make a relationship work and what wouldn't. They were both determined to settle for nothing other than the genuine article. Both concluded individually that it's impossible to find love when you're looking for it. Before they met each other they both had decided to quit the search for true love because they didn't seem destined to find it. Suddenly, there it was. "Roger," they tell me, "the only way to ever find love is to quit looking for it."

Love is like an elusive elf in the woods who loves to play hide and seek. It's so good at the game that when you feel you have it cornered it can make itself invisible. The harder you search for it, the more it redoubles its efforts to get away. When, in exasperation, you finally give up the game and go sit in a clearing in the woods simply to enjoy the evening, it will silently slip out of hiding, sit down beside you, and put its arm around you.

You can't embrace the concept of loving life and then deliberately go out and seek or create love. Love must come as a side effect of your other activities. Success is the same way. The most miserable people I know are the ones who set out with a deliberate drive and purpose to become wealthy. The happiest people I know are the ones who fell in love with the idea of doing something exquisitely well and found that a side effect of that activity was wealth.

DO WHAT YOU LOVE TO DO; THE MONEY WILL FOLLOW

Take young Boris Becker, for example, who can do one thing better than anyone else in the world. It's a dumb little thing at that. When standing on a grass tennis court, he can hit a tennis ball more accurately and faster than anyone else in the world. When he won at Wimbledon he couldn't play the rest of the game as well as others, but he took that little specialty and concentrated on doing it better than anyone else in the world. Now what if Boris had started out at the age of 10 and said, "I'm going to be a millionaire by the time I'm 20, from playing tennis. Then, because I'm wealthy and people admire me, I'll be happy." Isn't that the way most people set objectives? It doesn't occur to them that having material things so that people admire you for owning them is not what makes you happy. What if you became mature enough to get over the need for people to look up to you? You see, that approach is all wrong. Find something you love to do and for which you feel you have a talent and learn to do it better than anyone else in the world. Then love and happiness will find you.

Every super-successful person loves what he or she does. My friend Wayne Dyer has sold over 50 million books worldwide. He tells me, "Roger, I'm just doing what I love to do."

> *Find something you love to do, for which you have a talent, and learn to do it better than anyone else in the world. Then love and happiness will find you.*

They say that was the difference between Frank Sinatra and Bobby Darin. Back in the late 1950s and early 1960s they became very competitive. Darin determined to be more successful than Sinatra. If Frank booked into Vegas, Bobby had to get a date there too and see if he could outdraw Sinatra. He was a first-rate singer and extremely successful, but if you saw the two of them perform, the difference was subtle but obvious. Bobby Darin was doing it because he craved success. Frank Sinatra was doing it because he loved to sing.

> *If I'd have done everything I'd been credited with, I'd be talking to you from a laboratory jar at Harvard.*
>
> FRANK SINATRA

What a joy it is to watch someone doing something well, simply for the love of it. Watch the magic hands of Willy Shoemaker, who rode 10 or 15 years beyond the time when he could have retired from the sport a wealthy man, still trying to show those young fellas that there's only one place in the horse race where it matters, and that's at the finish post. When he won the Kentucky Derby on Ferdinand he got an unlucky break from the gate and trailed the other horses down the first straightaway. Counted out entirely by the commentators, he gradually coaxed his mount past the entire field to take the race on the finish line. Even the most hardened reporters were in total awe of Shoemaker's performance, calling it the most brilliant ride in the history of the sport. And horse racing has been around for almost 3,500 years! Did he do it for the money? No, he had more money than he could ever spend. For the recognition? No—if the sport lasts for another 3,500 years, he'd probably still be talked of as the greatest jockey who ever lived, even without the accomplishments of the last ten years of his career. He did it simply because he loved to do it more than anything else in the world. The fame and the wealth were a by-product.

Take Johnny Carson, living in a $9 million mansion on the cliffs overlooking Malibu and driving himself to work 4 days a week for 28 years to host his show. By his own admission he was not as successful in other areas of his life as he might have been. Divorced three times he said, "If I'd have put as much effort into my married life as I did into the show, I wouldn't have had any problems with my marriages." Although he made millions every year when he was hosting the *Tonight Show,* he probably could have done even better if he'd have branched out into other entertainment fields, but it's obvious he loved what he did.

THE BUSINESS OWNER WHO LOVES HIS WORK IS A JOY TO BE WITH

Occasionally you'll run into a restaurant that's run by someone who thinks this way, and it's a great experience. Such a place is Papadakis Taverna, down by the docks of San Pedro in Southern California. John Papadakis is a former football captain at the University of Southern California, who developed a burning desire to run his own business instead of work for a corporation. He's there every night greeting the customers and circling the tables to talk with them. He and his brother will occasionally break into an impromptu Greek dance for the customers, complete with wine glasses tossed over their shoulders. I'm able to get over there only about once a year, but he always remembers me and comes over to chat.

Another such place was Gianni Russo's State Street in Las Vegas. Unfortunately it's closed now, after the financial backer pulled out. Gianni was always on hand to talk to you and to present a red rose to the ladies in the party. He's incredibly handsome and would look vaguely familiar to you. If he saw your curious look, he'd tell you he was in the movie *The Godfather.* "I'm the one who beat up Sonny's sister," he'd explain with a bashful grin. He had a successful career going in Hollywood, but decided he loved running his restaurant more. The entertainers get tired of eating at the casinos, so State Street was a favorite place for them. You were likely to see Frank Sinatra or Tony Bennett in there, enjoying the fine Italian food; but with consummate class, Gianni would treat you with just as much deference.

> *The trouble with eating Italian food is that five or
> six days later you're hungry again.*
>
> GEORGE MILLER

However, restaurants such as these are rare, aren't they? When you find a restaurateur who's in it strictly because he or she loves the business, it's a real joy to be around that person.

You may not play tennis for a living, ride race horses, host a talk show, or manage a restaurant. It doesn't matter what you do. You'll become a Power Performer when the work gets into you so much that you develop a burning desire to do it better than anyone else in the world. Just as love will sneak up and put its arm around you only when you decide to stop looking for it, so will financial success and love of life overwhelm you the moment they are no longer your objective.

WORKING FOR MONEY IS DEPRESSING

The opposite point of view is downright depressing. These are the people who work only for money and do the very least they can to get by. To them increases in pay come only because they're able to squeeze them out of a spiteful employer.

> *Success and love of life overwhelm you the
> moment they are no longer your objective.*

Imagine a small copper mining town in Utah. The mine was the town's only major employer, so everybody in the town either worked at the mine or at a business dependent on the mine-workers' earnings—such as a store or restaurant.

The problems started when OSHA, the Federal Agency that oversees occupational safety and health, insisted that the mine install expensive antipollution devices at the same time that the workers started pressing for a substantial increase in pay. The union failed to accept the company's point of view that it wouldn't be good for either the company, the workers, or the town if the company were to be coerced into operating the mine at a loss. They offered the workers an increase in pay, but not as much as they were demanding. The workers said it wasn't enough and went out on strike. Since the mine was the only major employer in town, this put nearly the entire community out of business. The strike dragged on for two years. Every time the company made an offer to the workers, they said it wasn't enough. The company said if it couldn't reopen the mine soon, it would have to close it permanently. The workers didn't believe them.

Finally in desperation, the company closed the mine—reluctantly, because it would mean they would have to abandon this town of several thousand people that they'd created. Then all the people would have to leave, since there was no other employment. They were still sympathetic to the workers, so they set up a fund where each worker would get $3,000 in severance pay to relocate. Guess what the workers said? "It's not enough! It's not enough!" That kind of mentality is hard for Power Performers to comprehend.

MEMORIES OF THE COMMUNIST WAY OF LIFE

We all have to work at something. Not many of us have so much passive income that we can fulfill all of our financial needs without some activity on our part, even if it's just managing our investments. However, if you're working at anything strictly for the money, I urge you to reevaluate what you're doing and do it today. Make some changes and be thankful you're in a country where you have so many choices.

Can you imagine being in a country like Czechoslovakia when the communists controlled it? Back then there was only one employer. Under a communist system, everyone worked for the government. I mean everybody. There was no other employer. The man selling newspapers on the corner was working for the same employer as the maitre'd in the restaurant, as was the taxi driver who took you there and the manager of your apartment building. So there was virtually no sense of ambition in the country. You couldn't get better at what you did and change employers to earn more money, because there was no other employer. Of course, there was never any hope of opening your own business. There was no private enterprise of any kind, even for shining shoes or watching parked cars.

Not that there would be much point in having ambition, because there was nothing to spend money on anyway. Oh, yes, they might allow you to buy a house, a car, and maybe even a boat. Perhaps they would even let you rent out a room in your house, but they would not let you own another property and rent it out. There was no stock market in which to invest or any other investments you could make. The law didn't allow you to buy foreign currency, and your money was valueless outside of your own country. If you had money, you could put it only into a government-owned bank. A few of the stores in the center of town displayed items such as toasters and washing machines for sale, and the people pressed their noses against the glass and lusted after them, the way people on Rodeo Drive lust after $10,000 watches.

In Prague, Czechoslovakia, before the fall of communism, I had an interesting encounter with a group of three young East Germans. It opened my eyes to what life was really like behind the Iron Curtain and reminded me again of the value of the freedom we enjoy in this country. Westerners couldn't travel freely in Czechoslovakia in those days of course. Sonya, a government guide, met my daughter, Julia, and me at the border and stayed with us until we left the country, and lied to us every inch of the way. Remember there was only one employer, so she had to tell us exactly what the government had told her to tell us. Would you break many rules under the circumstances? For example, Sonya explained that we would be in Prague over a weekend, so not to expect to see too many people on the streets, as most people in Prague have a second home in the country they go to over the weekend. What nonsense!

Right in the middle of Prague, Wenceslaus Square, there's this guy throwing up. And this other guy comes along, takes a look at him, shakes his head, and says, "I know just what you mean."

MILAN KUNDERA

I determined to meet with someone who spoke English, so that I could get a truer picture. In the castle I noticed a young man who appeared to be straining to hear Sonya speaking English. I went over to him and introduced myself. His name was Gard, and he was from East Germany. His English was perfect, with a strong British accent, although he told me I was only the second English-speaking person he'd ever met. He and his friends had taught themselves the language by clandestinely listening to the BBC overseas service. They had no books or dictionaries and the only English writing they had ever seen was an old English newspaper. When I gave them the English books I had with me, they were ecstatic. They told me that they had studied what they heard on the radio, and if they had a disagreement about grammar they would take a vote to decide what they would adopt as correct.

I asked Gard and his two young friends to join my daughter and me for lunch, over Sonya's strong protests and the protests of the government restaurant manager, who tried to tell me there was no room.

At lunch my new friends told me that they were on a camping vacation but the East German government allowed them to go only as far as Czechoslovakia. They would allow only their most trusted citizens to visit Hungary, a country that was much looser in its controls. In 1989 we found out how justified their fears were, when 15,000 East Germans vacationing in Hungary escaped to the West. To further restrict the young people's movement, the government allowed them to bring only the equivalent of $5 a day with them.

They were desperate to get out of East Germany and seek freedom in the West. When they told me this with passion in their voices, I became skeptical. "Don't tell me you couldn't leave if you really wanted to," I said. "You're in this country on a camping trip. What's to stop you sneaking out through the woods and finding a way across the border?"

My naiveté amazed them. "You really don't think they built a wall through Berlin and left it so we could go around the end of it, do you? The communists have surrounded this entire country with two tall electrified fences placed in the middle of a 100-meter no man's land. Every 500 meters there's a machine-gun post. They shoot anyone trying to get out, without asking any questions."

They had camouflaged the fence at the West German border where we'd come into the country, but later on we saw what he was talking about at the Austrian border.

Gard was fluent in French and Egyptian, besides English and German, and was obviously very intelligent. However, he worked as a laborer in East Germany because he was unwilling to join the Communist Party, where he'd have to attend weekly meetings and swear against all religions, among other things to which he objected. It wasn't mandatory to join the Communist Party, but it was the only way to advance from being a laborer. Since he had one of the lowest-paying jobs in a country where working for the government is mandatory, he didn't work very hard, he told me. He told me that everyone he worked with also did as little as possible.

Later I was the keynote speaker at a meeting of small business people, and I related this story and told them how lucky they were to live in a country like America, which encouraged private ownership of business. Afterward an elderly lady came up to me with tears rolling down her cheeks. "I escaped from East Germany," she told me. "You told it exactly the way it is. I'm so happy to be here."

Under circumstances such as those existing in Czechoslovakia, the laissez-faire attitude Gard took toward his work was understandable. However, in this country—where we have so many options—it's a travesty for people to be working on jobs that are not inspiring enough for them to give it all they have.

START CONCENTRATING ON DOING WHAT IT IS YOU COULD DO BETTER THAN ANYONE ELSE IN THE WORLD

So to become a Power Performer, forget striving for success for its own sake and start concentrating on doing what it is you could do better than anyone else in the world. You'll find the success and love of life you seek will come and find you. I fought my way up the corporate ladder with the department-store chain for 13 years, with only modest success. When I quit to go into real estate strictly for the exposure to investment opportunities, not caring in the least about getting into management, it was amazing to me how management opportunities kept seeking me out and making me offers I couldn't refuse.

In my speaking business the smartest decision I ever made was to concentrate solely on making my talks the best they could be. When I first started I was trying to do everything myself, even though I had a highly paid company president back at the office. I was criss-crossing the country giving talks and then rushing back to the office to supervise the company. Then my president took me aside and said, "Roger, in your talks you're always preaching about concentrating on the highest and best use of time. When are you going to realize the highest and best use of your time is to make your talks better? Why don't you concentrate on that and let me run the company? I'll worry about whether we're making any money or not; you just concentrate on becoming the best speaker in the country." It was the best advice I ever received. When that became the thrust and making money became only secondary, we were able to start being selective about the opportunities that seemed to start coming to us from all directions.

It's a little like dating someone. I'm sure you've discovered that the less you try to make someone like you, the more you attract him or her to you. The harder you try, the worse it gets.

THE WORD *LOVE* DOESN'T COME CLOSE TO DESCRIBING WHAT LOVE IS

If we're to love life we should examine more closely what love is and what it isn't. If you've studied other languages you know that the word *love* is a glaring deficiency in our language. We use it to describe all kinds of emotions. How can we say we love escargot and use the same word to describe the feelings we have about our country—or our mother?

The Greeks do a little better with their language. They use two words: the first is *eros,* which describes the passionate kind of love men and women can have for each other, and which includes more than a touch of selfishness. You may love your girl friend, but catch her out with another man and that love can quickly turn to anger. Because of this love-hate aspect of the relationship, the opposite of *eros* is not hate, but indifference. As long as they are throwing plates at you, you have something there with which you can work. The relationship is over when indifference sets in and they're saying, "I really don't care what you do, go ahead. Be my guest."

> *When you are in love with someone you want to be near them all the time—except when you are out buying things and charging them to him.*
>
> MISS PIGGY

The other word Greeks use to describe love is *argope,* meaning the unselfish kind of love parents have for their children. I love my children, but if one of them calls me to say he or she can't come over because he or she has a date, I don't get jealous. To be a Power Performer you must be full of *argope*, or unselfish love.

LEANING TO DEAL WITH LIFE WHEN IT KEELHAULS YOU

However, when you love life, it can be a fickle mistress, can't it? There are times when you're absolutely convinced life must be dealing you every cruel blow in the book and rubbing salt into the wound, loving every minute of it. Now here comes the test: Do you still love the experience of living at those times? Do you still see it as a fascinating part of life's experience, or do you turn sour on life? Like a pouting teenager, you're thinking, "Well, if you're not going to be nice to me, I'm not going to like you any more."

Power Performers have learned *argope*—to love all of life's experiences, not just the comfortable or enjoyable ones. If things happen to them that turn their emotions upside down, they learn to ride the roller coaster and savor the feelings running through them, as out of control as they appear to be.

A few years ago I lost, in a little over six months, more than $2 million. It was almost all the money I had at the time. I didn't have to file bankruptcy, although it would have been a lot easier for me to have done so. For a while, however, just staying afloat was taking all my efforts. To make things worse, it was entirely my fault. If you've been through an experience like that, you know what it's like.

If you haven't, I'll try to describe it to you. Remember the old *Mutiny on the Bounty* movie? I'm talking about the one where Charles Laughton played the tyrannical perfectionist Captain Bligh. In those days they would punish sailors by keelhauling them. A charming habit. In the movie they tied two ropes around First Officer Christian's waist. One they held onto, and the other they looped under the bottom of the ship. Then they threw him overboard and slowly pulled him down through the water, under the ship and up the other side. It doesn't kill the offender, but it must seem as though it's going to.

Going through financial wars is like being keelhauled. You're convinced it's going to kill you. You wouldn't commit suicide, but you wish for a heart attack that would take you on to the next world honorably. It seems to drag on forever, and just when you think you can't take another minute of it, you pop out on the other side—to a world brighter and more colorful and more rewarding than it ever was in the past.

Looking back on that time in my life, I wouldn't trade the experience for anything. I wouldn't wish it on myself again, but it was a very rich and fascinating part of my life's adventure, and I'm certainly none the worse for it today. The race-car driver who narrowly escapes death in a crash or a hunter who outruns a polar bear must feel the same way. Now the challenge for the true Power Performer, who knows that loving life energizes his or her performance, is to appreciate it—while it's happening!

So Power Performers must learn to love all of life's experiences, not just when times are good and life seems to be loving them back.

LEARN TO BE NONJUDGMENTAL

There was a fascinating movie made a few years back called *Starman*. Jeff Bridges played a creature from another planet who had come to earth on a scientific investigative mission.

If this kind of story line seems a bit farfetched to you, let me tell you about a person I know who's made quite a study of this. He's absolutely convinced people from other solar systems have flown past Earth and observed us, but have decided not to land. He believes that there are thousands of planets with life on them, which I think is a statistical probability based on the sheer size of the universe. Our little galaxy, the Milky Way, contains 100 billion stars, and astronomers believe there are 10 billion other galaxies. Multiply those two numbers out and you may no longer think of Earth as the obvious place for space travelers to head toward.

On the wall of my office I have a painting of the universe. The Sun is a huge ball of fire on the left. Then the large planets stretch out across the heavens: Jupiter, Saturn, Uranus, Neptune, and Pluto. Between the Sun and the first large planet, Jupiter, is a tiny blue and white ball—Earth. Next to it I've put a little arrow that says, "You are here." Just to keep things in perspective.

My friend maintains the aliens took a look at Earth but didn't land because they just didn't have time to fool with a planet so primitive in its human relations: that we don't have one form of government to speak for all the peoples on Earth. Interesting observation, isn't it?

Another interesting theory to explain why space travelers haven't visited us is that our life span may be so much shorter than theirs. If their life span is a million years, for example, and ours is only 115 years, it must seem to them that we live for only a brief flash of time, far too brief for them to make contact with us.

Back to the movie. The Starman wasn't in human form, of course, but he genetically cloned himself, using a cell from a lock of hair he found in the heroine's photo album. Therefore he took on the human form of her dead husband. Bridges did an outstanding job of playing someone who was totally nonjudgmental, other than the respect he had for all living creatures. In one scene he runs across a dead deer strapped to the hood of a hunter's car and cannot understand why anyone would do that. So he uses his powers to bring it back to life. He's fascinated and thrilled by every aspect of life. Each nuance of everything he sees is of intense interest to him. He doesn't have any personal likes or dislikes that are constantly turning him on to the process of living or turning him off. That's an approach for which a Power Performer should strive.

Practice observing without judging. It's not as easy as it seems.

- ◆ "The man is eating alone in the restaurant," is an observation.
  "He must be lonely," is a judgment.

◆ "My son didn't mow the lawn as he promised," is an observation.
"Therefore he's lazy," is a judgment.

◆ "He doesn't smile much," is an observation.
"He's unhappy," is a judgment.

Try it—it will amaze you how many automatic judgments you make during a day. It's not an easy habit to break, but Power Performers know it's essential to getting the most out of life.

In the streets of India, I've seen children whose parents twisted the children's limbs at birth, to make them more successful beggars. Now it's easy to get turned upside down by that, and horrified and revolted. I think it's more productive to develop an intense curiosity in that. Why does it happen? What are the causes? How does the parent feel about doing that?

At the end of World War II millions of ordinary Japanese citizens were ready to kill their children and themselves, rather than face the disgrace of defeat. Winston Churchill once estimated that dropping the atom bombs on Hiroshima and Nagasaki saved over five million lives. It's easy to let a visit to the Peace Park in Hiroshima shock and disgust you. It's more important to observe, to ponder, and to seek an answer. As I signed the guest register at Hiroshima it fascinated me to see that a Japanese visitor had written in English next to his name: "God bless the heroic defenders of Hiroshima."

> *The war situation has developed not necessarily to Japan's advantage.*
>
> EMPEROR HIROHITO,
> AFTER LOSING HIROSHIMA AND NAGASAKI TO ATOMIC BOMBING.

At Heathrow Airport in London police arrested a terrorist who was trying to smuggle a bomb onto an El Al jetliner. The bomb would have killed him and all the passengers. It's easy to let that astound and terrify you and cause you to cancel your summer vacation in Europe, but it's far more valuable to see it as a fascinating part of life and ponder what causes someone to think like that. Of course, we do everything within our power to end it—I'm not preaching complacency, but we shouldn't let it sour us on life's experience.

So a Power Performer's love of life is an *argope* kind of love, which loves regardless of what happens, not an *eros* kind of love, which turns sour when things are not the way we would like them to be.

DON'T LET SELECTIVITY SPOIL YOUR ENJOYMENT OF LIFE

The other thing Power Performers understand about their love of life is that it can't be selective. You can't say you love someone when her hair is up, but not when it's down. You can't say you love someone when he's playing golf, but not when he's playing tennis. You either love somebody, or you don't. If your love is selective, then call what you feel about them something else, but don't call it love.

When I say I love this country, I mean I love it all, not just parts of it. Fifth Avenue at Christmas time, when the air is crisp and the shoppers wrap themselves up in their finest furs, is a wonderful place. But so is Grand Central Station with the sailors going home on leave, sleeping on the benches and using their duffel bags as a pillow.

I love Aspen at Christmas, when the affluent go out to play. Swooping off the top of Aspen Mountain on a sunlit day when the snow is perfect seems like a flight through heaven. But I also love Amarillo on an August afternoon, when heavy dust muffles the air and roads shimmer in the summer heat as they disappear over the horizon to the bottom of the sky.

When you first visit a country, as I first visited America in 1960, it's easy to be nonjudgmental. It's all new, it's all fascinating. However, the Power Performers never lose their love for their surroundings or their fascination for life, however familiar they may become with it.

Jack Nicklaus never loses the thrill of seeing a ball fly from his clubhead on a perfect trajectory, giving the illusion of gathering speed as it goes up and watching it appear to hover silently before it drops onto the green.

Willie Shoemaker never lost the thrill of urging his mount up the home stretch, feeling it gather a new reserve of muscle between his knees, and then smoothly gaining on the other horses as they glide in perfect harmony to the finish line.

Chuck Yeager never lost the thrill of lining up perfectly with the runway at 300 miles an hour, or standing a jet on its tail and zooming up through the clouds to the bright sunlight beyond—however many thousands of times he may have done it.

This enjoyment of life, this love of being a part of life's adventure, starts with your determination to find something in your life that you love to do so much that you're willing to devote your life to doing it better than anyone else.

Fill your days with an activity you enjoy doing so much that you'd do it even if you weren't getting paid for it. Then figure out a way to get paid for it, and work to become the best in the world at doing it.

◆◆◆

The Thirteenth Secret of Power Performers is:

They have learned to put love in their life.

◆◆◆

In the following postscript chapter, I'll put it all together for you. You'll see why Power Perfomers have developed these 13 secrets and how they come together to make you a Power Performer.

THE SEVEN TRAITS OF POWER PERFORMERS

We've come a long way haven't we? I'm sure I've offended your beliefs at times and I apologize for that. I'm sure I've bored you at times and puzzled you as we went off on seemingly irrelevant tangents. I probably confused you at times, and left you wondering why I was making a particular point. Believe me, it all had a purpose. The purpose was to bring us to this moment together. This graduating chapter! Not long now and you'll be ready to move on as a true Power Performer.

I realize that up to now I've asked you to buy an awful lot of blue sky—to just go along with me on some points and keep an open mind until you've had a chance to validate them against your own experiences. However, there's one thing I hope you haven't questioned me on. It's what I was telling you in Chapter Nine, that Power Performers don't do things for material reward. That's not my purpose in writing this book. What small financial gain or rise in notoriety that might come to me because of writing the book, is nothing compared to my concern that I'm able to share with you insights that may be just what you're looking for at this particular time in your life. I really do care about you, and I hope you'll write or call to let me know about your experiences.

My address is P.O. Box 3326, La Habra, CA 90631. My telephone number is (818) 854-3591.

So now it's just the two of us. Just you and me. We need to talk specifics about where we go from this day on to release the energy within you so that you can start to perform at the level of which you're capable. To be totally absorbed by the process of living. To be doing what you're doing because you love to do it. Never to wish that you were finished doing what you were doing, so that you could get on to something you really enjoy. There would be no such thing as quality time to you, because all of life would be quality time.

If you're to become that kind of Power Performer, there are seven things that you must make a part of your personal philosophy. These are the seven traits of Power Performers:

TRAIT 1. LET GO OF THE PAST

You must train yourself to live in the present and not to exist in the past or the future because both of those prevent you from fully enjoying the present. Here are the 3 things you must do to let go of the past and start living in the present:

1. Take full responsibility for your life.
2. Clean up past relationships.
3. Learn to forgive yourself.

TAKE FULL RESPONSIBILITY FOR YOUR LIFE

The first thing you must do is to start taking full responsibility for your life. This is such an essential fundamental that I made it a recurring theme throughout this book. If you are a person who is going around thinking you got fired from a job because your boss is an idiot or is picking on you, then you need to work that out until you truly understand and believe it wasn't that at all. In some way you didn't respond appropriately to the situation, and you set yourself up to be fired.

If you feel your business went broke because the competition behaved unethically or your banker had a grudge against you, you couldn't be more wrong. That doesn't make any more sense than an employee saying he or she is late to work because of a flat tire. You must take responsibility for your actions. You might be just as late to work as anyone else who got a flat tire, but you must understand that you're late because you failed to plan for the possibility of a flat tire, not because circumstances took control of your life. Accepting responsibility for your problems comes naturally to you as a Power Performer.

You're never really a failure until you start blaming someone else for what went wrong. Haven't you met people who can never see that they were at fault? They're always blaming other people for their problems. There's a reason for this. People who have no respect for themselves have trouble respecting others. If you think highly of yourself there's plenty of space there for you to think highly of others. In the same way, your ability to love others is in direct proportion to your ability to love yourself.

CLEAN UP PAST RELATIONSHIPS

The second thing that Power Performers must do to let go of the past and start living in the present is to take the time to clean up past relationships. The exercise of going back and making contact with the people involved in unpleasant situations in your past is one of the most powerful concepts in the field of human behavior.

I remember trying to persuade a young lady who worked for me to do this. She had a father in Oregon whom she hadn't seen for many, many years. She held inside her an incredible amount of bitterness toward him, with very good reason. When she told me the things he'd done, I thought of the line in the song, "How Can People Be So Heartless?" He was clearly a total jerk. Okay, Okay, that's a judgment, not an observation, but in his case I'll make an exception. I encouraged her to go to Oregon to meet him—not to forgive him or make friends with him but merely to make contact and complete the gap in this relationship—a gap that was affecting her enjoyment of the present moment so much.

She did, and when she returned she was positively glowing. Guess what she told me? Her father was still a jerk. However, now she could say it with a smile on her face. With this encounter, she had flushed away all the vitriolic feelings that had poisoned her system for years. She still didn't like him or choose to spend any time with him and, to the best of my knowledge, she never saw him again. However, the meeting cleaned up her life. I feel very strongly about this. You can't release the power within you and become a Power Performer as long as there's someone in your past who makes your blood boil when you think of him or her.

LEARN TO FORGIVE YOURSELF

The third thing you must do to let go of the past and start living in the present is one of the most powerful concepts I've ever heard. I got it from Maxwell Maltz, the author of *Psycho Cybernetics*. He told me about the power of learning to forgive yourself, which we talked about in Chapter Three. It's a wonderful concept.

Remember that all depression is caused by something that happened in your past. One of the best ways to avoid depression is to learn to let go of the past.

TRAIT 2.
ELIMINATE CONCERN FOR THE FUTURE

Having learned to let go of the past and in so doing avoid depression, you now have to ask the question—how can you teach yourself to eliminate concern for the future? All anxiety is caused by something that you fear will happen in the future. So if you eliminate concern for the future, you can say good-bye to anxiety.

The answer is the realization that living in the future is rooted in fear. Fear that you will lose your job. Fear that people won't love you anymore. Fear that you will retire in poverty. The people who fear like this are those who slave for 20 years at a job they don't enjoy to earn a nest egg for their retirement years and then retire and die of boredom and frustration within three years.

Victor Frankl's experience in Auschwitz taught us that, without purpose, we lose the meaning of life and set ourselves up to die. Most people set up a series of artificial purposes in their lives—to graduate from college, to get married, to become a vice-president of a company, to become president, to attend their daughter's wedding, to hold a grandchild, and so on. Instead, I want you to see as your purpose the very act of enjoying and appreciating life itself.

If you can eliminate fear from your life you've taken a big step toward learning to appreciate the present moment. That's why I included a chapter on facing fear in this book. There's a tremendous catharsis that takes place when you face and overcome your greatest fear. You'll see it as an explosion of repressed emotions, whether it's the fear of jumping from a plane, as it was for me, or the fear of walking through dangerous neighborhoods at night, or of confronting a hostile spouse or employer. Or your fear may be of quitting your job to start that new enterprise of which you've been dreaming.

When I was in the real estate business in California I became friendly with a man who had built quite an empire as a real estate broker. He owned 15 or so offices as well as several related companies. His community knew him as a wealthy and successful businessman. Real estate is a very cyclical industry, and he'd run into tough times. His biggest fear was having his creditors force him into bankruptcy. One day I saw his picture in the Los Angeles *Times,* along with an article explaining that he'd filed for bankruptcy. I sent him a note of encouragement, and he called me to say it really hadn't been as bad as he had feared. He felt great, and he was delighted that he'd finally faced it. That was exactly my reaction to my biggest fear—that of jumping from a plane. We all feel that way when we confront our greatest fear.

In a state of fear, we cling to things—whether it's someone who intended to kill himself or herself by jumping from a building and is now clinging to the edge of the fire department's net or a mountain climber trapped on a cliff, too scared to move in any direction. My friend was also clinging to things in his life. One was a marriage that hadn't been working for a long time, and the other was about 100 pounds of extra weight. But some tremendous changes took place in his life during the next few months. He went through a divorce that enriched both his and his wife's lives, and he joined Overeaters Anonymous to lose the weight. Now he's happier than he's ever been in his life.

Power Performers don't let fear stop them from enjoying their lives. They tend to open the door to strangers or to give rides to hitchhikers. While they're not necessarily thrill seekers, they're not afraid to drive racing cars or go zooming down ski slopes— because they understand something we'll all come to know before the adventure's over for us: It's not the length of life that matters, but the quality of our lives that makes the difference. So while Power Performers love life, they won't let survival fears inhibit their joy in the life experience.

Let me anticipate your question, if I may. If we live only for the present, isn't that irresponsible? What about the employer, or parent, who must sacrifice enjoyment of the present to secure his or her future and the future of the people toward whom he or she has responsibilities?

What about parents? Don't they have an obligation to subordinate their desires to give their children the attention they need?

My relationship with my children is this: We're separate individuals, running our own lives. I love them dearly and always will. However, I won't do anything for them that I consider a sacrifice, for which they'll owe me someday. True, they were all offered a college education and all the other things I can afford to give them, but these I offered freely, without any thought of reward. They don't have to repay me by promising to visit me on alternate Sundays for the rest of my life. Quite frankly, I'd be much too busy having fun living my life to sit around moping because they weren't spending time with me. As for an inheritance, if I die with any money left, it's because of poor financial planning on my part. I certainly don't plan on leaving them anything in my will. If I'm on my deathbed and I have $1.75 left in the world, I'm going to send out for a hamburger.

One of the key points I've tried to stress is how very destructive it is for you to think anyone or anything else can be responsible for your life, because it simply isn't so. Whether that other entity is a government, a union, a big corporation, or merely a mentor in your corporation, it's self-defeating when you no longer feel responsible for your own future and therefore your successes.

Power Performers know that only you can run your life and only you can make decisions. That includes your letting me do your thinking for you. Please don't blindly accept my ideas without applying them to your life. Remember we talked about the difference between intellectual and emotional belief? If you simply accept what I have to say, you may believe only intellectually in these ideas. Challenge what I have to tell you and go out and match it to your life, like a surgeon viewing two X-rays for comparison, and you'll come to believe emotionally that you really can raise yourself to Power Performance and do so much more with your life than you thought possible.

Power Perfomers are very conscious of this syndrome. Any time they start feeling responsible for somebody else, they start examining their true feelings. Is there real motivation to help that person or would they just get a charge out of controlling that person's life? The daughter who devotes her life to her sick mother, or the husband who devotes his life to caring for an invalid wife should never fall into the trap of feeling the other person is controlling her or his own life. Just the opposite may be true.

By confronting our biggest fears, we learn to overcome fear of the future.

So High Achievers have learned to live in the present moment by learning to eliminate guilt and regret over the past, which banishes depression, and fear of the future, which prevents anxiety.

TRAIT 3.
DEVELOP AN EVEN DISPOSITION

The next thing that will probably become clear to you is that Power Performers have remarkably even dispositions. So how do Power Performers avoid those periods of depression—what Winston Churchill called his "black cloud" days, when he felt dogged by a cloud of depression that appeared to hang over his head? Winston Churchill, as you might suspect, is my "main man." He was one of the great Power Performers of all time. However, he did display manic-depressive tendencies. "Manic" is a clinical term that refers to the unnatural highs people get. In a manic phase sufferers feel incredibly powerful, that nothing can stop them and that they can rule the world if they choose. Then they come crashing down to the depths of despair. Manic-depressives can get medication to temper these highs and lows, however, they seldom seek treatment because they're willing to put up with the lows to experience the highs. It's safe to assume many of the world's great leaders have been at least mildly manic-depressive.

Power Performers seem to live life on a fairly constant high, but only because they've learned to handle the lows. Here's how; and how I wish I'd learned about this 30 years ago. Depression, the black mood that most people suffer from time to time is, as I said, caused by something in your past. Live in the present and you can avoid depression. But more specifically depression is usually the result of unexpressed anger. If you get angry with someone, such as your boss, your wife, or your business partner, but you don't release that anger, it goes right into your biological system and surfaces an hour or a day later, as depression. My description may not be very scientific, but it's valid. By the time you start sliding into depression, you may have forgotten what caused it, but once you know this and examine what's been happening in your life, you'll probably be able to identify the cause.

You obviously can't go around yelling at people every time you get upset, even though it would be excellent therapy. Vince Lombardi was being very erudite when he said, "I don't get ulcers, I give them!" However, I do think we can let people know how we feel a lot more than we do, without causing problems. Just be careful that you let them know it was what they *did* that upset you, not who they are.

After my daughter graduated from USC with a degree in Business Administration, she went to San Francisco for a few days to visit a friend and called me to say she was thinking of getting a job selling statues in an art gallery. I told her it didn't seem worthy of someone who'd just invested $50,000 in an education. She told me, with the spirit and enthusiasm of a true Power Performer, that she planned to run her own life, and she hung up on me.

This miffed me, as you might imagine, and I tried to tell myself it was my concern about her making a mistake, not because it was my $50,000! However, instead of letting it ruin my day, I called her back and let her know that what she had said had made me angry. I wish I'd learned to get into the habit of doing that a long time ago. It would have saved me many restless nights. It's essential to find a release for anger. Exercise helps, because it purges the bloodstream of the toxins that anger creates, but nothing is as effective as expressing it to the person who created the anger.

Here's a strange technique that I've found incredibly power-ful. If I want to release anger at someone but it's just not appro-priate to do so, I'll write them a fierce letter telling them exactly how I feel about them and exactly what I'd like to do to them. I address the letter, put a stamp on it and walk it down the driveway to my mailbox. Then I don't mail it—because I'm too generous a person to ruin the person's day like that. It feels wonderful!

Just be sure that you don't leave the letter lying around for someone else to pick up. That happened to me once. I'd shared this idea with a woman whom I was dating. I got busy and forgot to call her, so she wrote one of these letters, and it was a doozie! Then she left it lying on her desk and a well-meaning coworker mailed it for her. I couldn't believe this letter when I got it. It real-ly surprised me when she called me later and was just as sweet as could be. I figured out what must have happened and was glad she got it out of her system; and I didn't tell her that I got the letter until months later.

TRAIT 4.
DON'T BE IN BUSINESS JUST TO MAKE A PROFIT.

Let me clear up one misunderstanding I may have created about Power Performers—a name which may conjure up an image of a super hero, controlling a huge corporation or running a nation. Or perhaps you think of a Type A personality—a hard driver who ruthlessly claws his or her way to the top. However, many Power Performers are ordinary business people. They're fun to be around, because they usually have objectives different from the average business person. They're not in it solely for bottom-line profit or for the feeling of power public success brings or to sur-round themselves with adoring employees. They start and build a business with much the same attitude as a recreational runner takes toward a marathon. They do it simply for the joy of doing it. They know it's going to be tough, a monumental challenge. Like the marathon runner, they know there'll be times when they wish they'd never even started the stupid thing, and they're convinced they'll have to quit in humiliation and defeat, but they carry on because they derive a unique joy from it. Once they've given birth to it, they'll move on or use it to accomplish some other purpose.

Take Walter Knott, for example, who started Knotts Berry Farm as a roadside fruit stand in southern California. He built it into a huge retail and amusement-park complex—the last I heard it was still the largest family-owned business west of the Mississippi. Even though Knott was very wealthy, he got such joy out of continuing to work hard at his business because a unique formula fascinated him. For every $15,000 of capital he invested, he could create work for another employee for the rest of that person's life. He didn't even have to come up with the $15,000. He had banks eager to lend it to him so that he could create even more jobs.

Another interesting example of a Power Performer in business is John Littlewood, an Englishman who became a millionaire by developing a chain of what we call five-and-dime stores. He was proud of his success, but found his friends would tease him about it and tell him he was just lucky or in the right place at the right time. So he set out to prove them wrong in an unusual way. He had all of his assets put into a blind trust and started out penniless again. Can you believe that? Since he didn't have access to any assets, he couldn't pledge them to borrow money. He was truly starting out from scratch. In a few years, however, he was a millionaire again. He had started a small football pool, which is a legal lottery in England, based on the results of soccer matches. It soon became the largest in the world, Littlewood Pools. Then he went out and did it a third time with a mail-order catalog, which supports Denis Waitely's theory that if we took away all the money in the world and distributed it evenly, soon it would be back in the hands of the people who had it before.

Trait 5.
Learn to Enjoy Life Now

Because Power Performers live in the present, not in the future, they're not very strong on building nest eggs. They're likely to spend their last dime on a trip up the Amazon or on a bus trip to Katmandu. Australians often have this delightful approach to life. They're the most fun-loving people I've ever run across. There are only 16 million of them. There are that many people in Tokyo, and Australia is as big as our lower 48 states. Even so, you'll find them all over the world, in the most unusual places. Run into them in the gambling casino in Monte Carlo and ask them what they're doing. "Oh, just taking a bit of a holiday," they'll tell you.

So you ask them, "How long will you be away from home?"

"Oh, about nine months I reckon, maybe more."

My favorite hotel in the whole world is Badrutt's Palace in St. Moritz. I was staying there once and got to talking to a group of Australians who'd come up to play tennis with their European friends. Can you believe that? That people would fly halfway around the world to play amateur tennis? These are not wealthy sheep ranchers, either. They're just ordinary people who know that their employer will understand when they return and will give them their job back.

That's why in Chapter Four, I stressed that the journey is the thing that matters, not the destination. You can't be a Power Performer if your need for security in the future is so strong it's stopping you from enjoying today.

It's why I stressed in Chapter Nine that wealth is not possessions; wealth is an income stream. King Edward VIII was immensely wealthy in 1936, after becoming king of England. Quite apart from the monarchy, the Royal Family has huge personal holdings in land, property, and works of art. In those days being king of England, and the British emperor, was really something. In those days you could go onto your royal yacht *Britannia* and set off to sail the world; and just about anywhere you landed, if you chose, you'd be in a country that you ruled. When love came into Edward's life though, in the form of Wallis Simpson, he looked around and said to himself, "What do I need all these things for?" When you become a true Power Performer, in love with life, you'll also wonder what you need all those things for.

TRAIT 6.
RISE ABOVE THE NEED TO HAVE PEOPLE LIKE YOU

The next thing you must overcome to be a Power Performer is the need to have other people like you. Power Performers tend to be equally at home spending the day alone at a deserted beach as they are going to a party. When you think about it we spend too much of our lives trying to get people to like us. Because of this we invite people to manipulate us. That was why in Chapter Three I warned about peer-group pressure and the negative effects it can have on our lives. We drive the kind of car that's socially acceptable, we dress to please other people, and we try hard not to be too obnoxious or in other ways stand out from the crowd. All of this drains the internal energy you must release to become a Power Performer. Power Performers on the other hand, will be found driving the car they most enjoy driving, even if it's 20 years old, and wearing the clothes they feel good about wearing, even if the clothes don't have designer labels. To become a Power Performer, you must surrender the need to have other people like you. As I explained in Chapter 13, on how to find love; when you quit being so concerned about whether people like you or not, you draw people to you.

TRAIT 7.
RISE ABOVE THE NEED
TO IMPRESS OTHER PEOPLE

The other weakness from which Power Performers have recovered is the need to impress anybody else. If they throw a party, it's because they'll enjoy the company of their friends for the evening, not because they're trying to impress anyone. They order caviar in a restaurant for only one of two reasons: Either they like caviar or they've never tried it and want to find out if they'll like it.

So they don't waste much time talking about money. I was in the club room at Narita Airport in Japan once, where they serve cocktails but no food, and started thinking about a hamburger. After a few days of rice and raw fish, such a thought is very potent, so I had to act on it. I slipped out to the snack bar for what turned out to be the worst hamburger I'd ever had in my life. They were doing their best, but this thing tasted as if they'd made it of mashed liverwurst.

When I got back to the club, a lady was talking to my girl friend. She couldn't have been there more than a few minutes, but already she was reciting a list of things she'd bought on the trip. My friend was wearing a Rolex watch. "Is that a real one, honey, or is it one of those imitations? I can tell you where to buy those in Hong Kong for $13." How dreadful!

So life's not going to be an adventure if impressing other people concerns you, and if, in desperation, you latch on to complete strangers so you can perform your act for them. This has to be insecurity run rampant. It'll ruin some people's day if the bank teller asks them for identification. They'll respond with, "Don't you know who I am!" What do I care if the bank teller thinks I'm hot stuff or not? That's why, in Chapter 10, I stressed the importance of setting meaningful objectives in your life—things that, deep down, you really care about. If you're lusting after that Mercedes simply so you can impress your friends down at the country club, you're going to be sadly disillusioned. What if they all pulled up in Rolls-Royces? Travel the world and indulge yourself in luxuries, of course, but do it because it gives you satisfaction, not so you can brag about it to other people.

WHEN YOU HAVE ACQUIRED THESE SEVEN TRAITS, WHAT'S LEFT IN YOUR LIFE IS LOVE

So Power Performers live just beyond needing other people to like them and just beyond needing to impress other people. If you can get past those obstacles, then what you have left in your life is love. Love of other people, and love of this thing called life. That's the Power Performer's true definition of the meaning of life.

HOW WAS IT FOR YOU?

Discovering the true meaning of life is an enigma brilliant people have pondered unsuccessfully since the beginning of time. I can best sum up my feelings about living life as a Power Performer with the following suggestion:

All across the country there's a tradition among people whose hobby is skydiving. The tradition is that the more experienced jumpers, who may be spending the afternoon in the club house at the airport, will come out to congratulate the people completing their first jump and welcome them to the sport. It's a wonderful feeling when you come in from your first jump and these people crowd around you. They're the only people who fully understand the experience you've just been through. They know exactly how scared you were, because they've been there. They understand the unbelievable exhilaration that sweeps over you when you hit the ground for the first time and realize you haven't killed yourself.

They crowd around you and slap you on the back and put their arms around you and say:

"How was it for you?"

"Did you enjoy it?"

"Wasn't it great?"

"Wasn't it beautiful?"

"Wasn't it an unbelievable experience?"

Here's how this relates to being a Power Performer. Throughout nearly all the philosophies of the human race there's a perception that there is indeed another life beyond this one, another world. For the sake of discussion let's just call it "heaven."

Imagine that our life's adventure is over and it's finally time to move on to the next world. Wouldn't it be something if all the people who'd been through the adventure before us met us at the gates of heaven? Then, in a blinding flash of light, all the secrets of the universe would be revealed to us. There would be no more mystery, there would be no more searching for meaning in life; it would suddenly become abundantly clear to us that our life on earth was just a very small segment of the whole process and that beyond us lay a thousand more exciting adventures just as marvelous as this one.

Everyone crowds around us with huge grins on their faces, enjoying our surprise and confusion. They're asking us about our life on earth and saying:

"How was it for you?"

"Did you enjoy it?"

"Wasn't it great?"

"Wasn't it beautiful?"

"Wasn't it an unbelievable experience?"

We say to them, "It really was. It was more wonderful, more exciting, more beautiful, more thrilling than I can possibly tell you!" If we can say that, then our lives have been a total success. We can claim the title Power Performer because we've derived the most we possibly could from the great adventure of being alive.

> *I'm not afraid to die. I just don't want to be there when it happens.*
>
> WOODY ALLEN

Here's a listing of Roger Dawson's audio and video cassette albums available from Roger Dawson Productions, P.O. Box 3326, La Habra, CA 90631.

You can order by calling (800) YDAWSON (932-9766) or by faxing (818) 854-3595.

AUDIO CASSETTE PROGRAMS

Secrets of Power Negotiating

6-cassette audio album with 24 flash cards. $65

This is one of the largest selling business cassette albums ever published, with sales of over $16 million. You'll learn 20 powerful negotiating gambits that are sure-fire winners. Then, going beyond the mere mechanics of the negotiating process, Roger Dawson helps you learn what influences people, and how to recognize and adjust to different negotiating styles so you can get what you want regardless of the situation.

Also, you'll learn: A new way of pressuring people without confrontation • The one unconscious decision you must never make in a negotiation • The five standards by which every negotiation should be judged • Why saying yes too soon is always a mistake • How to gather the information you need without the other side knowing • The three stages that terrorist negotiators use to defuse crisis situations, and much much more. *Also available: 228-page Synergistic Learning companion program in three-ring binder.* $99

Secrets of Power Persuasion

6-cassette audio album $65

In this remarkable program, Roger Dawson shows you the strategies and tactics that will enable you to persuade people in virtually any situation—not by using threats or phony promises, but because they perceive that it's in their best interest to do what you say.

You'll discover: why *credibility* and above all *consistency* are the cornerstones of getting what you want • You'll learn verbal persuasion techniques that defuse resistance and demonstrate the validity of your thinking • Step by step, you'll learn to develop an overwhelming aura of personal charisma that will naturally cause people to like you, respect you, and to gladly agree with you • It's just a matter of mastering the specific, practical behavioral techniques that Roger Dawson presents in a highly entertaining manner.

Secrets of Power Performance

6-cassette audio album. $65

With this program, based on this book, you'll learn how to get the best from yourself—and those around you! Roger Dawson firmly believes that we are all capable of doing so much more than we think we're capable of. Isn't that true for you? Aren't you doing far more now than you thought you could do five years ago? With the life-changing secrets revealed in this best-selling program, you'll be able to transform your world in the next five years!

Confident Decision Making

6-cassette audio album, with 36-page workbook $65

Decisions are the building blocks of your life. The decisions you've made have given you everything you now have. The decisions you'll make from this point on will be responsible for everything that happens to you for the rest of your life. Wouldn't it be wonderful to know that from this point on you'll always be making the right choice? All you have to do is listen to this landmark program.

You'll learn: How to quickly and accurately categorize your decision • How to expand your options with a ten-step creative-thinking process • How to find the right answer with reaction tables and determination trees • How to harness the power of synergism with the principle of Huddling • How to know exactly what and how your boss, customer or employee will decide, and dozens more powerful techniques.

The Personality of Achievers

6-cassette audio album. $65

You can learn how to go beyond your most ambitious goals with this breakthrough program. Life's high achievers know that there is no substitute for action—the positive, disciplined transformations of thoughts into deeds. This program identifies what makes people high achievers and shows you what—and how—these super-successful people think, how they act, and how they inspire others to help them succeed. It contains fascinating studies of personalities and behavior and transforms them into practical, common-sense strategies that will lead you to uncommon success.

VIDEO TRAINING PROGRAMS

Guide to Business Negotiations—70-minute VHS video $55

Guide to Everyday Negotiations—45-minute VHS video $55

If you're in any way responsible for training or supervising other people, these videos will liven up your staff meetings and turn your people into master negotiators. Your sales and profits will soar as you build new win-win relationships with your customers. Then use them to develop a training library for your employees' review and for training new hires.

Special Prices for Prentice Hall readers

Mention this book when you place your order and receive 20 percent off. All major credit cards accepted.

INDEX